The Poetics of Roman Ingarden

The Poetics of
Roman Ingarden

by Eugene H. Falk

The University of North Carolina Press   *Chapel Hill*

Manufactured in the United States of America

Library of Congress Catalog Card Number 79-29655

Library of Congress Cataloging in Publication Data

Falk, Eugene Hannes, 1913–
    The poetics of Roman Ingarden.

    Includes bibliographical references and index.
    1. Ingarden, Roman, 1893–1970—Aesthetics.
2. Aesthetics.   3. Poetry.   4. Literature—Aesthetics.
5. Semantics (Philosophy).   6. Husserl, Edmund,
1859–1938—Aesthetics.   I. Title.
B4691.I534F34   801'.93   79-29655
ISBN 0-8078-1436-9
ISBN 0-8078-4068-8 pbk.

photo of Roman Ingarden from *Analecta Husserliana*, volume 4,
courtesy of Professor Anna-Teresa Tymieniecka, editor

For Werner and Iris Friederich

Contents

Preface

It is one of the merits of René Wellek that he introduced Roman Ingarden to American scholars more than a generation ago. It is Anna-Theresa Tymieniecka, the editor of *Analecta Husserliana*, who has sparked studies of this great Polish philosopher's thought. In recent years, two of Ingarden's important works have been published in English translation.* On the whole, my terminology does not differ from that of the English translators. When obliged to deviate from the English text, I have supplied the translator's terms in parentheses with the notation "trans." before them.

This book is meant to introduce the serious student of *literature as art* to a subject he can no longer afford to ignore. Several classes of graduate students at Chapel Hill have furnished the incentive to prepare this work, and their inquisitive and critical minds have helped to fashion its composition over many years. Almost at the outset of this undertaking it became obvious that we could not achieve a sufficient understanding of Ingarden's poetics if we limited our study to the two works that have been published in English in the meantime. The notes to the following chapters specify some of Ingarden's sources and especially parts of his other writings which had to be consulted. In a few instances I felt obliged to develop some points that were left merely implied in Ingarden's texts, and to smooth out a few wrinkles that resulted from modifications in his evolving conceptions.

I must emphasize that my sole purpose here has been to give an exposition of Ingarden's works on literature. When the student has clearly grasped Ingarden's own position, he may wish to assess its merits in relation to different conceptions.

My first chapter contains formulations of basic problems and assump-

Das literarische Kunstwerk, 3rd rev. ed. (Tübingen: Max Niemeyer Verlag, 1965), translated by George G. Grabowicz, *The Literary Work of Art* (Evanston: Northwestern University Press, 1973), with a useful introduction and selected bibliography; and *Vom Erkennen des literarischen Kunstwerks* (Tübingen: Max Niemeyer Verlag, 1968), translated by Ruth Ann Crowley and Kenneth R. Olson, *The Cognition of the Literary Work of Art* (Evanston: Northwestern University Press, 1973).

tions, and simplified definitions of terms. It is meant to provide information similar to highway markers indicating principal routes and to the colored lines that explain road classifications. It also contains a geometric theorem which will frequently be used to illustrate some of Ingarden's typical analyses and syntheses and his conception of structure. The first chapter also hints at the reasons why Ingarden asks certain questions and why he seeks answers that will reveal the essential nature of a literary work of art—of any literary work of art—and what obligations this essential nature imposes on the reader. All the other chapters trace the map (or blueprint) of the "anatomical" structure of the literary work of art, of the functional relations of its elements, of its layers, and of its order of sequence. They also describe the attitude and the procedures a reader of a literary work of art should adopt when he has become acquainted with that map. Literary scholars and critics will find their own functions mapped out.

I should like to express my sincere appreciation to Paulette Jones, who prepared the typed copy of my manuscript with exemplary care; to Laura Oaks of The University of North Carolina Press for her perceptive editorial assistance; and to Professor Werner P. Friederich for his constant encouragement and helpful suggestions. Very special thanks are due to Professor Iris Friederich for her expert and patient assistance throughout my struggles for precision and clarity.

Introduction

The principal aim of scholarship is to provide knowledge of a cohesive system of ascertained data, to show the method that has led to its discovery and may lead to its expansion, to preserve that knowledge, and to transmit it. Literary scholarship has evolved as a branch of history and especially of the history of language and civilization. The subject matter and methods of literary scholarship have in many respects been determined by exigencies of historical scholarship. Therefore any written work can be seen as primarily a literary "historical document." Works such as a novel, a poem, a play, a historical or philosophical treatise, a political pamphlet, diaries, letters, and accounts of travels have all been considered as literature. In garden, however, reveals essential differences between a literary work of art and works that intend to present and refer to the real, independently existing, world. By establishing that distinction, he has ensured the emancipation of literature as art from other writings and provided literary scholarship with a ground of its own from which a system of essentially related works of literary art can emerge as a distinct branch of knowledge. This is based on a grasp of what the literary work of art is, i.e., of what constitutes the identity of this object and how it should therefore be cognitively approached. Without a clear recognition of this identity there can be no systematic knowledge showing the general operation of the functions of essential constitutive elements of all literary works of art. Ingarden has shown that if there is to be such knowledge, two other conditions need to be fulfilled. First, the object of that knowledge—the literary work of art—must be intersubjectively accessible on the ground of its mode of existence. Ingarden has demonstrated the intersubjective accessibility of the literary work on the ground of its heteronomous existence. Secondly, the systematic knowledge of objects of any kind requires that one should be able to reduce them to a basic model containing the essential features found in every object of that kind. Just as there is no science or practice of medicine without a model of man, i.e., without anatomy and physiology, there is no systematic knowledge or competent treatment of literature as art without a knowledge of the "anatomical" structure and of the "organic" functions of the basic model of the literary work of art as such—of its general idea. Ingarden's work supplies that fundamental knowledge.

Literature and the other arts belong to our cultural heritage. Their competent cultivation can and does improve the quality of our lives. In some of the pages of this book there will be occasional references to the "naive" reader, the "consumer" of literature, who likes to "enjoy" a literary work, to indulge vicariously in the experiences of presented characters, to be carried away with enthusiasm, to rejoice, to hope, or to suffer with them, to gain practical lessons from these experiences, and sometimes to remember a phrase or a poem that captures a "quintessential" insight. He has more faith in his spontaneous enjoyment of literature than in theories that are supposed to enhance his understanding and pleasure. At some points in our lives this reader is in all of us. It takes patience and effort to learn that knowledge of what art is enhances our enjoyment, opens our eyes to aesthetic values, and heightens our sense of living. Naive responses to art are usually conditioned; competent responses are governed by cultivated insights. For the cultivation of art, exposure to it is indispensable, but without a knowledge of what it is that we respond to—and especially what we should respond to—we may never rise beyond the mentality of the onlooker who may be captivated by his perceptions without ever achieving the contemplation of the aesthetic qualities of the perceived object.

When we perceive an object, let us say a rose, we may respond to it in many different ways. We may, for instance, wish to know its name and origin or use it as a decoration, or we may simply experience its aesthetic qualities, find delight in the color of its petals, and become absorbed in its shade and purity. Then we look again at the rose as a whole, note the arrangement of its petals, and become absorbed in that. Then we turn again to the perception of the rose and yield to the quality of its fragrance. We may go on repeating these exploratory moves from the perceptions of the rose to the intuitive experiences of its various aesthetic qualities until in the end we reach the contemplation of their harmonious unity, which is called the "aesthetic object" of the rose we have perceived. We can say that this aesthetic object is founded in the material object we call a rose. As a rule, though we may not be always conscious of it, each of those affective qualities elicits an appreciative acknowledgment from us, and when we have reached that phase of our experience at which our contemplation of the aesthetic object occurs, we frequently give expression to our valuation—by which we confer a value to an object that we have thus experienced—and use such terms as "beautiful," "perfect," or "exquisite."

Each rose is the carrier of its particular aesthetic object, but however varied the aesthetic objects of roses may be, we recognize that the constitution of each of these aesthetic objects is determined by a characteristic configuration which only roses have. To put it differently: the constitution of these aesthetic objects is determined by the essential configuration of roses in general, or the rose as such. The same applies to the aesthetic objects of all objects of a certain kind, and thus also to those of the literary work of art. Every individual literary work of art has its own particular assortment of aesthetic qualities (its aesthetic object), but whatever the assortment may be, it is of that kind which can be grounded only in the characteristic configuration of the literary work of art as such. That characteristic configuration is the fundamental condition for the appearance of literary aesthetic qualities, but of course these qualities can actually appear only in an individual literary work of art. We have seen that aesthetic qualities can appear only on the basis of experienced sensory data of a perceived object; in this instance, the perceived object is the presented world of the literary work of art, which means that this world must be perceptible if it is to be the carrier of literary aesthetic qualities. Consequently, the presented world must be so constituted that it can appear in our imagination, that it can be imaginationally perceptible. To sum up: literary aesthetic qualities can appear only on the basis of an imaginationally perceptible presented world which is founded in a structure that is modeled on the characteristic configuration of the literary work of art as such. Whatever the material differences that distinguish one presented world from all others, and therefore one literary aesthetic object from any other, the basic structure of all literary works of art must be the same and its elements must be selected in such a way as to render the presented world imaginationally perceptible and capable of carrying congruous aesthetic qualities whose harmony permits the competent reader to constitute an aesthetic object. It is our familiarity with that essential structure that enables us to know what kind of qualities we may expect and should look for, to recognize the artistically effective elements that carry literary aesthetic qualities, and to savor their harmony when we have constituted the aesthetic object which they found.

Every literary work of art is a cohesive structure of elements culminating in the presentation of a self-contained presented world. Every element participates in the founding of the presented world. Some elements have the function of founding or linking other elements; some participate directly in the presentation of that world, while others have the function of bringing about its phenomenal appearance; and some elements fulfill several functions at the same time. The elements can be assigned to four different layers of the literary structure, but these cannot be identified with the inert layers of, for instance, a geological sedimentary formation, because in a literary work the elements within each layer and the layers themselves are functionally interrelated. As in a musical composition, this stratified structure is extended in that it has an order of sequence, and each phase of this sequence contains all the layers. This, then, is the structure of the elements in the unfolding layers of a literary work of art that culminates in the *layer of presented objects*.

To begin our discussion of the layer which is the immediate foundation of the layer of presented objects, I should briefly draw attention to a condition of our perceptional processes which we know from experience. When we look at a real object, for instance, a box, we recognize it for what it is, but we never see the whole box. Regardless of our perspective, we can see at any given moment only what we call an aspect, an adumbration; yet through that or any other of its aspects, we perceive the emergence of the box as a whole in its so-called phenomenal appearance. It is, then, the function of the aspects to bring about that object's phenomenal appearance. We may draw three important conclusions from this recognition. First, the adumbrational elements constitute the *layer of aspects* in a literary work of art. Second, because the phenomenal appearance of objects may be brought about through a variety of their aspects (e.g., visual, auditory, intellectual, emotional), the preponderance or the variety of the types of aspects an author selects determines the adumbrational style of his work. Third, because the primary function of the layer of aspects is to bring about the phenomenal appearance of presented objects, we must recognize again that a literary work of *art* demands that we experience imaginationally the presented objects, and that we do not limit our reading to a mere absorption of information about their existence and destiny.

Once again, a few preliminary observations drawn from experience may be necessary before we consider the *layer of meaning-units*, which from the point of view of founding, plays the most important role in the literary stratified structure. When two persons speak of an object that stands before them, they pay little attention to its name because they "fill in" its meaning with their perception of the object seen in the concrete unity of its various perceptible determinations. If, however, one person seeks to describe that object to another person who cannot see it and does not know it, a number of descriptive sentences may be necessary to enable the other person to gain some notion of that object. Naming it does not help much, for if that object were, for instance, a desk, the interlocutor could, on that basis alone, not know its color, shape, style, width, etc. Every name, in fact every word, is in that sense skeletal: it is only a *schema*. Even descriptive sentences are schematic, because no real object can ever be described exhaustively, and also because every description is bound to contain some points of indeterminateness. Since every word, sentence, and complex of connected sentences can furnish only a schematic projection, the presented world itself is only schematic, and the aspects, which are also projections of sentences, are necessarily schemata. Depending on our attitude, we may read and apprehend a text only within the range of the skeletal information contained in it, or we may complement some of the points of indeterminateness of the schematically presented objects and fill in some of the gaps in the progression of presented events. All these complementations are acts of *concretization*. Our concretizations are usually spontaneous and mostly they serve the purpose of getting a better grasp of what we hear or read. Sometimes while we listen to what we are told, we concretize the statements somewhat freely and we may be told by our interlocutor that we have misinterpreted his words or that we have inferred details that distorted his account. The text, too, is an interlocutor and we must follow its directives, remain within the range of admissible complementations, and sometimes refrain from "interpretations" when the text means to preserve its "opalescence" through ambiguity. As long as we do not concretize it, the literary work of art itself is an intersubjectively accessible schematic structure.

Sound-formations carry word-meanings and form a layer in the stratified structure of the literary work of art. As carriers of meanings, word-sounds are indispensable, but their importance lies in that their aesthetic (phonic) qualities can enhance the effect of individual word-meanings and of sentences. In some poems they determine the mood of the presented world by their melody or rhythm. A literary work, in the broad sense of the term, may be read merely for its so-called content, but a literary work of art engages our imagination and should be read aloud—in the original language if possible. Within the system of every language there evolve correlations between word-sounds and the meanings they carry, correlations which are, in a sense, untranslatable.

To sum up: The basic ("anatomical") structure of the literary work of art consists of four layers, and this structure has an order of sequence. The elements contained within this structure have the function of welding the work into what may be called an "organic" unity which founds the presented world. However, we have so far mentioned the functions of only three layers: the layer of sound-formations, which carries the layer of meaning-units, which in turn projects the layer of aspects, through which the presented world appears. The functions of these layers are essentially presentative, and their confluence culminates in the fourth layer, the layer of presented objects. What, then, is the function of the layer of presented objects *within* the literary work of art?

It may seem that the function of this layer is directed outward: from the presented world into the world of our lives. Normally it is assumed that the function of the presented world is to enrich our lives by the ideas, truths, and ethical and aesthetic values contained in it. There is no doubt that a literary work of art fulfills one or several of these functions, but the problem we have raised pertains to its function within its own structure. To determine that function we must first recall that this structure is only schematic and that the presented world contains points of indeterminateness and gaps in its order of sequence. Unless we concretize the work, the qualities of the presented world cannot become imaginationally perceptible. To put it differently: the sound-formations, the meaning-units, and the aspects present a skeletal world, but in a literary work of art the elements of each of these layers (and the structural order of sequence, too) must contain potentially perceptible—aesthetic—qualities which we must be able to intuit in our concretization. It is on the strength of these potential qualities that the schematically presented world is "exhibited" and thus prepared for our imaginational perception. Throughout our acts of concretization we furnish actualized aesthetic qualities of concretized elements to the constitution of the aesthetic object of the evolving phenomenally appearing presented (exhibited) world. Consequently, it is in the layer of presented objects that the aesthetic qualities of the founding layers and of the order of sequence are assembled. This layer serves to channel the confluence of those aesthetic qualities. It is this layer that demands of the writer, if he is an artist, that he make the aesthetic qualities congruous, so that we may be enabled to constitute the aesthetic object which the presented world is to carry.

We can see that in the schematic structure, which we call the literary work of art, aesthetic qualities exist only potentially. In an aesthetic concretization the potentialities are actualized and the concretized presented world displays them to our imaginational perception. We must therefore distinguish the work of art itself from its concretization—or rather, from its concretion.

We have suggested earlier that we sometimes concretize the schematic work to gain a better understanding of it. In this instance, our acts of concretization are primarily interpretive and they may reveal to us the thoughts, the truths, the ethical values—the view of life—contained in the work. Such a concretization is necessary. A literary work of art, however, also demands that we concretize it aesthetically. To be achieved, an aesthetic concretization must be carried out in a sensitive aesthetic attitude during a competent reading. Competence means here the ability to recognize and heed the directives of the qualitative potentialities embedded in the schematic structure of the work of art. Each layer contains its aesthetic qualities and so does the order of sequence. Aesthetic qualities are apprehended directly, i.e., intuitively, but they strike us only when we assume an aesthetic attitude, when we are open to their affective force of suggesting themselves and of evoking in us an emotionally colored response, which is imbued with our appreciative acknowledgment of their presence. From the beginning of an aesthetic concretization, every discovered aesthetic quality incites us to look for other congruous qualities that are carried by artistically effective elements of the unfolding structure. To achieve that attitude, we need to suspend the praxis that governs our lives and yield to the affective qualities perceived in a presented object. We must not dwell on our perceptions of this or another object of the presented world any longer than it is necessary to explore them while we search for a succession of revealed aesthetic qualities. We must savor these qualities and also the modifications they undergo on account of the functions of other congruous qualities. Sometimes we experience modifications of qualities because in the structural order of sequence they suddenly appear in a foreshortened perspective while new elements carrying new qualities move into the foreground and engage our intuitions by the dynamics of their interplay.

When our literary investigations are historical, it is not only legitimate, but necessary that we establish the authenticity of the text, that we explore and, if possible, ascertain its historical and contemporary setting, its genesis, its political, social, and economic determinants, its place in the literary and cultural tradition, its impact and life in its various concretizations at different times and in different cultural communities. But, it must be emphasized, a literary work of art demands first of all a cultivated aesthetic reading, cognizant of the artistic effectiveness that constitutes its artistic value and capable of a sensitive concretization during which the work's aesthetic value is revealed. Without that competence, we may not be aware of the truly important principles that determine the place a work occupies in a hierarchy established by literary-artistic and aesthetic values. We must also emphasize that a cultivated reading demands philological sophistication, a knowledge of the language as the carrier of a culture, a keen recognition of what the text conveys explicitly and what it implies by its semantic nuances and cultural allusions.

From what we have seen so far, we can say that Ingarden's conception of literary structure is governed by the principles of founding and of reciprocal functional relations. This clearly applies to the structure of layers. For instance, the layer of aspects is founded in the layers of meaning-units and sound-formations and fulfills its founding function with respect to the layer of presented objects. However, we have seen that layers are also functionally interrelated, so that, for instance, the layer of aspects fulfills certain constitutive functions with respect to the layer of presented objects, but its own determinations must be fashioned by the writer in the light of the presented world he seeks to exhibit.

We have also seen that though the elements of each layer found their aesthetic qualities, the author-artist must select and arrange the elements in the light of aesthetic qualities with which the presented world is to be endowed. Finally, we have seen that the aesthetic qualities carried by the literary work of art found in turn that work's aesthetic object.

Throughout Ingarden's explorations we find the demonstration of a basic fact: the sum of functionally interrelated units which achieve unification form a whole that is not merely the sum of its constitutive units, but a new entity. We have seen the emergence of new entities within the schematic structure of the literary work of art and also within the concretized work whose aesthetic qualities constitute its aesthetic object. We still need to point out that each aesthetic object differs from every other, not only because it is constituted by a different assortment of aesthetic qualities, but also—and especially in great works of art—because the arrangement of aesthetic qualities endows the aesthetic object with a configuration, a *Gestalt*, that is all its own. It is this *Gestalt* that emerges from the functionally interrelated aesthetic qualities of an aesthetic object, but only if we have appropriately concretized a genuine literary work of art. Ingarden has prepared the ground for our informed and sensitive reading and for our appreciation of artistic and aesthetic values. At the very core of his explorations is the investigation of presented human experience and of the means by which it is presented. He demands that we not become riveted to the merely perceptive apprehension of human experience, but that we learn to recognize and to assess its *quality*, which is just another way of saying "its aesthetic value." Ingarden's lesson does not at all point the way to aestheticism, but rather to a keen recognition of the potential quality of our lives. Is not that what the study of the arts and of the humanities in general is supposed to teach us?

The Poetics of Roman Ingarden

Chapter 1

1. Notes on the formulation of problems

The story of human consciousness may be described as the story of man's encounter with the world. He has been seeking to fathom the world in relation to himself, himself in relation to the world, and objects of the world in relation to other objects of the world. These relations point to various perspectives from which man has sought to discover the sense of the world, and his own purpose. At the same time, he has been examining these perspectives and has been paying increasing attention to the methods of inquiry by which sense and purpose may be revealed to him.

In response to exigencies of individual and social needs, and sometimes of survival, although for purely intellectual reasons, too, man has been formulating varied and changing views of the world and of his place within it. These views have yielded systems which serve collective and individual purposes. Collective purposes brought forth, for instance, traditions, customs, and religions, as well as social, legal and political institutions. Philosophical and scientific systems evolved from individual quests. All those views and systems have been changing in the course of time in response to man's heightened awareness of himself and of the world, and as a result of changing forms of inquiry which he has adopted. The purpose and the course of our explorations depend on the sort of questions we ask when we seek to understand on the one hand the objects (the world) and on the other hand ourselves (the subject), either as an entity which is part of the world or as one which is at the same time to be distinguished from the world. Depending on the target at which these questions are primarily directed, we may distinguish four broad domains of inquiry: the object of inquiry, the subject of inquiry, the process of inquiry, and the purpose of inquiry. It is not our intention here to survey these domains or to show in what divers ways they may be interrelated (which would prove to be a most difficult task, for each anticipates the others). We shall focus on these domains only when they pertain to our explorations. Let us consider a number of questions that may be raised within these domains of inquiry, and it will become apparent that every question relates at least implicitly to every domain. Our distinction of domains of inquiry should prove useful, however, when the complexity of questions is to be clearly grasped.

What, for instance, does "matter" mean when we point to an object? Is matter something real, or is it an ideal notion that evolves in acts of perception and cognition? What are acts of perception and cognition? What kinds of cognition are there? Is not every perception already the result of some mental coloration that affects the nature and the properties of the object depending on the subject that confronts it? Are not some of these mental colorations necessarily different even in a single subject at different times? Do perceptions and cognitions all necessarily reflect personal attitudes, or are they only subjective, i.e., performed by an individual consciousness but not necessarily personal? How can anything become an objective and intersubjectively identical object of cognition? Are scientific processes the only ones by which the necessarily subjective cognition is overcome and valid proof offered? And what does a scientific demonstration prove and what does it tell us about the objects of the world? Are the "natural laws," according to which cause-effect connections are shown by verifiable proof to govern recurrence, actually valid? (The assumption according to which these laws are mere statistical generalizations does not completely invalidate them: it only places a limit on their validity.) Besides, is it not by us ourselves, or rather by the law of our reasoning, that causal chains in the process of cognition are formed? Does it make any sense to seek so-called generative causes, when all that we can really hope to discover is the circumstances or conditions under which certain manifestations occur and recur? What do we achieve when we define an object within a deterministic system of cause-effect connections? Can we, within this system, "clarify" what an object *is*, or do we merely "explain" the causes (conditions, circumstances) of its occurrence (and recurrence) to provide a basis for its predictability within the scheme of its spatial and temporal existence? What is the process of cognition, what questions must be raised if, instead of explaining an object, we should seek to clarify it, and what kind of knowledge would that process yield?

Before we address ourselves to this last question, or rather this complex of questions, it may be of some interest to note that Max Scheler relates man's search for scientific laws to a deep-seated attitude of the inquiring subject, to one of man's basic manners of cognition intended to serve his desire to exert mastery over the world and himself, a mastery for which predictability based on uniform recurrence in conformity to natural law is necessary.[1] Further, and in close connection with what we have just noted, he maintains with cogent arguments that sensory perception is itself governed by a "law" which causes us to seek out uniformity of manifestations in preference to those which are singular in nature. We may conclude that man's primary (and natural) desire for mastery determines his search for regular recurrence and scientific law, and that it also affects the selective process of his sensory perceptions, and ultimately his natural inclination to pursue knowledge derived from recognized reliable cause-effect relations.

We should note, however, that there is another element in sensory experience which may be linked to our inclination to seek causal explanations. All perceptions based on sensory data are inseparable from the spatial and temporal realms within which they occur. In the spatial realm, we perceive an object in its extensions, or we apprehend it in relation to other simultaneous elements either static or in an actual or potential displacement. In the temporal realm, we apprehend not only the sequence of different objects (in the broadest sense of the word) but also the changes which under given circumstances certain objects undergo. While it is possible to limit one's apprehension to sequential manifestations alone, it stands to reason that our natural propensity to seek out cause-effect connections will induce us to look also for causal explanations of a sequence in time. Sequential data may at times presuppose cause-effect relations, but chronological sequences may be followed without any awareness, and sometimes even without any possible knowledge, of cause-effect underpinnings.

The direction of our inquiry becomes radically different when we do not approach the object of our intended cognition with questions pertaining to various established systems, i.e., when we do not ask to know the object's spatiotemporal relations, the circumstances under which it may have been the effect of generative agents; or why, when, and where it has undergone the changes that have led to its present manifestation; or what its original, present, or future function, effect, or purpose may be: when we only ask *what* an object is. Obviously, the questions pertaining to the various kinds of inquiry that we have just enumerated are valid and relevant. It is, for instance, a fact that the nature of certain objects is actually codetermined by the purposes for which they have been produced, and that some objects have their existential foundation in the functions they perform by virtue of their relation to other objects. Nevertheless, neither the purpose, nor the

---

1. Max Scheler, *Philosophische Weltanschauung* (Bern and Munich: Francke Verlag, 1968), pp. 7ff.

function, nor its cause can provide an adequate answer to the question of what the nature of an object is, i.e., what the reciprocal functions of the formal and qualitative constituents of its configuration and structure are.

Nor can we answer that question by pointing to our personal relation to the object. Each of us may differ in his responses to the same object, and even one person's responses to it may differ at various times. Consequently one and the same object cannot elicit such a variety of responses unless the diversity of responses is rooted in our own diversity, which is based on the differences that distinguish one person from another, or one and the same person from himself at different times. That we respond in diverse ways to the same object should be a sufficient indication that we are either not responding to the objective nature of that object, assuming of course that we have agreed on what that nature is, or that we ourselves have not freed our cognitive process by removing the self from its involvements and by freeing ourselves from our inclinations to pursue certain habitual (and often, at the same time, natural) interests, and thus from certain old-established, and commonly pursued directions of inquiry; that we have not made it possible for our consciousness to apprehend an object without the prepossessions originating in and developed by our existence within the world, and without asking questions that are not relevant to the identification of what really constitutes the configuration and the structure of an object. Normally, we do apprehend objects without any particular concern for their nature, and our cognition and responses adjust to the functions they perform or to the place they occupy in systems within which we have been accustomed to view their existence. Thus we are wont to inquire about the various possible relations an object may have to some other object or objects, or about its historical antecedents, and often we seek at the same time the causes which explain the object's existence. In doing so, we may sometimes show no regard for the fact that the sum of causally related elements that account for the existence of the object does not constitute the nature of that object, for it is a new and different entity with respect to its founding elements.

If, instead, we wish to apprehend an object as a structure of the various determinants of its configuration, we disregard those modes of inquiry; i.e., we reduce the object to its nonsystematized existence in an effort to *see* what its structure essentially is, what constitutes its essential—invariant—being. This is Ingarden's primary aim in his first major work, *The Literary Work of Art*. His earliest attempt to determine an effective mode of inquiry, which, I believe, provides the pattern for his investigation, may be found in his paper "Essentiale Fragen: Ein Beitrag zu dem Wesensproblem."[2] First, however, it should prove useful to offer a few terms whose highly simplified definitions may shed some light on the direction of our explorations.

As a point of departure we should state that consciousness is always consciousness of something. To put it differently, we may say that consciousness always means, *intends*, something, it is always directed at something, it is always *intentional*. Normally, as we have pointed out, our disposition to assume that all objects belong to some already established system of investigation, affects the intentionality of our consciousness; i.e., it affects the manner in which we *mean* the object. Our disposition to focus our consciousness on the object in its "nonworldly" existence, i.e., apart from those established systems, is a disposition to see "without prepossessions," i.e., without the prepossessions which are the result of dealing with objects within any of those systems, or of perceiving them with a personal bias. The disposition to see without prepossessions may be described as the disposition of "pure consciousness." Not all objects lend themselves to being readily seen without any prepossessions, and this clearly applies to every object produced to fulfill a practical purpose: a shoe, a shoehorn, a grapefruit knife, etc. And yet, regardless of the purpose for which these objects are produced, they do have a formal structure and are constituted by a configuration of determinants which may be apprehended without regard for their practical functions.

The directedness of our consciousness, after we have "bracketed" (i.e., set aside) the systems of the "world," may be called the *intentionality of pure consciousness*: we *mean* or *intend* the object and only the object as it essentially is. Briefly stated, this intentionality consists initially of a grasp of what is given to our perception: the presence of an object in its self-givenness. This grasp may culminate in our "directly seeing" that object's essential configuration, i.e., in our *intuition* of its essential identity.[3] As a procedural step in early stages of exploration one may have to bracket the "context" by which an object may, when seen within a context, be endowed with a certain "coloration." We shall see that in his examinations

2. *Jahrbuch für Philosophie und phänomenologische Forschung* 7 (1925): 125–304.

3. To avoid any possible confusion, we must remind ourselves of the distinction between the meaning of the term "identity" as signifying *what* an object essentially is, and that other meaning of "identity" which signifies sameness in the sense that one object is "identical" with another. Identity in the first sense denotes the *essential* being of an object; in the second sense it denotes the sameness of objects, which (as we shall repeat later) presupposes an *ideal* identity (the *idea*) in respect to which objects are considered to be the same.

Ingarden brackets the context whenever he first seeks to establish the constitutive nature of an object. We shall see that this is an important procedural step, for it permits us to establish, for instance, the nature of the meanings of individual isolated words and to examine, on that basis, their "contextual significations."

As we aim to achieve the disposition to see without prepossessions, we first perform what may be described as two complementary acts of a single process. We seek to bracket the systems ("the world") and thus *reduce* (in our consciousness) the object to its nonworldly existence. The object thus reduced in our consciousness is called a *phenomenon*, and we shall call this process *phenomenological reduction*. As we carry out this reduction our worldly self is necessarily suspended and freed of those prepossessions which we derive from established systems of investigation. This concurrent suspension of our worldly self (which may never be complete) is called *epoché* and should be distinguished as an identifiable facet of the phenomenological reduction, because we might neglect—concerned as we are with the reduction of the object in our consciousness—to suspend acquired residual worldly attitudes which we have mentioned and which may still persist and mar in some respect the prepossessionless intentionality of pure consciousness that we seek to achieve.

It is only when this twofold process has been carried out that the intentionality of pure consciousness can directly see—*intuit*—the phenomenon. In this act we may intuit the object's *essential (eidetic) constitutive nature*, as distinct from its variable traits, whose variability is revealed to us when we happen to perceive two objects that are "essentially identical"—except for certain traits that from the point of view of the two objects' essential identity, appear incidental; they are "variable." The process that leads to our intuition of an essential (eidetic) nature may be called *eidetic reduction*. Ingarden's "Essentiale Fragen" is an attempt to show the problems and procedures of constitution by which we may arrive at the essential identity, i.e., the essential being, of an object.

Finally, it must be emphasized that the essential identity of all kinds of objects cannot be apprehended in the same manner. Provisionally, we may divide objects into *real* empirical objects, such as table, bed, house, trout, terrier, and *ideal* objects, such as square, circle, squareness, circularity. Real objects have temporal and spatial extension, and an end. In the course of their existence they may undergo certain changes. Ideal objects, however, have no temporal existence, and they are immutable. We shall see later that there are types of objects which we cannot, on the basis of these criteria, simply assign to either real or ideal existence, for they do not quite fit either of these categories.

2. The relation between propositions and questions

A. *Propositions*

In his "Essentiale Fragen," Ingarden seeks to identify those questions which he considers *essential* because they may be answered by propositions about the essential identity of objects under consideration. A proposition is a judgment whereby we mean to affirm (or to deny) some *state of affairs* pertaining to an object. We should note that a proposition which is a judgment must be distinguished from the declarative sentence by which it is affirmed. We shall see that questions which ask *what* an object is may be answered by various propositions, and that only certain special propositions are judgments about the essential nature of the object. Before we can consider what an essential question is, and what a proposition affirming the essential nature of an object means, we should first note the material of a proposition. Let us consider the proposition "The diagonals of a square are of equal length." The *material* of the proposition consists of the subject of the proposition ("The diagonals of a square"), the copula ("are"), and the object of the proposition ("of equal length"). Similarly we may state: "The earth is the center of the universe," or "The city of X is the cultural center of the world." All of these propositions have a subject, a copula, and an object. While their material structure is thus the same, their form is not. *Affirmation* is the *form* of a proposition, but the affirmations in these propositions are different, because of the differing manners in which we mean to affirm the states of affairs. Although all affirmations make "a claim to truth," we cannot mean to affirm all states of affairs with the same degree of certainty. The fact that the diagonals of a square are of equal length is evident to anyone who knows what a square is. When we make the judgment, we know that its validity can be proved, i.e., that the state of affairs which we mean—*the intentional state of affairs*—is provably identical with an objective state of affairs.

At one time the affirmation of the judgment that the earth is the center of the universe was no doubt meant to be valid, but in the course of time this judgment proved to be false. It follows that affirmations about *some* nonideal states of affairs may, in spite of their claim to truth, sooner or later prove to be false, regardless of how obvious their truth may seem to anyone. The truth of my judgment that a certain city is the cultural center of the world may be obvious only to me, and yet, personally, I may mean that judgment to be valid. Nevertheless, if I am aware of the limitations and thus of the relative validity of some of my judgments, then I must be aware also of the degree of certainty with which I mean to affirm a state of affairs. If my affirmation is meant to be absolutely valid (if the state of affairs which I mean is meant to be provably identical with an objective state of affairs), then that affirmation is an *assertion*. Consequently, every assertion is an affirmation, but only an affirmation about a state of affairs meant to be provably objective is an assertion.

We have stated that the validity of a proposition depends on whether or not the affirmed intentional state of affairs is provably identical with an objective state of affairs. However, we shall now see (1) that a proposition remains valid even if the *extent of this identity* is not complete; and (2) that *asserted* propositions may not all be meant to be valid in quite the same manner. With regard to point (1): I can assert a proposition when I describe a square as a parallelogram. Not all the *moments* (dependent parts, not portions) of a parallelogram can be found in a square, and yet the statement as worded is true. For the proposition to be valid, it is enough that no moment of the objective state of affairs should contradict any of the moments of the proposition. With regard to point (2): Let us first consider what is called an *apodictic* assertion, such as "The diagonals of a square are of equal length." In this assertion the function of the copula is to imply that we *mean* the diagonals of a square to be *necessarily* of equal length. Clearly, this state of affairs happens to be ideal, for a square has no temporal existence, and the validity of a proposition about it cannot be changed by any modifications due to empirical existence. On the other hand, when we make the *categorical* assertion that all men are mortal, we mean that in human experience they are mortal *without qualification*, which is not the same as to say that all men are necessarily mortal. Categorical assertions are valid, but since they are not founded in necessary states of affairs, they may, however valid they are at a certain time, be disproved by unforeseeable developments in our experience. (Perfectly valid categorical assertions about man's never reaching the moon might have been made only a short time ago.)

We may state, then, that assertions may not all be of the same type in spite of the indisputable validity of the propositions at the time of assertion. The difference between the *types of assertions* is not affected by the degree of our certainty about the asserted state of affairs, but rather by the type of proof pertaining to it. When we examined the three propositions mentioned earlier ("The diagonals of a square are of equal length," "The earth is the center of the universe," "The city of X is the cultural center of the world"), we sought to determine which of the affirmations were meant to be assertions; we were concerned primarily with the degree of our certainty about the validity of our judgments. Consequently, our affirmations, whatever they may be, depend on how *we mean* the proposition, i.e., on what sort of relation we mean to establish between the subject and the object of the proposition. The intentionality of this relation is quite striking, not only because we can and often do use the same copula (e.g., is, are) and have it perform different functions, depending on how we mean to establish that relation, but also because in some languages the copula is in certain cases not even used explicitly, but is only implied.[4]

We pointed out that a proposition must be distinguished from the declarative sentence by which it is affirmed. Consequently, declarative sentences are able to convey different types of affirmations regardless of what sort of claim to truth—if any—is made. It is, in fact, possible to utter a simple declarative sentence, a so-called *pure declarative sentence*, without meaning in the slightest to suggest that it is to be understood as a genuine affirmation about a true state of affairs. We frequently find such pure declarative sentences in language textbooks (e.g., "This car is an American product"); they appear to be affirmative sentences, but given the context, we clearly do not mean them to convey genuine affirmations.

From all our considerations it follows that, consciousness being always the consciousness of something, any object or state of affairs of which I am conscious is always intentional: I mean it; and I *may also* mean it to be objective. Thus, when I form a proposition about an object, I am making a judgment about a state of affairs that pertains to the object, and when I formulate a statement about that state of affairs, I convey, by means of a declarative sentence, an affirmation which is the form of my judgment. The affirmation may or may not be genuine. The declarative sentence is, then, a reflection of my intended judgment. It is worth mentioning that no statement is a "direct expression" of my feelings or of my experiences, for my feelings and experiences do not express themselves in sentences. I may of course fathom my feelings and experiences as objects toward which my consciousness is directed and affirm something about them. This is mentioned because it is the basic condition for any sentence's being able to mean the same to two or more subjects or to one and the same subject at

4. For a discussion of the functions of the copula, see Alexander Pfänder, *Logik* (Halle: Max Niemeyer Verlag, 1929), pp. 128ff.

various times. This, as we shall see later, does not mean that a declarative sentence, as a formulation of a judgment, may not also "manifest" certain features of the frame of mind of the speaker. However, if we wish to know only what an affirmation (or an inquiry) *means*, i.e., what state of affairs is affirmed or inquired about, we bracket the context and any concomitant mental states of the person who is formulating the proposition or the question. If, however, we wish to apprehend that meaning with the manifestative characteristics of the uttered statement and with its signification, then we must take into account the situational and linguistic context in which the statement is embedded.

B. Questions

Like a proposition, a question is an act of consciousness which must be distinguished from the interrogative sentence by which we ask the question. Inquiry is the form of that act of consciousness just as affirmation (or assertion) is the form of a proposition. The material of a proposition has no character of indeterminateness, for the relation between its subject and object is considered to be established. Consequently, the term "state of affairs," which implies that the relation between the subject and the object of the proposition is established, cannot properly be used to designate the intended material contained in a question; instead the term "problem" is used. A certain indeterminateness always pertains to some elements of the question, and therein lies one of the basic differences between the material of a proposition and the elements of a question. Another difference lies in the fact that whereas the intentional state of affairs of an affirmation may be identical with an objective state of affairs, the problem, whose solution depends on an affirmation of a state of affairs, cannot, for it exists only intentionally in the question.

Depending on the elements that are indeterminate, two kinds of questions may be distinguished: *Existential questions* and *factual questions* (pertaining to unknown elements of a state of affairs) (*sachhaltige Fragen*). An existential question (such as "Does water boil at 100° C?") may be answered by simple affirmation or negation. Every element of this question is known. What remains indeterminate is the existence or nonexistence of the state of affairs which the answer is expected to determine. A factual question pertaining to one or more unknown elements of a state of affairs (such as "What is the pace of erosion of this material?") cannot be answered in the same manner as the former question because it contains an unknown element which the answer is expected to reveal. For such a question to be correctly formulated, the unknown element must be clearly identified; which means that the problem must be stated unequivocally. There are certain conditions under which a question may be judged to be correctly formulated even before the true answer has been given. Using Ingarden's example, let us ask this question: "What angles are formed by the diagonals of a square?" Every element in the question is "objective" in that it refers to an object of existential independence. Secondly, all elements of this question are connected into a whole which is based on presupposed connected elements of an objective state of affairs (a square can have only two diagonals, diagonals form angles, etc.). This means that the elements of this problem presuppose, by virtue of their objectivity and arrangement, an objective state of affairs. Finally, it should be noted that a problem is stated unequivocally when all elements admit of only one interpretation. The problem pertaining to only one unknown element is to be distinguished from that posed in a *complex question*, which consists of more than one unknown, as, for instance, "When and for what purpose will he go there?" The important fact to remember is that the problem of a correctly phrased question presupposes a state of affairs, and that it is this presupposition that gives a question its direction.

3. Basic terminology: essence, idea, schema[5]

A. *Essences*

Assuming *epoché* and phenomenological reduction have been carried out and that we are ready to constitute the essential identity of objects, we seek what makes them what they are, what their invariant constitutive nature is. The constitutive nature of an ideal object is a *concretized* quality: e.g., the constitutive nature of a square is concretized squareness, that of a circle is concretized circularity. These qualities, which we call *essences* (*Wesenheiten*), constitute—when concretized—the nature of an ideal object. The constitutive nature of a real object is the *realization* of a characteristic ("typical") *configuration* of the object's determinants, which is merely analogous to a concretized essence; but a concretized essence and a realized characteristic configuration of determinants both have the function of constituting the invariant nature, the essential identity, of the objects. We

5. Ingarden's terms are based mainly on Jean Hering's "Bemerkungen über das Wesen, die Wesenheit und die Idee," *Jahrbuch für Philosophie und phänomenologische Forschung* 4 (1921): 495–543.

should point out that whereas a concretized essence can be intuited as a *unity*, the realized characteristic configuration of the determinants of a real object can be apprehended as a *whole* only on the basis of *recognitions* derived from experience. We should recall that the concretized essence of ideal objects is timeless and immutable, whereas the realized characteristic configuration of real objects may undergo various modifications over a period of time and is therefore only relatively constant; but the measure of quasi-permanence which it does have also permits us to consider it analogous to essences.

From what we have just said we may conclude that the invariant constitutive nature of an *individual ideal* object is a *concretization* of an essence. Thus squareness is concretized in the constitutive nature of any individual square, regardless of the lateral dimension the particular square may have. The invariant constitutive nature of an individual *real* object is a *realization* of a characteristic configuration. Thus "tableness" is realized in the constitutive nature of any individual table, regardless of what traits a particular table may have.

B. Ideas and schemata

When we intuit the essential identity of any object, we do so on the basis of acts whereby we constitute its invariant nature as concretized essence or as realized characteristic configuration; we ignore its variables. Because the same essence is concretized in the invariant constitutive nature of every square regardless of lateral dimension, we say that all squares are essentially identical. However, that does not mean that all squares are essentially identical *in respect to* the essence squareness. Individual squares can be essentially identical only in respect to their ideal correlate, *the general idea of the square as such* that allows for the variable of lateral dimensions; whereas the essence squareness is a quality, an immutable unity that can have *no variables*. A characteristic configuration (e.g., tableness) that constitutes, when realized, the nature of real objects is not immutable, but it is at least a relatively constant unity. Only in respect to the general idea "the table as such," which allows for variables, can individual tables be "essentially" tables, i.e., can they be essentially identical *as* tables. Most general ideas have at least one variable.[6] The square has one variable: lateral dimension. Other general ideas may have more variables; e.g., the triangle has the variables of lateral dimensions and of the size of inner angles.

6. We should at least note that the general idea "the point as such" has no variables.

What, then, is the relation of essence and general idea? Every individual square is ultimately an individuation of the general idea—the square. Only an individual square has a nature, whereas the general idea of the square can have no nature; it can have only an ideal correlate of that nature, the so-called *constant qualitative moment*. Thus the constant qualitative moment is to the general idea as the invariant constitutive nature is to the individual object. We may state, then, that squares of various sizes are essentially identical in respect to the general idea under which they fall, because the same essence which is concretized in the essential constitutive nature of every individual square is also reflected in the constant qualitative moment of the general idea of the square. Furthermore, it follows that all objects that fall under the same general idea can be *grouped essentially*; i.e., they can be grouped on the basis of their essential identity and not merely on the basis of certain traits (features).

A general idea needs to be distinguished from a *particular idea*. A particular idea is that ideal correlate which contains all the properties and traits of an individual object. For instance, an individual square of a given lateral dimension is an *individuation* of its particular idea. All squares of equal size fall under the particular idea of which they are the individuations and are therefore not only essentially identical, but identical in respect to that particular idea. However, the identity of objects in respect to the particular idea of which they are individuations does not extend, for instance, to their localization in space and time.

We may describe the relation between a particular and a general idea in the following manner: an individual object is the direct individuation of its particular idea, but only its (essential) constitutive nature (and not its particular traits) may be considered as "derived" from the constant qualitative moment of the general idea under which it falls, because the general idea does not contain any of the object's variable particular traits. Consequently, the particular idea is an intermediary ideal correlate between the individual object and its corresponding general idea, and is therefore subordinate to that general idea. Finally, the particular idea of an object may also be regarded as a point of reference whose identity permits us to consider all objects that fall under it to be *grouped as identical* (except for their localization).

When we intuit an essence, such as squareness, we intuit it as a unity, for it has no distinguishable dependent moments. Once squareness is concretized in an individual square's constitutive nature, we distinguish the constitutive moments of that nature, i.e., the right angles, the sides of equal length, and parallel opposite sides. These three constitutive moments in the nature of an individual square are absolute, for without any one of them the object would not be a square. Because the general idea "the square" is the ideal correlate of an individual square, these absolute moments of an individual square are also distinguishable in the general idea.

If we consider an individual square and limit our apprehension to the moment of the parallelism of its sides, we may say that it is a parallelogram. It is because of this one absolute moment that a square is a parallelogram. If we then consider an individual rectangle or an individual rhomboid, we note that these objects reveal the same absolute moment in their nature; and we conclude that they too are, when seen from this perspective, parallelograms. Because of this absolute moment of their natures all these objects can "be," or "play the role of," or be apprehended from the perspective of the *schema*—the skeletal structure—of a parallelogram. The constitutive nature of square, rectangle, and rhomboid contains four angles. On the basis of this moment they may be apprehended under the *schema* of a quadrangle. Consequently, all of these objects may be apprehended either as parallelograms or as quadrangles. When we apprehend essentially different objects such as squares, rectangles, and rhomboids, under the schema "parallelogram," i.e., on the basis of this one absolute constituent perceptible in each, we are carrying out a grouping according to a schema.

From what we have said about a schema so far, it follows that, for instance, a parallelogram is a skeletal structure consisting of certain absolute moments: it has four sides and the opposite sides are parallel. However, the schema of the parallelogram does not contain any specifications with regard to the angles formed by the sides, nor with regard to lateral dimensions. As long as these specifications are not determined, the schema "parallelogram" remains *potentially* either a square, or a rectangle, etc., of various sizes, and the constitutive nature of an individual square cannot be actualized solely on the basis of the absolute moments of a parallelogram. If an object is to be a parallelogram, it must have four sides and the opposite sides must be parallel, but the object can be individuated only if the variables (the size of angles and sides) are actualized either in accordance with specific indications, or if the object's other schemata (e.g., the schema of a rectangle and that of an equilateral) are indicated to guide our actualizations. Let us assume that we are presented with successive different schemata of an object whose nature is not known to us, but which we are supposed to project while one schema after another is given to us. First we are told that the object is a parallelogram. We may—to a certain extent—visualize a plane figure that has four angles and four sides, but we must wait for the next schema, or some concrete specification, or make a decision of our own before we can "fill out" the details that are left indeterminate by the first given schema. When we are then told that the object which we are supposed to project is also a rectangle, and later that it is also an equilateral, new actualizations are thus made possible at each step until all constituent schemata become actualized and we come to apprehend the object as a square. That square may finally come to light as an individual square when the lateral size is either specified or determined by us and thus actualized. It should also be noted that the first given schema determines the initial range of our projection. The second given schema narrows that range, and finally, after the actualizations of all potentialities are carried out, the projection is narrowed down to the individual object which we can now apprehend as an equilateral rectangular parallelogram—a square—of a certain size.

Essences, general and particular ideas, and schemata affect our cognition of the constitutive nature of objects. The three types of questions that we shall now consider presuppose our understanding of what is meant by the constitutive nature of objects, and the distinctions we have discussed should therefore facilitate our grasp of what we may call the targets at which the questions are directed.

4. Types of questions

A. The question whose target is a determinative proposition (Bestimmungsurteil): *What is that (this, it)?*

The question "What is that?" should be understood as pointing to some individual object, real (oak) or ideal (square). The answer to this question is inadequate if we are told the name of the object, and the name happens to be one we have never heard. The name is meaningful only if we already know what the constitutive nature of the named object is, for the name "oak" is the name of all objects whose essential constitutive nature is identical. Consequently, that nature is the condition for an oak to be named "oak"; and it is the object itself, and not the condition, that is so named. We must conclude that the unknown to which the question seeks an answer is the essential nature that constitutes the object, that makes it what it is, and not the name.

An answer indicating what *kind* of an object we are pointing to is also inadequate, because this answer presupposes our knowledge of the constitutive nature of that object and thus of the essential grouping to which it may be assigned. Besides, our question does not in any way imply a connection or relation to other objects.

Before proceeding with the analysis of the question, we should note that the object to which the word "that" points is at least to some extent a "known." It may be known to us as a result of our perception or from a reported perception, we may know some of its traits or properties, or its functions, or at least some of its relations to other objects, but as long as we do not know the determining property (quality) that makes it what it is, all other determinative moments it may have will not suffice to establish its constitutive nature. The problem of the question is, then, the determination of the constitutive nature of the object.

If my answer is stated in a determinative proposition ("That is an oak"), it implies that I have already apprehended the constitutive nature of the object to which the "that" of the question and the "that" of my answer point; and that any object with that essential constitutive nature (regardless of variables) is named "oak." Consequently, the determinative proposition affirms the essential identity between the constitutive nature of the object pointed to and that of any object called "oak."[7] A determinative proposition has, then, a twofold function. First, it determines the constitutive nature of the object. Second, it points to the distinctiveness of that object's essential identity; which means that the object's constitutive nature contains the necessary constituents for our recognition that it *differs* from all other objects whose constitutive nature is not essentially identical with its own.

B. The schema question: What is an X?

When we ask "What is an X?" and do so with the knowledge of what the constitutive nature of that X is, we are obviously seeking to establish a schema under which the object may be apprehended. The schema ques-

---

7. The special function of the copula in this proposition must be distinguished from that used in statements such as "This is red" or "This is a plant." In these statements the copula does not mean to establish identity between subject and predicate. In the first case it refers to the *quale* of the subject, and in the second case to a classification. It is of course possible, depending on the context, that the copula in "This is an oak" may actually refer to a specimen, and not to the particular constitutive nature of the object. In this case, however, we are not dealing with a determinative proposition.

tion, as we would expect, implies one or more absolute moments which govern the grouping of an object with other objects. "A square *is* a parallelogram," or "A terrier *is* a mammal (or a vertebrate)" is a proposition affirming a grouping based on a schema which is an absolute moment. It may seem that the same state of affairs is being affirmed when we say: "A terrier *belongs* to the class mammalia." In everyday language such a wording is assumed to carry the same meaning as that in which the copula "is" is used. In actual fact, however, mere *belonging* to a class does not necessitate that all objects within it have in common a constituent property that is *absolutely* related to their constitutive nature. To belong to a class may at times mean nothing more than an arbitrary grouping of objects on the basis of so-called "relative traits," i.e., features they have in relation to other objects without any regard to their constitutive nature. We may form a class of objects even because they simply belong to one and the same proprietor. Clearly, some constituent, i.e., an absolute property, is fundamental for an object to be grouped by *necessary connection*, which is not to be confused with mere *relations* between objects, relations based on relative traits. Relative traits suffice, then, to form a class, whereas an absolute moment is necessary for an object to be grouped according to a schema. If we answer a schema question, we must recognize that the proposition "An X *belongs* to the schema Y" is valid exactly because an X *is* also a Y, which means that an absolute moment codetermines the nature of X and entails its being apprehended under the schema Y. It follows that no single schema can reveal the constitutive nature of an object, whereas the constitutive nature of an object does reveal a schema. This is an important implication of the proposition "An X is a Y." It is worthy of note that in a different context Ingarden touched on the same question many years later and actually spelled out the implications of the above analysis.[8]

To sum up: In asking the question "What is an X?" we are seeking a proposition affirming a grouping according to a schema. We are dealing with an object whose constitutive nature is known to us. We are actually seeking the unknown—the schema Y—with the assumption that Y is something "internal" in relation to X, that it is "inherent" in X, that whenever X exists Y exists too, and that Y is "entailed" by X as its coexistent. Most importantly, we further assume that the knowledge of the constitutive nature, and hence of its necessary existential connections, determines the schema under which the specimen can be apprehended.

8. "The Hypothetical Proposition," *Philosophy and Phenomenological Research* 18, no. 4 (1958): 435–50.

The main purpose of a determinative proposition is, then, to arrive at a determination of an object's constitutive nature and thus of its absolute moments. On this basis the object may then be apprehended under one or another of its schemata. If the principle of grouping does not take account of the constitutive nature of the classified objects (elements of the class), and is governed, let us say, by the presence (or sometimes absence) of features irrelevant from the point of view of the constitutive nature of the elements but dictated by some expedient purpose, all that we can learn is the *relation* of objects to other objects, but nothing about the *necessary connections* with other objects, connections which cannot be ascertained without an analysis of their constitutive nature and its absolute moments. Consequently, a grouping according to a schema presupposes a knowledge of the object's constitutive nature and thus of its absolute moments; it is the result of this knowledge.

C. *The question whose target is an essential proposition* (Wesensurteil): *What is the X as such?* (Was ist das, das X?)

Since we aim to present an exemplary demonstration, we shall assume that the X is an ideal object. Following Ingarden, we shall analyze the nature of the square. If we ask the question "What is the square as such?" we are expecting an answer which is a proposition that will reveal the absolute moments of the constitutive nature of every individual square. That nature is, as we know, reflected in its ideal correlate, the constant qualitative moment of the general idea of the square. Only when such a question has been adequately answered, can we, in the logical sequence of inquiry, know the (essential) constitutive nature of the square and its absolute moments, and thus answer the question whose target is a determinative proposition, and finally the schema question also.

The answer to the question "What is the square as such?" is, as we expect, the proposition "The square is an equilateral rectangular parallelogram." By the subject of the proposition (the square) we mean the general idea "the square" which is the ideal correlate of any individual square. The squareness which is concretized in the particular constitutive nature of an individual square is reflected in the ideal correlate of the constitutive nature, i.e., in the constant qualitative moment of the general idea of the square. Thus, through the particular constitutive nature of an individual square, we apprehend the constant qualitative moment of the square; we intuit in it the concretized essence squareness. Because the constant qualitative moment of the square is a reflection of concretized squareness in the nature of every individual square, the *subject* of the above proposition means "the square as such" and reflects at the same time the concretized squareness which we intuit in every individual square.

The absolute constituents of the nature of an individual square (right angles, sides of equal length, and parallel opposite sides) are concretizations of the essences rectangularity, equilaterality and parallelogramness. These constituents have also their ideal correlates in the general idea of the square; they are reflected in its *constants*. We can see, then, that the *object* of that proposition consists of the constants of the square. We may conclude by stating that that essential proposition affords, in its subject, an apprehension of the general idea of the square and an intuition of the essence squareness; in its object, an apprehension of the absolute constituents of the nature of any individual square.

Clearly, the constitutive nature of all objects cannot be thus apprehended, and therefore essential propositions can, strictly speaking, be formulated only with regard to the general idea of objects whose constitutive nature is the concretization of an essence. The general idea under which such objects fall is called an *exact idea*; the general idea under which real objects fall is called an *inexact idea*. As we have already mentioned, the constant qualitative moment of an inexact idea is the correlate of an essential configuration which is a synthesis of properties and traits in the nature of real objects that fall under this idea. If, for instance, we consider the nature of the object "bed" and ask what constitutes it, we can enumerate the traits of objects so named that we have encountered so far and form in our minds what we may call an open-ended configuration. Open-ended, for we cannot possibly foresee the potential number of determinants that may constitute the nature of beds in the future. (Who could have foreseen the contemporary waterbeds?) Consequently, the constitutive nature of any individual bed is merely the concrete correlate of a configuration of traits that determines the constant qualitative moment of the inexact idea "the bed." Because of the variable constitutive nature of empirical objects it is impossible to formulate an essential proposition about them.

5. Existential moments

So far we have assumed that objects may be adequately distinguished according to their real or ideal mode of existence. There are, however, objects, such as literary works, whose mode of existence does not quite fit that distinction. Different distinctions are needed, and Ingarden established criteria for existential description,[9] criteria that we shall note as four pairs of contrasting *existential moments* which, for our purposes, will provide the information we shall need for future reference.

(1a) Existential autonomy   (1b) Existential heteronomy

(2a) Existential originality   (2b) Existential derivation
     (*Seins-ursprünglichkeit*)   (*Seins-abgeleitetheit*)

(3a) Existential self-sufficiency (3b) Existential connectivity
     (*Seins-selbständigkeit*)   (*Seins-unselbständigkeit*)

(4a) Existential independence   (4b) Existential dependency
     (*Seins-unabhängigkeit*)   (*Seins-abhängigkeit*)

   (1a) *Existential autonomy*. An object has existential autonomy
        if its nature and subsistence (continuing existence) are im-
        manent: e.g., an essence, a real object, an act of con-
        sciousness. These objects contain within themselves all the
        determinants for what they are.
   (1b) *Existential heteronomy*. Objects have existential heteron-
        omy if they are purely intentional in their formal structure
        and material determinants: e.g., correlates of sentences,
        mental images.
   (2a) *Existential originality*. Objects have existential originality
        when they cannot be produced by any other object. All
        objects that have existential originality also have existential
        autonomy.

9. See "Bemerkungen zum Problem 'Idealismus-Realismus,'" in *Jahrbuch für Philosophie und phänomenologische Forschung, Ergänzungsband: Husserl Festschrift* (Halle: Max Niemeyer Verlag, 1929), pp. 159–90. This essay should be read in conjunction with his paper "Les modes d'existence et le problème 'idéalisme-réalisme,'" in International Congress of Philosophy, Tenth, *Library*, 2 vols. in 3 (Amsterdam: North Holland Publication Co., 1949), 1 : 347–50. A detailed analysis may be found in Ingarden's *Der Streit um die Exiztenz der Welt*, 2 vols. in 3 (Tübingen: Max Niemeyer Verlag, 1964), 1 : 65–123.

(2b) *Existential derivation*. Objects produced by other objects are existentially derivative: e.g., heteronomous objects.

(3a) *Existential self-sufficiency*. (In his French paper, "Les modes d'existence," Ingarden called this existential moment *distinctivité*.) Objects have existential self-sufficiency if they do not require, for their subsistence (continuing existence), the coexistence of any other object with which they may form a whole distinct object: e.g., essences that are not concretized, or individual real objects.

(3b) *Existential connectivity*. This is the existential moment found, e.g., in a concrete color which demands for its existence a certain intensity; also, every determinant of an object has this moment.

(4a) *Existential independence*. Objects are independent when they do not require for their subsistence any other object. They are thus independent with regard to an act of cognition directed at them.

(4b) *Existential dependency*. This moment is found in objects which, though self-sufficient, still require another materially appropriate object for their subsistence: e.g., correlates of sentences, man and oxygen.

6. Expression and meaning

In Ingarden's terminology the word-sound is endowed with our intentionality and it thus means (intends) its correlate. By virtue of this function, it may be considered a meaningful sign. This function must be distinguished from that which the word-sound may fulfill when it is a sign that indicates the frame of mind of the speaker. A brief exposition of Husserl's analysis of *expression* and *meaning* [10] may serve as a helpful introduction. Here, we shall consider the sound-formation of a word as its "expression." The "word" thus comprises an expression and a meaning of which the expression is the carrier. Every sign is a signifier that signifies something. We now wish to know what sort of sign an expression is, what it signifies, and in what sense it "signifies." Let us first consider some signs

10. Edmund Husserl, *Logische Untersuchungen*, 2 vols. (Tübingen: Max Niemeyer Verlag, 1968), Investigation I; translated by J. N. Findlay, *Logical Investigations* (London and Henley: Routledge and Kegan Paul; New York: Humanities Press, 1976).

that are *not* expressions. A sign may be an *indicator* (*Anzeichen*) when it is, for instance, a mark (a brand, a stamp, a flag), or a commemorative sign (a memorial, a monument), a trace (a fossil), or a symptom (heartburn). When such an indicator becomes the intentional object of my consciousness, i.e., when I am conscious of it, and I recognize it in its indicatory function, I formulate a *unified* judgment. This, however—for purposes of analysis only—may be broken into two judgments. In one of these judgments, the indicator is constituted as the *signifier*; in the other, the indicated object is constituted as the *signified*. The essential characteristic of this unified judgment is my subjective empirical certainty or assumption that the sign, which I have recognized as an indicator, indicates, on the strength of my experience, a certain or a presumable presence of a signified object. Furthermore, when I make that judgment, I do not make any deductions and conclusions, although in some cases my experience may be logically based on a previous deduction and conclusion. The fact that a sign, which I recognize as an indicator, elicits my unified judgment, in which the signifier is constituted in its indicatory function together with the signified object, clearly points to *association*. Association consists in one object's "pointing toward" another as if that other "belonged" to it. Husserl characterizes the productive effect of the associative function as turning coexistence into correlation.

Under certain circumstances and in a special sense, an expression can be recognized as an indicator. Its indicatory function must, however, be distinguished from its function of being a carrier of *meaning*, a *meaningful sign*. An expression has at all times a meaning and is therefore always a meaningful sign, but what does an expression signify when it is an indicator?

Suppose I utter a statement before a person in a language which he does not understand. Although he cannot understand the utterance, he does recognize the manifestation of my intention of making a statement. The act whereby I utter an expression *indicates* (or *manifests*) to the listener my intention of communicating. When he understands my utterance, he may concentrate on what I mean to say, but that does not alter the fact that my expression functions at the same time as an indicator of my intention of communicating; i.e., it still fulfills *this manifestative function*. This, then, is what is signified by an expression as indicator; it does not indicate the object which the expression means, i.e., which is the correlate of the *meaning* of the expression. Gestures and the play of features, which may accompany communicative speech, do not normally indicate that object either; they are, however, indicatory manifestations of, for instance, how the speaker feels about the object. We should distinguish manifestative functions in a narrow sense from those in a broad sense. Expressions that manifest the speaker's intention of making a statement constitute a manifestation in the narrow sense. We speak of a manifestation in the broad sense when we attribute to the speaker such mental states as joy, pain, or sorrow. We may observe similar instances of manifestations in the broad sense when we apperceive the speaker as a person who is thirsty when he is asking for a glass of water, or as the person who is wishing, doubting, proving, when we hear a statement of appropriate expressions communicating a wish, a doubt, or a proof. Indicatory manifestative characteristics cease when the speaker has completed his speech. After that, all that remains is the statement itself. Indicatory manifestative characteristics are fleeting, whereas the meaning of the expressed statement is objective in the sense that it may be repeatedly uttered as the same by anybody who speaks the same words.

We shall now turn our attention to expressions as meaningful signs. Obviously, expressions do not occur in isolation, but if we wish to explore the meaning an expression carries, we must do so by isolating it and thereby removing it from the broader setting in which it is normally found and where the meaning is always affected, sometimes considerably modified, by the contextual and situational functions the expression is made to fulfill. As we stated earlier, an expression has at all times a meaning, and, for instance, in communicative speech it also acquires manifestative characteristics. We should repeat that an expression retains its meaning even when it acquires, in addition, certain "significations" that are the result of contextual and situational functions it fulfills. We distinguish, then, between the meaning of an expression and its manifestative characteristics on the one hand, and the meaning of an expression and its signification on the other. Because we wish to explore the expression as meaningful sign, i.e., what it means, as well as the basis on which it can carry out the function of meaning and referring to our intentional (i.e., intended) object, we must bracket those functions of an expression that are indicatory (manifestative) and significatory (revealing the effects of the setting on the meaning).

Every expression, considered in isolation, is, then, a sound-formation that carries a meaning. The meaning is usually conferred on the sound-formation by convention (unless we coin an expression). Every time we use or hear an expression we actually confer its conventional meaning on it again: we mean it to have this meaning. This is our "intentional" act, whereby an expression acquires a meaning and forms with it a unity. It is on this basis that I choose an expression with a (conventionally) conferred meaning, and I use it to refer to an object or to a state of affairs which I "have in mind," i.e., to an intentional object or to an intentional state of affairs. Consequently we can distinguish two different intentional acts whenever we use an expression. By the first of these acts we mean directly our intentional object or state of affairs, and by the second intentional act we mean that intentional object (or state of affairs) indirectly through the intermediary of a meaningful sign which is its appropriate expression. Why, then, do we choose a certain expression to refer to our directly intended object? We do so because we recognize that whatever the meaning of the expression "intends" is more or less, or sometimes even essentially identical with, what we mean, what we intend, what our intentional object is. We could say that the "meaning-intention" of the expression means an object—which is its own intentional object, its intentional correlate—and that that object is essentially identical with our intentional object. It is because of this essential identity of the two intentional objects— an identity that is possible only in respect to the general idea under which the two intentional objects fall—that the expression refers to *our* directly (originally) intended object. This is the manner in which the referential connection occurs.

When we hear an expression, we become aware of its potential meaning-intention, we actualize it, and we usually seek to realize the referential connection between the intentional correlate of the expression and an intentional object (or state of affairs) that we mean. The referential connection is realized when we can intuit in the reflection of a general idea the essential identity between the correlate of the expression and the intentional object which we supply. A distinction must therefore be made between expressions in whose case a referential connection is realized and those whose meaning-intention is "empty." Whenever the meaning-intention of an expression is more or less actualized by our acts of "meaning-fulfillment," the referential connection may be realized.

An analysis of our experience of apprehending an expression as a meaningful sign shows that while the sign itself, i.e., the sound-formation, keeps its perceptible presence, it provokes our meaning-conferring act, and our interest shifts to the meaning-intention of the expression, to its own intended correlate which we seek to actualize by our acts of meaning-fulfillment. These are some of the moments of our intentionality which are welded in the unity of our experience. It may be useful to add a brief comment about our meaning-conferring act that leads to our apprehension of the sound-formation as a meaningful sign. The mere sensory datum of a sound-formation cannot by itself induce our meaning-conferring act, just as the mere sensory datum of the bark of a dog cannot become a percept without our first knowing from experience what these objects are. This means that if we are to recognize the sound-formation as a meaningful sign, we must perform this *objectifying interpretation* on the basis of experience. When an interpretive grasp of an expression occurs, the sensory datum of the sound-formation normally recedes or vanishes. The sensory datum of the sound-formation is therefore only a fleeting basis for the apprehension of the meaning of an expression.

Since the meaning-intention of an expression parallels our direct intending of an intentional object and since the meaning-intention can refer to our intentional object only because the correlate meant by the expression proves to be essentially identical with the intentional object as we mean it directly, it follows that one must never take the directly intended referential object for the meaning (i.e., the correlate) of the expression. By way of illustration, the expression "this horse" means a correlate which happens to be essentially identical with any one of a multitude of instances in which any horse may be meant to be thus determined. Husserl speaks here of a "sphere of different meaning-fulfillments." Consequently one and the same meaning-intention may refer here to different individual objects (horses), and this could not be the case if the meaning-intention of that expression were to refer directly—and therefore exclusively—to a single referential object. Conversely, the meanings of different expressions may refer to the same object. For instance, it is to Napoleon that we refer in the expressions "the victor of Jena" and "the vanquished of Waterloo." Finally, we should at least note that the expression "the square circle" is not without meaning, but that its meaning-intention does not permit any meaning-fulfilling act because there can be no corresponding intentional object, and no referential connection can conceivably be realized. If the meaning-intention of the expression accords with any object (or state of affairs) that we mean, then our meaning-fulfilling act *covers* the range of the meaning-intention and the referential connection between the meaning-intention and the object we mean makes sense, even if the object is fictive (a gold mountain).

We may sum up our analysis by stating that the term "covering" suggests a mutual fitness between (a) the object as we mean it and on the basis of which we fulfill the meaning-intention of the expression, and (b) the manner in which the meaning of the expression projects its correlate. This situation is analogous to one in which two persons perceive one and the same object. Each has his perception, and to the extent to which both mean the same object, the content of one perception is identical with the other. In the same way the object as it is intended by the meaning of the expression may be essentially identical with the object as we mean it. In other words, the content of the meaning-intention and the content of our meaning are essentially identical in respect to the idea of that object. Consequently, every act of meaning-fulfillment implies our directedness not only to our intentional object (or state of affairs) and to the correlate of the meaning-intention of the expression, but also to that ideal correlate—the general idea—in respect to which both are essentially identical. This, then, is what we must understand if we speak of the referential object of an expression; the latter can indeed not be identified with the meaning of the expression.

Chapter 2

1. Introduction

In his "Essentiale Fragen" Ingarden aimed above all at determining the essential nature of an object and its idea. Similarly, in *The Literary Work of Art*, he again seeks to determine the essential structure and the idea of the literary work. Here he is not directly concerned with questions about the author, artistic creation, aesthetic stance, and value judgments. All of these questions, he rightly argues, should be raised only when the essential structure of the literary work, its idea with its constants and their interrelations, has been adequately established. Consequently, up to a point he ignores the reader, especially one who would apprehend the literary work with such worldly prepossessions as those derived from personal bias, or from social, political, or religious convictions. Obviously, he cannot bracket the relatively "neutral" mental operations that are necessary for bringing structural elements or aesthetic qualities of a literary work of art to light.

When we consider *The Literary Work of Art*, we find—in addition to his main concern of determining the invariant structures of a literary work—three themes running through Ingarden's exploration. One of these follows the differences that distinguish the heteronomous existence of the world presented in the literary work of art from objective reality. The second follows the path of inquiry in respect to the interrelated structural functions within the unfolding stratified literary work. The third leads us consistently to the recognition of an ascending structural pattern: the basic configuration of functionally and cohesively interrelated elements always founds a new entity. If this new entity is also constituted by a configuration of functionally interrelated elements, it too founds a new entity, and so on until the new entity—an essence—emerges as the culmination of the total structure.

An analysis of the idea of the literary work cannot begin with any one literary work of whatever kind. When we speak of the idea of the literary work, we postulate a literary configuration as an ideal correlate of which any one literary work is an individuation. The literary work is thus conceived as a structure whose interrelated heterogeneous constants are fused into a configuration by the reciprocal functions they fulfill. This conception brackets the variables of individual works and focuses on an investigation of the literary structure itself. For this reason the creative processes, the "value" of a work derived from its relation to other works, and the multiplicity of "formal" and "thematic" variables resulting from social, psychological, intellectual, and other developments are not taken into consideration within this investigation.

According to Ingarden, every literary work of art is an organic structure of interrelated "layers" of sound-formations, meaning-units, schematized aspects, and presented objects. The structure of each layer is first examined in isolation so that its constitutive moments may be identified and their connections and functions established. Thus Ingarden turns his attention to words before examining them in the context of a sentence, and to sentences before considering them in the larger context of connected sentences. This is the characteristic pattern of analysis that is based on successive phenomenological reductions. It focuses on the determination of the constitutive configuration of objects, the general idea under which they fall, and the necessary connections entailed by their essential nature. No doubt Ingarden chose the term "layer" from polyphonic composition, where heterogeneous layers individually contribute their respective melodies to the whole organic structure. The layers of the literary work differ from each other in that each has its own particular material components. Each layer also plays its part with regard to every other layer and within that new entity which emerges, as we shall see, from the work's structure as a whole; but every layer does not play the same part in every literary kind. Furthermore, by virtue of its special features, each layer brings its own qualities of aesthetic value to the aesthetic value of the whole work. Quite apart from the structure of layers, we shall have to consider the structural dimension of the literary work that causes it to have an extension from a so-called beginning to a given end, i.e., its structural order of sequence.

2. The layer of sound-formations

A. *The word and the word-sound*

In every literary work we encounter words, sentences, and connected sentences. Each of these formations consists of a unity of phonic material and meaning. We shall begin by asking what we mean when we say that we hear repeated pronunciations of the "same word." Actually we never hear the same phonic material when a word is pronounced by different people or even by the same person several times. Strictly speaking, in every instance we hear new and different phonic material, and yet we believe that we hear the same word even when it is mispronounced. It is obvious that our impression of sameness does not stem from the phonic material, but from the word's essential sound-configuration which is reflected in the constant qualitative moment of the general idea in respect to which the several utterances of the word are considered the same, in spite of the variables in pronunciation. It is on the sound-configuration that we confer a meaning, and a sound-configuration is thus concretized in any utterance of the phonic material. On that basis the variably uttered phonic material is recognized as the carrier of one and the same meaning regardless of whether we pronounce, for instance, "tomato" in the American or the British manner. By *word-sound* (*Wortlaut*) Ingarden designates a word's *essential* sound-configuration which we endow with meaning. We may describe a word-sound as a sound-configuration that carries a meaning and imposes it on the phonic material in which it is concretized. Obviously, a word-sound cannot be equated with the concrete phonic material in which it happens to be concretized.

It may seem, then, that a word-sound is an ideal object of a distinct kind. Indeed, if we could show that the sound configuration and the meaning carried by the word-sound are constant in the sense of being immutable and timeless, we could consider the word-sound to be ideal. The fact is, however, that the sound-configuration as well as the meaning with which it is endowed are only relatively constant, for they change under various conditions in the course of time. Mutability is the reason for rejecting the notion of the ideality of word-sounds. Nor may we claim that they are real, for as we have just noted, a word-sound cannot be equated with any of its concretizations.

What, then, is the relation between the word-sound and the *word*? The word is a concretized word-sound endowed with meaning, and normally occurs in some form of discourse. When used in speech, the word may be endowed with manifestative qualities such as tones of sharpness or mildness which indicate, in a broad sense, the speaker's frame of mind. Clearly, *these* tonal qualities are not moments of the word-sound, though some word-sounds may have potential tonal qualities of their own that emerge in the course of any concretization and do not depend on the manner in which they are uttered.

Under certain circumstances manifestative qualities do not emerge. This is most obviously the case within a terminological (for instance, scientific) system where the meaning carried by the word-sound is all that matters and the frame of mind of the speaker is of no relevance. Ingarden calls words of this kind "lifeless." Even in the language of social communication we may find lifeless words or phrases—for instance, clichés. "Vivid" words or phrases, on the contrary, possess tonal characteristics that do not depend on manifestative qualities supplied by the speaker, but suffuse the sound-configuration itself, as onomatopoeic words do. Some vivid words evolve in the course of the social, intellectual, and spiritual development of a shared life within a language community. For instance, certain terms can sometimes assume in political discussions a tonal quality of abuse, ridicule, or invective. Some obscene words are also vivid; i.e., their sound-configuration is capable of evoking, for instance, a visual representation of the object which they designate. A neutral (e.g., scientific) or socially more acceptable word normally precludes such a meaning-fulfilling act. When Ingarden claims that a word-sound itself may contain aesthetic qualities which are due to a special relation between its potential tonal quality and its meaning, he is suggesting that in certain cases, within a given language, we may find a sound-configuration possessing a special adequacy for the realization of the meaning in a given tonal unity. This fact becomes quite striking when we compare the tonal quality of certain words in one language with that in another language, or in different local pronunciations of the same language in which a special pronunciation is considered to be the "proper" one.

B. Phonic configurations of higher rank

Words, as we know, do not occur in isolation; they are always dependent elements of the broader context of a sentence. When a word does seem to occur in isolation (e.g., "Help!"), it is essentially a compressed statement. Even a sentence is only relatively independent, because it is normally a link in a chain of meaningfully connected sentences. We noted before that no formation is ever the mere sum of its components, but a whole new entity that has its own being. The same holds true of a sentence whose words merge into a unity of meaning and sound-formation ("melody"). The phonic aesthetic quality of a word in a sentence is affected ("colored") by the proximity of other words, but the melody of the sentence does not depend only on the phonic quality of the words within it but also on the function that the sentence is meant to serve. Of course, individual words do not lose their identity in a sentence, but they acquire secondary characteristics, so-called "relative characteristics," which pertain at the same time to their phonic quality and to their meaning; at this point, however, we are focusing on the sound-quality of aesthetic value alone. For instance, we may consider the effect of the contrast produced by the immediate succession of words with soft sounds and words with harsh sounds. The effect of juxtaposed contrasting colors may illustrate the distinction between the unaltered identity of a word and the relative sound-characteristics it may acquire in a sentence. These characteristics may sometimes result from the sequence of vowels of a certain pitch. Wherever these melodic characteristics come to the fore in a literary text—and particularly, though by no means exclusively, when the text is intended to be heard—the author's art may be appreciated by the manner in which he exploits such potential aesthetic effects. Rhyme and assonance play, of course, a major role in the constitution of these aesthetic characteristics. Melodic characteristics are always conspicuous in spoken language, especially in dialects. Characteristics of feeling or mood (e.g., sad, gay, powerful) may be brought about by manifestative qualities of speech, but they may result also from the phonic material itself, as we know from listening to music or to a foreign language we do not understand.

Rhythm also furnishes a special aesthetic characteristic to the word in context. It is *based on* a recurrence of accented and nonaccented sounds, but it cannot be equated with this recurrence (just as the word-sound cannot be equated with the phonic material in which it is concretized). Rhythm is, then, an aesthetic quality which is founded in, and emerges from, a configuration of accented and nonaccented sounds which recur in a pattern. Regular rhythms require the recurrence of the same pattern of accentuation, whereas free rhythms are found in free verse and prose. A certain variation of rhythms forming a unified pattern of greater or lesser complexity accounts for rhythmic characteristics of a higher rank. The sequence of word-sounds has an immanent rhythm which determines the rhythmic qualities of a text and prescribes the manner of recitation. If we disregard these exigencies, we may impair the quality of the layer of sound-formations. The immanent rhythm of a text determines a certain pace of recitation. Obviously, one may increase or decrease the actual pace of delivery in a given recitation without affecting the rhythmic configuration of the sequence of words, but we must agree that within broad limits, a certain pace is more appropriate than another, exactly because the rhythmic configuration demands it.

Some rhythmic qualities do not depend solely on the phonic components of a sequence of words, but on the full meaning of sentences. Words perform various functions in a sentence, and some functions demand that certain words receive special emphasis. Other functions make it necessary that certain groups of words be made to form separate cohesive phonic units. These units are marked, for instance, by commas, colons, or periods in the written language; in the spoken language, they are marked by pauses and by a special emphasis on the word preceding a pause, whereas the words which constitute the unit follow each other without interruption according to immanent rhythmic qualities, and not according to the whim of an individual recitation. Both regular and free rhythms prove the interdependence of the phonic components and of the meanings of words in a sequential order.

According to Ingarden, the function of pauses is to separate the unity of meaning of a set of phonic units from that of another set. Although this statement is valid, we ought to add that the separation itself serves a more complex purpose, and the pause is the means by which this purpose is achieved. Every single word contributes its individual meaning and the signification it derives from its contextual position to the phonic set to which it belongs. Consequently the phonic units constitute a set when their unity of meaning is established. At that point we perceive not only the individual meaning-units, but also the unity of meaning of the phonic set as a whole. Hence a pause is a necessary device by which the unity of meaning of a number of individual phonic units merging into a set may be apprehended. The pause is, then, a gathering-point at which the meanings of word-sounds concretized in a phonic set emerge as a unity of meaning. Pauses are indispensable for the apprehension of larger meaning-units which themselves are constituted by smaller units whose relations and connections need to be welded, during appropriate pauses, into ever larger units of coherent meanings. It is during the silence of a pause that we can grasp the full import of preceding connected expressions as we allow their unity of sound and meaning to emerge.

Since the concrete phonic material is different in every individual utterance, it is obvious that it cannot be part of the literary work, whereas the configuration of a word-sound is an indispensable part of it. Although the manifestative quality is not a moment of the word-sound, it necessarily characterizes certain literary works, especially a stage play. The same holds true of rhythmic patterns, pace, and melody when these characteristics emerge in certain works as a direct consequence of a particular arrangement of words.

C. The role of the layer of sound-formations in the structure of the literary work

As constitutive elements of the structure of a literary work, sound-formations contribute a special material, as well as particular aesthetic qualities, to the polyphony of the work. Their role in that polyphony may be instantly recognized in the transformation of a work when it is translated. Even though the aesthetic qualities of the sound-formations of a literary work in two different languages may reveal some moments that both versions have in common, it is not those moments that concern us, but the polyphony of all the layers, because it is the synthesis of the aesthetic qualities of all layers that constitutes the polyphony of a given work and determines its uniqueness and aesthetic value. That synthesis is bound to be different if the aesthetic quality of one layer is appreciably changed, as is the case in a translation.

Ingarden states that the existence of a literary work might not be impossible if the layer of sound-formations—insofar as it enriches and modifies the polyphony—were omitted. This, we hasten to add, does not mean that the layer itself is dispensable; it does mean that its functions of enriching and modifying the polyphony are less important than its ontological function of providing a material base for the structure of the other layers, and of revealing them, which is its phenomenological function. The ontological function of the layer of sound-formations is to provide a material base for all other layers, and most immediately for the layer of meaning-units. The phenomenological function of the layer of sound-formations is to allow us to apprehend word-meanings carried by word-sounds.

3. The layer of meaning-units

A. Basic assumptions

The layer of meaning-units plays a determining role in the constitution of the other layers of a literary work. The material of this layer has properties which we have to consider by themselves before the constitutive functions of this layer in relation to other layers can be analyzed. It is the material of this layer that determines the nature of the presented objects, which are very different from those our consciousness projects without the intermediary of meaning-units. Furthermore, it is only through a rational comprehension of the material of meaning-units that the projected presented objects become accessible to our consciousness. Our comprehension depends largely on the clarity, the transparency, of the structure of individual sentences and on the clarity achieved by the manner in which sentences are connected. This means that clarity depends on the unambiguity of the components of an individual sentence and on their arrangement with such precision as to permit their reciprocal functions to constitute an immediately comprehensible unity of meaning. The same holds true for sentences that are components of a complex of sentences whose clarity again depends on the transparency of its cohesion. The choice of components and the manner of their arrangement may result in ambiguity or precision, in complexity or simplicity, and in a variety of other characteristics whose combinations constitute the overall aesthetic character, the *style*, of the layer of meaning-units in a given work. The style of this layer must be in harmony with that of the layer of schematized aspects, for where this is not so, the presented objects projected by the meanings may fail to come to the fore. The overall stylistic character of this layer is a new qualitative—aesthetic—entity which is based on, but not reducible to, its varied characteristics. Like any formation, it has its own being which is irreducible to the mere sum of its components. Consequently, the layer of meaning-units has its own aesthetic characteristics which it contributes to the polyphony of the work as a whole.

The role of a word in a sentence and the characteristics derived from its position in a context can logically be considered only after we have established its essential configuration. Ingarden therefore temporarily brackets the context which a sentence (or a sequence of sentences) may establish. Before we can focus on the configuration of the word-meaning and on the purely intentional object that the meaning-intention of the word projects, we must first review the relation between *our* intentional object and the intentional act of consciousness by which we mean it, and the relation between the meaning-intention of a meaning-unit and *its* intentional object.

The term "intentional," as we noted earlier, is used to describe our *acts* of consciousness. They are intentional in that an object is our directly intended target, and we mean to reach it without the intermediary of meaning-units. The term "intentional" is also used to describe the intended *object* which is the target of our act of consciousness. Every object, i.e., every thing, property, condition, process, activity, etc., toward which our consciousness is directed—which is intended (meant) by us—is an intentional object. In a so-called simple act of meaning (sometimes called a simple act of projection), we have in mind an object *as schema* (for instance, a table), without its individual particular determinants. Such an object obviously has no real existence. It is a projection of our intentional act of consciousness wherein the object's *purely intentional* existence and nature (in this example, an indeterminate table) originate. In a sequence of subsequent discrete acts we may *mean* a somewhat particularized table (without, however, *imagining* it at the same time), but we may still not mean that this object is in any way real; we may still mean it to be purely intentional. With each new discrete act we may supply an additional feature to the already projected and now heteronomously existing purely intentional object. Although it derives its existence and its intended nature from the intentional act, it does become the intentional correlate of this act as soon as it is projected. In a sense, it "transcends" the projecting consciousness—it *confronts* it—and becomes a target of the originating act of consciousness and of any subsequent one (such as the discrete acts we have just mentioned, or the recall of the projected object): in brief, *intentionality entails confrontation*. This is why the purely intentional object cannot be a moment of our act of consciousness by which it is projected.

A real (and also an ideal) object has existential independence; i.e., it does not require for its subsistence (continuing existence) the existence of any other object. It *may*, if my consciousness is directed toward it, become the target of my act of consciousness; in this case the independent object becomes "also intentional." A heteronomous purely intentional object, on the other hand, does depend on an act of consciousness for its existence (for its coming into being) and its subsistence. All objects, be they purely intentional or independent, are *originally intentional* if they are *direct* targets of our intentional acts and thus confront our acts of meaning. If, on the other hand, we mean an object *indirectly through the intermediary of meaning-units*, we say that such a target is a *derived purely intentional object*. We call it that because it is really the intentional object of the meaning-intention of a meaning-unit whose intentionality may be said to derive from and, so to speak, reflect our original acts of meaning, our original intentionality. We have already seen that no referential, i.e., originally intentional, object can ever be the direct correlate of a meaning-unit and we may now add that the derived intentional object of a meaning-unit is necessarily purely intentional, even if the referential (originally intentional) object to which it refers is independent. To sum up, we may state that our intentional act of consciousness must be distinguished from its target, the intentional autonomous or heteronomous object that confronts consciousness; that a purely intentional object is heteronomous, whereas an independent object is autonomous and only "also intentional"; and that an object which is the direct target of our consciousness is originally intentional, whereas an object intended through the intermediary of meaning-units is a derived purely intentional object.

Depending on whether an originally intentional object is meant to be existentially independent or purely intentional, *our intentionality* (i.e., the way we mean it) reveals a different *formal structure* and also a different capacity (trans. "content"), i.e., a different capability of containing the formal structure and the qualifications of the intentional object. If we project an *independent* object, we mean it as we must mean it, because the autonomous object imposes its formal structure on our intentionality. Besides, our intentionality comes into play only if our intentional act happens to be directed at the object. Because the particular constitutive nature of an independent object is already established before the act of meaning occurs, the capacity of our intentionality is determined by the immanence of that object's constitutive nature, which no intentional act of ours can change. For this reason an autonomous object cannot be "carried" by the intentionality which projects (means) it. Such an object is itself the carrier of *its own* capacity, which we must distinguish from the capacity of the projecting intentionality. The capacity of an autonomous object contains: (1) the formal structure of the object, i.e., the formal structure of, for instance, a thing, property, condition, process, or activity; (2) within this formal structure, the particular constitutive nature of the individual object; and (3) the existential character (for instance, the object may be real).

Let us now consider *our intentionality* by which we project a purely intentional heteronomous object whose existence and nature originate directly in our act of consciousness. Suppose that a purely intentional object is being projected and that we mean it to have the formal structure of a thing. Within the bounds of its *intended* formal structure, we mean it to have certain purely intentional features that should constitute its nature. However, as we stated earlier, we can vary, alter, or take away the features with which we endow the purely intentional object's constitutive nature. The features of such an object are contained in our intentionality—in *its* capacity—before they are projected to constitute the nature of that object. The existence (and hence the formal structure of a certain thing) and the nature of that object are in fact carried by pure intentionality. To put it differently, its formal structure (for instance, that of a thing) is "subordinate" to the formal structure of pure intentionality that projects it. And yet, once the formal structure of the purely intentional object has been projected, it *seems* as if it were the carrier of the intended constitutive nature. Thus, for instance, if the purely intentional object is meant to have the formal structure of a table, that intended thing seems to be the carrier of its properties and traits. In a sense this carrier is like the one that carries the constitutive nature of an autonomous object called "table," but the difference lies in that the "carrier" of the intended constitutive nature of a purely intentional object is itself carried by the formal structure and capacity of pure intentionality. Therefore we must repeat that this is a "carrier" only in appearance, for the *thing* and its *nature* are those of a purely intentional object which "draws its seeming existence and nature from the projecting intention of the act of meaning." [1] A purely intentional object is thus a mere *semblance* and depends in its "entire existence and existential qualifications [*Sosein*]—in spite of its transcendence ["confrontation" in our terminology]—on the existence and nature of the appropriate act of consciousness." [2] It should be emphasized that we are normally unaware of pure intentionality as the carrier of such a heteronomous object, and that we therefore mistakenly assume that the purely intentional object is constituted by its own capacity. This is one of the reasons for what we may call, in Coleridge's words, "a semblance of truth sufficient to procure for these shadows of imagination that willing suspension of disbelief for the moment, which constitutes poetic faith." We may conclude by summing up that the capacity of the purely intentional object is a projection of pure intentionality. It has only the appearance of containing the object's formal structure, constitutive nature, and existential character.

We noted the distinction between an originally intentional object which we mean directly through an intentional act of consciousness, and a derived purely intentional object which we mean indirectly through the intermediary of meaning-units. When an originally intentional object becomes the referential object of a meaning-unit, we know that this referential function is possible because of the essential identity of the correlate of the meaning-unit with the originally intentional object; the originally intentional object is, as it were, meant twice: by the intentionality of the act of consciousness that projects the object directly and by the intentionality of the word-meaning that derives from the intentionality of the act of consciousness. Ingarden calls the *word-meaning* (the meaning-intention, but not its correlate) a "mirror image" of our intentional *act* by which we *mean* an object directly. We must remember, however, that no meaning-unit can, for the reasons we have already discussed, mean an object in quite the same fashion as it is meant by the direct intentionality of the act of con-

1. *Das literarische Kunstwerk*, 3rd rev. ed. (Tübingen: Max Niemeyer Verlag, 1965), p. 128; George G. Grabowicz, trans., *The Literary Work of Art* (Evanston: Northwestern University Press, 1973), p. 123. Hereafter cited as *LK* and trans.

2. *LK*, p. 127; trans., pp. 121–22.

sciousness. A meaning-unit projects only a schema of the object's capacity. Furthermore, Ingarden constantly stresses the disparity between, on the one hand, the intensity of lived experience accompanying original projections, and on the other hand, the derived intentionality of the word-meaning. An originally projected purely intentional object is "subjective" in the sense that it is accessible only to the projecting consciousness. The "experiential background" that surrounds such an original projection is inaccessible and may be only inferred from a corresponding projection effected through the intermediary of intersubjective meaning-units.

B. *Word-meanings*

I. THE INTENTIONAL DIRECTIONAL FACTOR

So far we have dealt with word-sounds, phonic configurations of higher rank, the role of the layer of sound-formations in the structure of the literary work, and with the relation between word-sound and word-meaning. We shall now turn our attention to *isolated* word-meanings. Depending on the moments of their configurations, there are different kinds of word-meanings. *Nominal word-meanings* (names of objects) or *nominal expressions* (such as "the center of the earth," "red ball," "colored paper") need to be distinguished from other word-meanings because their configurations reveal a special cohesion, a unity of meaning, within which the constitutive moments depend on each other in various ways.

The *intentional directional factor* is the moment of the nominal word-meaning to which we shall turn our attention first. The intentionality of the nominal word-meaning reflects our intentional act directed toward our originally intentional object. The intentional directional factor of a nominal word-meaning mirrors the direction of that act, although its immediate target is the purely intentional object projected by the word-meaning itself. Obviously, if the target of the meaning-intention is a single object, the intentional directional factor follows a single radiating line: it is "single-rayed." If the meaning-intention is directed toward several objects, the intentional directional factor is "multi-rayed," and it may be so in a definite manner, as in "my three sons," or in an indefinite manner, as in "people"—to use Ingarden's examples.

Depending on the existential moment of the originally intentional object to which the word-meaning refers, the intentional directional factor may be *constant* and *actual* or *variable* and *potential*. It is constant and actual if the referential object is meant to be autonomous and its particular constitutive nature is therefore meant to be determinate. If the originally intentional object is meant to be heteronomous, it is projected as a schema whose intended constitutive nature is meant to be a configuration to which potential and variable traits may be added by discrete acts. The intentional directional factor is here therefore variable and potential, but it may be stabilized by appropriate discrete acts. The intentional directional factor of such word-meanings as "red" or "small" is meant to be variable and potential as long as they are not applied to an object and the shade of "red" or the size of "small" is not yet meant to be determinate. This brief discussion of the intentional directional factor of nominal word-meanings is sufficient for our immediate purposes. We shall soon see that intentional directional factors of verbal word-meanings have different functions.

2. THE MATERIAL CONTENT OF THE NOMINAL WORD-MEANING

The capacity of every object, as we know, comprises the object's formal structure, constitutive nature, and existential character. Since the intentionality of a word-meaning reflects our intentional act directed toward an object, the word-meaning also parallels the manner in which we mean the capacity of that object. The moment of the nominal word-meaning called the *material content* reflects the *intended constitutive nature* of the intentional object. The intentional directional factor is constant and actual when the projected object is meant to be autonomous and its constitutive nature established. When the projected object is meant to be heteronomous, its particular constitutive nature is meant to be fluctuating before it is stabilized (assuming it *is* stabilized), and the intentional directional factor is therefore potential and variable. Accordingly, the material content of a nominal expression such as "colored paper" does not reflect a determinate constitutive nature because "colored" is variable, and hence the particular nature of that object is not meant to be stabilized. For this reason the intentional directional factor of this nominal expression is variable.

3. THE FORMAL CONTENT OF THE NOMINAL WORD-MEANING

The capacity of an intentional object comprises an intended formal structure, and this intention is reflected by a corresponding moment of the nominal word-meaning, a moment called the *formal content*. That the intentional object is intended to have the formal structure of, for instance, a thing, or a process, or an activity, is normally not meant in quite the same explicit manner as the material content is intended by the word-meaning. Ingarden calls this implicit manner of intending *functional*, and speaks of the *formative function* of the nominal word-meaning.

4. THE EXISTENTIAL CHARACTERIZATION AND THE
EXISTENTIAL SETTING OF THE NOMINAL WORD-MEANING

The capacity of an intentional object comprises its intended existential character, and the nominal word-meaning reflects that intention by the moment of *existential characterization*, whereby the object is meant to be, for instance, real or ideal. This moment is usually meant in a functional manner. The moment of *existential setting*, which should be distinguished from the moment of existential characterization, may already be reflected in an isolated *nominal expression* even without specifications provided by a sentence. In the example "the capital of Poland," the meaning contains not only the characterization (the object is one of those whose character is of the type of real objects), but also the real setting: the object really exists *as a fact*. When we project the object "the character Hamlet," we recognize that while its existential character is that of the type of real objects, it has no real existential setting in spatiotemporal reality, although it does have a setting in the fictive "reality" of Shakespeare's play.

We noted the dependence of the intentional directional factor on the material content. It is easy to see that any intended modification of the material or of the formal content is bound to affect all the moments of a nominal word-meaning because they constitute a unified configuration and thus perform jointly the function of projecting an object. It now remains to point out that the object that is projected by a nominal word-meaning is, regardless of its formal structure, something that is meant to have a self-contained unity, something that is meant to be a carrier of its properties and traits. Hence not only a thing (table), but even a process (fermentation), or an activity (writing, walking) is projected as *static*, whereas acts are projected in their unfolding or becoming. It is, then, toward a static target that a nominal intentional factor is directed. It is the formal structure of a static target that is meant functionally by the nominal formal content, and it is the intended constitutive nature of a static target that is meant by the nominal material content.

5. SOME DISTINCTIONS BETWEEN FUNCTIONS

So-called "functional words" (e.g., this, that, here, there, and, to, by, etc.) are used to perform certain syntactic functions in respect to objects designated by other words, especially nouns, and also in respect to sentences. When they are used in respect to nouns, they cause them to form more or less complex meaning-units ("the boy and his father"), and at the same time, they establish functionally certain intentional relationships between the objects projected by the respective nominal word-meanings.

Strictly speaking, there is no material content in the meaning of functional words, but there is a moment that Ingarden considers analogous to it in words such as *next to* or *under* which characterize the intentional object with regard to its localization, without of course determining its nature. Because they have no material and formal content, functional words cannot project an intentional object. Consequently, they can perform their functions only with regard to those objects that are already projected formally and materially.

Another type of function may be noted in the meanings of adjectives in nominal expressions. Using the example "a red, smooth sphere," let us first consider the adjectives *in isolation*. "Red" (similarly "smooth") has a variable and potential directional factor that points implicitly to some object with which "red" is meant to be connected. Although this object is not yet determined with regard to its constitutive nature, the isolated adjectives point functionally to its material content at least insofar as they imply that the object is red and smooth. However, the object's nature must be formally so constituted that it can be red and smooth, and to this extent at least the adjectives in that nominal expression determine functionally a formal content also. When we now consider the *isolated* word-meaning "sphere," we note that it is meant as a schema in this case. Thus "red," "smooth," and "sphere," considered in isolation, have directional factors with certain bounds of variability. When we then consider the unified expression, and still mean "sphere" as a schema, we note that the three directional factors are converging on the same schematically projected object-correlate. In the course of this convergence their bounds of variability become restricted by virtue of the reciprocal functional effects they have on each other. Thus the object becomes stabilized at least to a certain degree of determinateness while the converging directional factors of "red" and "smooth" fuse with that of the nominal word-meaning "sphere." Consequently the main function of adjectives in nominal expressions is to bring to a certain degree of specificity some of the determinants of the constitutive nature of the intentional object which is the correlate of the whole expression.

6. THE ISOLATED VERBAL WORD-MEANING

The formal content of the isolated purely verbal "writes," "wrote," "walks," "walked" [3] implies an activity, but not an activity of the static

---

3. In the case of an isolated finite verb the personal pronoun has the sole function of indicating the person and number of the verb. In some languages it may be omitted.

type projected by a nominal word-meaning. The purely verbal function of a finite verb implies that the activity is *dynamic*, for it is meant as an unfolding, a becoming, a happening. It is the formal content of a verb that accounts for its having a temporal quality, so-called *tense*, whereas a nominal word-meaning projects an object which, *by itself*, is devoid of any temporal dimension. The material content of "writes" and "wrote" is the same but differs from that of "walks" and "walked" because it intends materially different activities. Finally, the connectivity of the isolated finite verb reveals the verbal directional factor because the latter calls for and points to a needed complement: some subject which is to carry out (active form) or to undergo (passive form) the projected activity. This complement is of course provided in the sentence. The verbal directional factor of the isolated finite verb is potential and variable, even though in some languages the subject is determined at least with regard to the number (singular or plural) and in others with regard to the gender also. The unique and most important feature of the verbal directional factor, as distinct from the nominal one, is that it does not point to the projected activity but to the subject that carries it out or undergoes it.

7. ACTUALITY AND POTENTIALITY OF NOMINAL WORD-MEANINGS

It may be useful to recall at this point our discussion of the essential proposition where the distinction between our direct apprehension of the subject of the proposition and the apprehension of the constants of the general idea was stressed. We shall now seek to determine that distinction from the point of view of the *meaning-intentions* of the nominal word-meaning "square" and of the nominal expression "equilateral rectangular parallelogram." If we assume that an individual square is given, the meaning-intention of the word-meaning and that of the nominal expression both refer to it. In this case the intentional directional factor of the word-meaning and that of the nominal expression aim not only at their respective purely intentional correlates but also at one and the same single referential object. However, the material content of each projects a qualitatively different purely intentional object, and the same referential object is therefore meant in two different ways. The previous analyses have led us to recognize that the formal content and the material content of a nominal word-meaning (or nominal expression) project an intentional object *jointly*. Thus the formal content, which is meant functionally, does not project the object only as, for instance, a thing, but also as a thing with certain properties and traits. This is so because simultaneously with the formal content the material content plays its own role in the projection by the manner in which it means the nature of the object. For instance, the material content of the word-meaning "square" projects the constitutive nature of its intentional object (object-correlate) as concretized square-ness, whereas the material content of the meaning of the nominal expression "rectangular equilateral parallelogram" means the nature of its object-correlate to be constituted by the properties of concretized rectangularity, equilaterality, and parallelogramness. Consequently these two meanings designate one and the same referential object in different manners both materially and formally, but the intentional directional factor of the nominal word-meaning (square) and that of the nominal expression (rectangular equilateral parallelogram) ultimately point to one and the same referential object. However, because this object is in each instance actualized *materially* in a different manner, the *meanings* of "square" and of "rectangular equilateral parallelogram" are not identical. What we can see here again is that one and the same object may be apprehended in different ways, and that the correlate of the nominal word-meaning may actualize and render explicit the object as the concretization of an essence, whereas the nominal expression actualizes the same referential object in terms of the constants of its essential constitutive nature and makes them explicit.

Our example shows that this ideal object may be meant either in the light of a concretized essence or in the light of its constant moments. The nominal word-meaning projects the object as an essential unity, whereas the nominal expression projects the same object as a unity of constitutive constants. To put it differently, we may say that these are two different projections made possible by our apprehension of the *concept* of this object. Thus by its material content the nominal word-meaning "square" means *actually* only one part of the concept of the object, whereas by its material content the nominal expression "rectangular equilateral parallelogram" means *actually* another part of the same concept. For reasons we have already mentioned, the formal content of the word-meaning and that of the nominal expression actualize different formal structures of one and the same intentional object. The concept of an ideal object such as the square contains, then, its essential constitutive nature (concretized square-ness) as well as its constants and implied variable determinants. In the case of a real object, the concept contains the object's essential configuration (as reflected in the general idea) and all its properties and implied variable determinants. Our apprehension of the configuration of real objects is based on cognitive acts performed in the course of time. Similarly, the configuration of a character in a novel emerges in the course of the story and can be apprehended only in retrospect. We may conclude that the concept of any object is the *ideal entity* that contains within its range all the potential correlates of any possible material content of nominal word-meanings or expressions by which that object may be projected. Thus every nominal word-meaning or nominal expression presents an actualization of a "part" of the concept.

The more we know about the constitutive nature of an object, the more the range of the concept of that object expands for us. Thus one and the same nominal word-meaning which by way of its correlate may at first actualize the nature of an object only sketchily assumes for us increasingly richer potential meanings as we become better acquainted with the nature of the object that that word-meaning designates. Of course, these potential meanings by which our apprehension of the simple nominal word-meaning is enriched remain *implicit* as long as new nominal expressions do not make the actualizations explicit. What we now need to know is how we are to assess the implicit presence of the potential elements of a concept in a nominal word-meaning when we can have no recourse to our original cognition of the object, i.e., when we have only the literary text to guide our apprehensions. Normally, we are guided by the semantic range of a nominal word-meaning within a given language, i.e., by its semantic range in relation to other similar word-meanings whose range may in part overlap its own. The identification of the range of the implicit semantic potentialities of a word by which a concept is to a certain extent actualized depends on our knowledge of the language. Ingarden calls implicit potentialities of a word-meaning "empty" when they are circumscribed only by the particular language. He calls the implicit potentialities in a word-meaning "ready" when they are suggested by the context in which the word is found in the text of a literary work. Finally, we should note that the empty potentiality of a word-meaning may be readied by the context in such a way as to lead to ambiguities and sometimes even contradictions. For instance, a context may cause the semantic range of a word to encroach on another word which actualizes a different concept, so that a *separation of the concepts* is therefore in order.

8. WORD-MEANINGS AS ELEMENTS OF SENTENCES

So far we have considered word-meanings almost exclusively in isolated words. We shall now consider at least some modifications that occur in the meaning of a word or nominal expression according to the functions it performs in a sentence. *Structural shifts* may be exemplified by juxtaposing (a) "Every. Body. Is. Heavy" and (b) "Every body is heavy." In the first instance every word-meaning is an isolated self-contained whole, whereas in the second the "rigid delimitation" of isolation and self-containment is broken. What, we must ask now, are the structural shifts that ensue in word-meanings as they move from self-contained isolation to their integration into a sentence? While the individual words remain identical with those found in self-contained isolation, the word-meanings, as elements of a sentence, *connect* and *unite*, form a unity of meaning, and make the constitution of sentences possible.

Structural shifts are, however, not the only modifications one may observe when isolated word-meanings become elements of a sentence. Far-reaching modifications, due to *syntactic functions*, appear especially in nominal word-meanings. Although I shall use Ingarden's examples, a different order of presentation seems preferable. We shall consider the modifications of the nominal expression "the Roman consul" when it fulfills certain syntactic functions.

(1) The Roman consul exerted great political influence in the
    Roman state.
(2) C. J. Caesar, the Roman consul, crossed the Rubicon.
(3) M. J. Brutus killed the Roman consul.

The intentional directional factor of the *isolated* nominal expression "the Roman consul" is variable, and it remains so when it fulfills the syntactic function exemplified in the first sentence. The material content determines in both instances the bounds of variability of its intentional directional factor. Although the formal content of the expression projects in both cases an intentional object which is an independent carrier of its properties, the formal content is in the first sentence at the same time modified by an explicit predicative statement.

In the second sentence the variable intentional directional factor of the isolated expression becomes actualized, because in this (appositive) syntactic function, its target is the same intentional object as that of the intentional directional factor of "C. J. Caesar," although the material content of "C. J. Caesar" and that of "the Roman consul" are different. We noted that the formal content of the isolated expression "the Roman consul" and that of the same expression in the first sentence project an intentional object which is an independent carrier of its properties. However, when that expression is in an appositive position, its formal content can no longer project an object which is an independent carrier, because this syntactic function limits the expression to the role of a mere determinant of the truly independent carrier "C. J. Caesar." This modification results, then, in reducing a nominal expression to a function which is analogous to that of adjectives in the composite nominal expression "the red, smooth sphere."

In the third sentence, the directional factor of "the Roman consul" is actual, provided of course that we place the sentence in a context with other sentences that reveal the intended object, or in the context of our historical knowledge. In this sentence, the nominal expression is a direct object and its syntactic function modifies its formal content in that the correlate is at the same time projected as the target of an action. Thus the carrier of its own properties becomes also the bearer of actions directed at it, and consequently, not only the formal but also the material content is thereby modified. This modification is so far-reaching that the nominal expression, as a direct object, loses the independence it would have if considered in isolation. Since the English nominal word-meaning retains its unaltered word-sound regardless of whether it is the subject or the direct object in a sentence, and derives its function as an object from the position it occupies in the sentence, let a Latin example prove the point: *bonus amicus* (good friend) can stand in isolation as an independent carrier, but as a direct object it becomes *bonum amicum* and reveals, in isolation, its dependence; it could not stand by itself as the name of an object without calling its connectivity to our attention. We see, then, that when a nominal word-meaning or expression is a direct object, its meaning is transformed and it demonstrates its belonging to a meaning-unit of a higher (more complex) rank.

In these three instances we have found modifications that do not exist in the isolated nominal word-meaning or expression. More importantly, we may now also recognize that the formal structure of the projected intentional object is modified or even transformed as it moves from being the intended correlate of an isolated word-meaning to become an element of a state of affairs that is the intended correlate of a sentence.

9. THE MODE OF EXISTENCE OF MEANING-UNITS

Let us now return to the problem of the existential mode of word-meanings and review some of the insights we have gained so far. We noted that the derived intentionality of a word-meaning which projects an object is only a mirror image of the intentionality by which our consciousness projects that object; that a word-meaning cannot be real; and that it is not an ideal object, being neither timeless nor immutable. Semantic changes are sufficient proof that the meanings carried by word-sounds are not timeless. Structural shifts, modifications, and transformations of word-meanings in a sentence clearly prove their mutability. Although the structural shifts, modifications, and transformations pertain to the word-meaning, their existence and their qualifications depend on certain acts of our consciousness. We know that a word-meaning, carried by the phonic material of a concretized word-sound, means its purely intentional correlate and that it may be at the same time functionally directed at an independent referential object. Since phonic material cannot engender any one of a word's intentions, and since no word can of itself adjust its intending and govern its modifications, it stands to reason that the intentionality of a word-meaning and its modifications that occur in the formation of sentences must be the result of subjective operations that could not be undertaken if word-meanings were ideal entities, which, as we know, cannot thus be affected by acts of consciousness. These subjective operations are intentional acts of our consciousness. The word-sound as a characteristic configuration is itself the result of an intentional act on the basis of which we determine the meaning carried by the respective phonic material. The phonic material means whatever the intentional act of consciousness wants it to mean, mostly of course on the basis of convention. Our consciousness must project an object directly if that object is to be meant indirectly through the intermediary of a word-meaning. Consequently, as already stated, the meaning-intention carried by a word-sound can have only a derived intentionality. The difference between the intentionality of the act of consciousness and that of the word-meaning is that the former is truly a moment of the act of consciousness, whereas the intentionality of the word-meaning confronts the intentionality of the act of consciousness and is derivative.

We know that a purely intentional object draws its seeming existence and nature from the projecting intentionality of the act of consciousness. Likewise, the derived intentionality of the word-meaning draws its existence from the intentionality of the original act of consciousness, which it confronts. It seems to be the intentionality of an act of consciousness, but it is merely a reflection of it. Thus a word seems to intend its object-correlate, but because its meaning-intention is conferred on it, that correlate is ultimately meant by an act of consciousness. Although we shall have to amplify our findings later, we may say that these acts of consciousness constitute one of the ontic foundations of the existential heteronomy of a word-meaning, and thus of a sentence, and of connected sentences as well.

C. Sentences

I. THE SENTENCE-FORMING OPERATION

The operation whereby the intentionality of consciousness projects its mirror image upon the restricted field of an isolated word-meaning is rare. It consists of numerous discrete acts in the course of which the elements of the word-meaning are gradually welded into a unity. This unity endows the word with its identity, on the strength of which it may be repeatedly used for the formation of complex meaning-units, for instance sentences, for language provides us with a ready supply of established word-meanings. It is in the formulation of a sentence that we can observe most clearly the complexity of discrete acts of consciousness, i.e., those subjective operations by which we choose, connect, and unify word-meanings in view of the intended sentence-correlate; and it is in this operation that the shifts, modifications, and transformations we have discussed actually originate. The operation becomes more extensive as we move from the formulation of sentences to more complex structures of connected sentences that we mean to weld into a thematic whole.

For every sentence there is an "established formal schema" that needs to be filled in by a formative operation which may be of either of two types. If the operation is carried out in a more or less strict adherence to the schema, in a sort of reactualization, it differs from a truly original operation, which is a creative act. Whichever sentence-forming operation is performed, both are normally mere phases of a broader operation that encompasses a larger topic, such as a story—the "theme" which we seek to develop. Our orientation toward the topic calls for a broad operation in the light of which every individual sentence is constructed. The extent of our grasp of the topic may, of course, differ according to the degree of our awareness. Thus the clarity with which we fathom the topic affects the operation by which a sentence is formed and the sequence of sentences is arranged. Furthermore, each sentence affects the formation of any subsequent sentence and thus affects the formation of the sequence of the sentences that follow. Conversely, each operation is also affected by the anticipated sentence and sequence of sentences that are to follow. Consequently every sentence-forming operation is carried out, on the one hand, under the impact of the topic as a whole and, on the other hand, under the thrust of preceding and the counterthrust of anticipated formative operations. This formative pattern is the normal one, but one may form a sentence without reference to any conceived topic. However, even in that case, a sentence may contain the germ of a potential development of subsequent related sentences which, if developed, may yield a complex of coherent interdependent sentences that may produce a unified topic.

The structure of a unified topic depends on the type of coherence within each sentence and on the type of coherence resulting from the disposition of the sentences. Both these structural features rest throughout their formative process on subjective operations and vary therefore in every instance; i.e., the "same topic" is treated differently according to the subjective operations that produce it. These operations do not exclude other factors, such as emotions, that affect the mental operation by which sentences are formed. What matters is the recognition that regardless of other factors, the mental operation is indispensable in the sentence-forming process. Since each of us can tell a given story in various ways, it may seem that we are completely free in this operation; this is, however, not so, for we are still tied by the exigencies of the nature of the story.

All these considerations show that word-meanings, meanings of sentences, and meanings of connected sentences that yield meaning-units of higher rank are correlates of subjective intentional operations; that they depend on these operations in their formative process and during their seeming existence, which is neither real nor ideal but heteronomous; that they confront the intentional acts that project them; that their meaning-intentions reflect our intentionality; and, finally, that the purely intentional correlates of meaning-units are intended to conform, to the point of essential identity, to our originally intentional objects—regardless of whether the latter are purely intentional or independent.

2. CHARACTERISTICS OF THE STRUCTURE OF SENTENCES

In the light of previous analyses, a sentence consists basically of a sound-formation and of a unity of meaning derived from the connection and unification of a number of word-meanings. There is of course no sentence-sound that could correspond to the nature and function of a word-sound. Just as every word-meaning points to an object other than itself, namely an object-correlate, the unified meaning of a declarative sentence also projects its correlate, which is a *state of affairs*. Since the unified meaning of a sentence is not merely the sum of its constitutive meaning-units, the function of the meaning of a sentence cannot be merely the sum of the functions of its units. The meaning of a sentence as a whole fulfills the functions dictated by its intended purposes. However, we must first determine what the structure of a sentence is. The following analysis will focus on the simple, *the pure declarative sentence*, regardless of functions which it may serve. We should also remember that just as a word-meaning has a derived purely intentional object, the correlate of a sentence is purely intentional regardless of whether it may *also* refer to an objective independent state of affairs.

The pure declarative sentence "A car is passing by" consists of at least two separate but unified meaning-units. What process accounts for the structural shift from their self-contained isolation to their connection and unification which assure the possibility of a sentence? We are witnessing here an interaction (in the figurative sense of the word) between the separate units. We know that the nominal word-meaning ("car") projects an object both materially and formally, and its intentional directional factor is directed toward this object. The verb ("is passing by") projects an "unfolding" (again in the figurative sense) dynamic activity, and its intentional directional factor finds in the projected object ("car") its complement which stands there "ready" to carry out the activity. Consequently, the activity is presented as effected by the projected object which thus becomes the subject that carries out the activity. (That is not the case in the expression "a passing car," because "passing" serves here merely as a trait.) So far, then, we may state that upon reaching its ready complementary object, the *verbal* intentional directional factor brings about the connection and thus a unity of meaning between the nominally projected object and the unfolding activity, a connection in which the projected object can now be seen performing the activity projected by the verb. Because of the connection, the nominal word-meaning undergoes a major transformation, for its function lies in the projection no longer of a simple intentional object, but of one that is now also the *carrier of an activity* projected by the verbal word-meaning. In the syntactic setting of the pure declarative sentence "This rose is red," the function of the predicate "is red" is to *attribute a trait* to the correlate of the name, but the manner in which the attribution occurs in what we mean to be a pure declarative sentence is verbal; i.e., the having of a trait is meant as an unfolding of an activity.

The syntactic function of the verb in a simple declaration means the object is ready to carry out an activity or to assume a trait, whereas in a declaration that is also intended to fulfill the function of an affirmation, and sometimes keeping the same wording, the verb *also* means to recognize the object as being already the *de facto* carrier of the trait. It is that readiness of the projected object that enables the verbal directional factor to reach the object which is its target, and thus to satisfy the verb's connectivity. Without that readiness the finite verb could not carry out its syntactic function, which is to *unfold an activity* so that it may be carried out or assumed by the subject. Here we see the reciprocal functions of the name (the subject) and of the finite verb waiting for each other to connect so that each may effect its actualization. Thus they establish the *unity of meaning* in a pure declarative sentence, a unity which may then permit this sentence to fulfill its broader function. In conclusion, the meaning-intention of a pure declarative sentence consists of the synthesis of a nominal and a preponderantly verbal meaning-intention.

3. THE CORRELATE OF THE SENTENCE

We should first note again that the correlate of the unified meaning of *any* sentence is purely intentional, even though it may also refer to an objective (independent) state of affairs. We should also recall that the correlate of an interrogative sentence cannot be a state of affairs, but must be a "problem." Because the correlate of an interrogative sentence is not a state of affairs, there can be no counterpart in the sphere of objective existence to which this correlate could *correspond*; consequently this correlate is purely intentional and existentially tied to the meaning-intention of the sentence that projects it. A question cannot be an affirmation of a state of affairs: only its answer can. Similarly, when we consider the correlates of imperative (or optative) sentences, we realize that they cannot be states of affairs either, for only the carrying out of a command (or the fulfillment of a wish) may result in the realization of a state of affairs about which an affirmation in a declarative sentence may be made. It follows therefore that only the correlate of a declarative sentence *may* correspond and refer to an independent state of affairs. We must also remember that a state of affairs is meant to have its existential foundation *within* the object to which it pertains ("This iron is hot"), or in relations of an object to another object ("My son loves his dog"), regardless of whether or not that state of affairs also happens to become the intentional target of our direct (original) act of consciousness and is referred to by the correlate of a declarative sentence. It should of course be clear that the correlate of a declarative sentence has no corresponding independent state of affairs if that sentence is meant to be purely declarative, or if it reflects a false judgment, or if we do not mean to lay a genuine claim to truth. We must, then, always distinguish between our original intentionality, by which we mean a state of affairs to be independent or purely intentional, and the derived intentionality of a declarative sentence whose correlate is always purely intentional but may, if the affirmation contained in it is genuine and valid, also refer to an independent state of affairs. Consequently, the nature of the relation between the purely intentional correlate of a declarative sentence and a referential state of affairs depends ultimately on whether we mean that correlate to be essentially identical with an objective state of affairs.

Before proceeding, we should remind ourselves of the distinction we drew between the projected capacity of an independent object and that of a purely intentional one. We saw that the formal structure of our intentionality projecting an originally intentional independent object is imposed on us by this object's autonomy; that the capacity of this object contains the object's formal structure, including its particular constitutive nature and existential character; and that the formal structure of such an object (for instance, this table) is the true carrier of its particular constitutive nature and of its existential character (of being real). We noted, on the other hand, that the capacity of a purely intentional object, be it projected by an original act of meaning or by a meaning-unit, depends for its formal structure, including its nature and existential character, on our purely intentional acts that carry it. Thus its formal structure is only seemingly the carrier of its nature, for we know that we can, by discrete acts, modify or change it; in fact, we can think it away.

Within the capacity of an object, we distinguished three elements: the formal structure, the particular constitutive nature, and the existential character. Similarly, within the capacity of the correlate of a sentence we distinguish *the formal structure*, *the matter*, and *the existential character*. The formal structure within the capacity of an object may be, for instance, that of a thing, whereas the formal structure of the correlate of a sentence may be that of a state of affairs, a problem, a command. When we compare the existential character of a derived purely intentional object, i.e., the object-correlate of a word-meaning, with that of a derived intentional state of affairs (which is the correlate of a sentence), we find that the existential character of the object may be meant to be of the *type* of real objects and that the existential character of the state of affairs may be meant to be of the *type* of objective states of affairs. However, because such an object and state of affairs are purely intentional, their "reality" is a mere semblance. Let us now note the *matter* in the capacity of the correlates of two sentences: "Is iron hard?" and "Iron is hard." The matter is the same in both correlates, although in the first instance the formal structure is that of a problem, and in the second that of a state of affairs. However, we may also note that while the formal structure of two correlates may be the same, their matter may be different: "This rose is red" and "This dog is brown." As we can see, the formal structure of the state of affairs really comes to light when we vary the matter.

We should now recall that the correlate of a declarative sentence is a state of affairs and that its unified meaning consists of a synthesis of nominal-verbal meaning-intentions. With this reminder we shall now continue our exploration of the correlate of a declarative sentence by contrasting its *formal structure* with that of the correlate of an isolated nominal word-meaning. When an object is projected by a nominal meaning-unit, for instance "this rose," it is given to us as something that is enclosed within itself, that subsists in its unified self-containment. Thus we apprehend in one single grasp the correlate of the projection "this rose" in its self-enclosed *objectified givenness*, so to speak "from without." Now let us see what happens when this correlate of an isolated nominal meaning-unit becomes, in the course of a sentence-forming operation, an element of the projected state of affairs: "This rose is red." First of all, this declarative sentence is of the type in which a statement is made about a determinant of an object ("rose"), and consequently the state of affairs as a whole is meant to be situated within that object. Secondly, as already mentioned, the nominal meaning-unit ("This rose") fulfills the function of enabling the verbal directional factor to reach it as its target, and also that of being ready, as a subject, to carry out the unfolding of an activity (of *having* a trait). If we now consider "this rose" as an element of the correlate of that sentence, we find that while the object is still meant as a unity, it is no longer self-enclosed, as it would be if it were the correlate of an isolated nominal meaning-unit. As soon as the object becomes an element of a state of affairs, its formal structure is meant to be marked by a certain openness; in a figurative sense, we open up the object as we seek to fathom a state of affairs that is lodged within it. When we form a sentence whose correlate is a state of affairs of this type, we break through, as it were, the self-enclosed bounds of the object-correlate of a nominal meaning-unit.

The element of redness is just as much a component of the state of affairs as the object "this rose," but the two elements are differently contained in the state of affairs. The element of redness, like any constitutive property or any variable trait, is marked by existential connectivity and depends on the object by which it is carried and in which it is contained. The object ("This rose"), as carrier of its properties and traits, is thus qualitatively determined by that element, that trait: "this *red* rose." If we wish to grasp the functions of the two elements in the state of affairs, it may be useful to resort to figurative terms and speak of their "interaction" in an "unfolding" state of affairs, although the relation of the two elements is of course static. It is in the light of this fact that we must understand the statement that the object-correlate "this rose"—though meant as a unity—

is no longer self-enclosed when it becomes an element of the state of affairs "This rose is red." We shall now explore the functions of these elements while remembering that the nominal word-meaning "this rose" projects an object that is a unity of "enfolded" determinants. What, then, are the functions of the two elements in that state of affairs?

We know that the particular constitutive nature of things consists of an essential configuration of certain constituent *properties* and of variable *traits*. Color is one of the properties in the nature of a rose, and one of the traits of that property is its hue, which determines the name of the color. Depending on the other traits of color, i.e., chroma (which is its purity or saturation) and brightness (value), we qualify colors as, for instance, dark, bright, light, pale, dull. The traits of color being variable, any one trait may be a determinant of the *particular* constitutive nature of the individual object "this rose," but no trait can be a constituent of its *essential* configuration of properties. In our state of affairs we consider the object ("rose") first of all as fulfilling the function of the carrier of the properties of its essential constitutive nature, but as the state of affairs unfolds, the object also emerges as the carrier of a variable trait (red) that determines one of that object's constitutive properties (color). During the very unfolding of the state of affairs we see its two elements (rose–red) interact as if they faced each other on opposite sides. However, it is an essential characteristic of a sentence-correlate of the type "This rose is red" that it is an unfolding state of affairs within which that opposition of elements is seen in the state of being resolved, surmounted, by the functions of the elements: (a) by that function of the object (as carrier of the properties of its constitutive nature) whereby it becomes also the carrier of any one or of several of its determining traits; and (b) by that function of the trait which effects its becoming a determinant of the object's particular nature. During the resolution of that opposition the trait of redness is seen as if it were being drawn into the existential sphere of the object, but it is not yet meant to be included in it, as it would be in "the red rose," where the resolution of the opposition is meant to be completed. The unfolding of the state of affairs "prepares" our eventual apprehension of that inclusion. This is the reason why "this rose" still appears in a *potential-actual mode* when it is an element of such an unfolding state of affairs. By the potential-actual mode of the object we mean that during the state of affairs in which the opposition between the two elements is being resolved we do not yet apprehend *explicitly* the actuality of the rose's being red, as in "this red rose," but only as potentially red, although *we know* that it is already actually not only red but also the carrier of many other traits.

These considerations recall what we said about "*the* rose," whose constant qualitative moment reflects the essential constitutive nature, the unity of constitutive properties, that account for the rose's being a rose. The carrier "*this* rose," this individual rose, is, in addition, implicitly the carrier of all the traits of its constitutive properties. However, the correlate of "this rose is red" does not mean *explicitly* that this rose is also, for instance, soft and fragrant. Thus potentially explicit states of affairs lie implicitly behind every property and trait of an individual object and wait to be unfolded so that the implicit determinants that are still enfolded and concealed in the *concept* of the carrier may be revealed and, as we shall see, sometimes even "exhibited" as the implicit potentialities embedded in it. Consequently, a word-meaning that projects an object-correlate (an object of the type of autonomous objects) as an element of a sentence-correlate should be meant as an actualization of only a part of the concept of the respective object and as the carrier which the states of affairs enfolded and coexisting within its unity have in common. After all, an autonomous object has its independent existential range, its individuality, exactly because of the function it fulfills as the carrier of its particular constitutive nature. As we penetrate into this nature we bring forth by each cognitive act a new state of affairs within which a property or a trait of that nature is unfolded and thus revealed.

So far our discussion has focused on a state of affairs contained within the object, and thus on the opposition of a trait to its carrier. In the light of an unfolding state of affairs, we broke through the self-enclosed bounds of the projected object, which opened up through our sentence-forming operation that sought to unlock and reveal a trait of its nature. To what extent may we, however, speak of unlocking the nature of an object and of discovering a state of affairs within it, when we consider the correlates of sentences such as "A car is passing by" or "My dog is barking"? In these instances the object does not unfold in the same manner as in "This rose is red," but it does reveal a "trait" by carrying out an action. Strictly speaking, these objects do not become carriers of traits, but they unfold in that they become carriers of an activity particular to their range of effectiveness. Also, the potential-actual mode of these objects is the same as that of "this rose" in the state of affairs we have just discussed, because the implicit potentiality in the state of affairs of, for instance, "A car is passing by" points to the actuality of the nominal projection "a passing car."

Ingarden's analysis of the formal structure of a state of affairs that is the correlate of a declarative sentence reveals our acts of *perceptional constitution* as we seek to fathom the self-contained nature and the range of effectiveness of an intentional object. If the purely intentional state of affairs projected by a declarative sentence is intended to correspond to an objective one, our intentionality is, as we know, fashioned by the autonomy of that objective state of affairs. Consequently, our latitude in projecting it through the intermediary of a sentence-correlate is restricted by the formal and material constituents of the object, but of course also by the nature of our perceptional faculties, and, as we shall see, by certain characteristics of sentences and of connections between them. In any case, when we mean to affirm the correspondence of the state of affairs of a sentence-correlate to an independent state of affairs, the correlate cannot be ambiguous. When, however, the correlate is not meant to be projected in reference to an independent state of affairs, the capacity of the purely intentional state of affairs may contain elements that from the point of view of empirical reality may appear to be contradictory (particularly in the realm of the fantastic) and may lend themselves to various "equally valid" readings. When the ambiguity resulting from the "opalescence" of the correlate is intended, i.e., when contradictory elements are mingled with those that might correspond to experientially known elements, we should not seek to "translate" the correlates of such sentences into alternative correlates, for the ambiguity is intended to induce suspense. This stance is, of course, possible only if we recognize the formal structure of pure intentionality that projects the capacity of a purely intentional state of affairs. Once again, then, we must never ignore the distinction between the formal structure of the projecting intentionality and the structure of the projected capacity of the state of affairs.

4. THE CONNECTION OF SENTENCE-CORRELATES

We shall now consider some of the differences between directly (originally) perceived objective states of affairs and those which we project through the intermediary of sentence-correlates. Because we wish to examine the formation of connected sentences, i.e., the connection of sentence-correlates, we shall no longer limit ourselves to single states of affairs. When we perceive an independent object *directly*, we find that it is given to us in its self-contained unified wholeness; i.e., we perceive it in its concrete (in the original sense of "grown together") structure, in the "original state of coalescence" of all its constitutive properties and traits at that given moment of its existence. If we mean to apprehend any single state of affairs which is embedded in the unity of that object, we can do so only by an intentional act which isolates and separates it from the concreteness of the object and from all other states of affairs within the object's existential range. While we bracket all other states of affairs, the object emerges within the separated state of affairs not only as the carrier of its constitutive nature but also as that of the determinant which faces it. However, our consciousness does not remain riveted to that single state of affairs; we do in fact continually glide from one perceived aspect of the object to another or from the one intentionally apprehended state of affairs to another. We may say that we cross over the line of demarcation by which our intentional act separates for a moment one state of affairs from another, and that we displace that line when we apprehend simultaneously two or more states of affairs. Thus we realize that these demarcations do not belong to the object but are the effects of our purely intentional acts of apprehension. In the course of these direct fluid apprehensions we can at all times refer to the original concrete structure of the object, to the original state of coalescence of its constituents and other determinants.

These characteristics of an original fluid apprehension of states of affairs within an object, this crossing over or displacement of lines of intentional, momentary demarcation by which apprehended states of affairs are first isolated and then perceived in varied combinations, this constant shift from apprehension of individual or complex aspects of an object (or of its range of effectiveness with regard to other objects) to the concreteness of the object itself, cannot be duplicated through the intermediary of sentence-correlates. The unfolding state of affairs which is the correlate of a sentence is a rigidly discrete unit. The connections and coherences that tie together the correlates of a sequence of sentences cannot by themselves eliminate the effects of the rigidity of meaning-units through which an object is presented fragmented into states of affairs that are caught, as it were, in a "net" of connected sentence-correlates. Clearly, we must recognize that the reflection of our original intentionality in the derived intentionality of meaning-units of higher rank (i.e., of the complexes of connected sentences) is not exactly a "mirror image"; it is not a faithful replica, but rather what we may call a series of juxtaposed discrete snapshots of our original projections. These snapshots elicit by their order and their particular functions connections and coherences that lack the fluidity of our original perceptions; they make us unable to keep in sight the object's concreteness, the coalescence of its constituents and determinants which an originally intentional apprehension affords.

Let us now consider the nature of connections of sentences and the conditions under which they occur. We noted earlier that a sentence-forming operation is normally a mere phase of a broader operation by which we mean to develop a topic, and that the formation of a sentence is therefore carried out under the impact of a topic and under the thrust of preceding and the counterthrust of anticipated formative operations. When we face a text we find the sentences in an established sequence of connections, so that the meaning of any individual sentence is modified by that of a preceding sentence. For these reasons we proceed necessarily from one sentence to another in a sequential order with an eye to the gradual apprehension of meaning-units of increasing complexity. To simplify our task of assessing what connections between sentences are, and also to avoid a possible misunderstanding, I prefer to point out at once the difference between the connection of two sentences used in reference to a real and perceptibly given object, and the connection of the same two sentences when their purely intentional correlates are not meant to correspond to any independent referential object. "My typewriter has forty-three keys. The keys of my typewriter have a light touch." When these sentences refer to this typewriter on which I am writing, the intentional directional factor of "my typewriter" is in both sentences meant to reach the same independent object that is before me, for I mean to make an *affirmation*, in fact two affirmations, about it. It is the intended affirmation about one and the same independent object to which both sentences refer that establishes the connection of the sentences in my mind. If, however, I were to isolate the two sentences, they would become pure declarative sentences, and I would not even know whether these were statements made by the same person, or whether they pertained to the same typewriter. Thus their connection would be invalidated. Nevertheless, if I found these two pure declarative sentences occurring in succession and without any apparent reference to an independent object, I would consider them to be connected, but not on account of any independent object to which they might pertain. (We shall soon see on the basis of another example that succession does not by itself account for the connection.) In all similar examples we find a *material connection* between the consecutive correlates, because the second state of affairs depends materially on the first. The carrier ("my typewriter") of the first state of affairs establishes its existential sphere within which the carrier ("the keys") of the second state of affairs can materially fulfill its function. Thus the second state of affairs is implicitly drawn into the existential sphere of the first and both states of affairs are made to belong to the same purely intentional object projected by the nominal expression "my typewriter" without any reference to any independent object.

What, then, is the connection between the sentences and how is it brought about? (For the sake of easy distinction we shall henceforth use the term *meaning-unit* when we refer to the meaning of a word, and the term *sense-unit* when we refer to the meaning of a sentence.) It is obvious that there is no connection between the following two consecutive sentences: "Cars make an unbearable racket. Chapel Hill is in North Carolina." The reason for the absence of a connection lies here in the fact that no single meaning-unit of either sentence reaches over into the sense-unit of the other. Consequently, both these sense-units are enclosed. Let us now consider a sentence such as "He is very happy and is playing merrily in the garden." The intentional directional factor of the word-meaning "he" is in this isolated sentence potential and variable, and thus calls to be stabilized; it reaches over into some already established meaning-unit which we seek to find in an antecedent correlate. If we place the sentence "My son received a good report-card" in front of that sentence, the intentional directional factor of "my son" determines the target for the intentional directional factor of "he" (in the second sentence), which can thus be actualized. We see, then, that a connection has been established here because a meaning-unit of the second sentence could successfully reach over to a meaning-unit of the preceding sentence. The connection we have just described is, however, not the only one that links the sense-units of the two sentences: if we were to add the expression "for this reason" at the beginning of the second sentence ("For this reason he is very happy, etc."), the connection would be effected not only between the two meaning-units (my son–he); the connection would explicitly actualize what is already implied in the second sense-unit, namely the connection between the entire state of affairs ("He is very happy, etc.") of the second correlate and the entire state of affairs of the first correlate ("My son received a good report-card."). What we consider to be a connection between two sentences is, then, the successful reaching over of a meaning-unit or a sense-unit of one sentence-correlate into another with the result that a tie is effected between the correlates whereby, in turn, they modify each other and yet retain the individuality of their sense-units. It should be noted that the reaching over need not occur only from one correlate to the other, that it can be reciprocal, and that several sentences may be thus connected. We know already that the immediate succession of sentences does not necessarily establish a connection, but we should add that the place of a sentence in relation to other sentences in their sequential order does play a role. If we were to reverse the order of the two sentences we used ("He is very happy and is playing merrily in the garden. My son received a good report-card."), the connection would fail to be established, because the stabilizing of the intentional directional factor of "he" requires a previously actualized intentional directional factor to whose established target the "he" could then point and on which the two intentional directional factors could thus converge.

Connections between sentences may be of various types. They may be explicit or implicit, direct or indirect, tightly knit or loose; further—and this is to be particularly noted—the connection may be purely material, or it may at the same time be effected by some explicit *logical* function. Let us consider Ingarden's example: "The square is an equilateral rectangular parallelogram. Its diagonals intersect and are equal to each other *because* every equilateral rectangular parallelogram has such diagonals." In the light of the logical function of the word "because," the material connection is explicitly turned into a logical, a necessary one. This is the sort of connection of sentences by which we may mean to prove the validity of our affirmations, of our judgmental claims to truth. The importance of this observation can readily be seen when we realize that different types of connections between sentences result in different compositional structures, such as stories, theories, proofs. Depending on the type of connections that we find to be prevalent in a compositional whole and also depending on their sequential order, we can discover the characteristic *dynamics* in a given work.

5. QUASI-MODIFICATIONS OF SENTENCES IN A LITERARY TEXT

The preceding statement about various types of connections which affect the character of the new entity (story, theory, etc.) may serve as at least one hint that there are some recognizable indices to distinguish a "literary text" from, let us say, a theoretical treatise. Sentences found in a literary text are neither purely declarative nor genuinely affirmative. Affirmative sentences in a literary text have only a quasi-affirmative character, i.e., they have the external appearance of affirmations, although they are not meant to be, nor in fact are they, genuine judgmental propositions. Before presenting Ingarden's argument, I propose to review very briefly some of the materials covered previously.

A proposition is a judgment whereby we affirm (or deny) a state of affairs by expressing it as a declarative sentence. Every affirmation makes a claim to truth, but affirmations differ according to the degree of certainty with which the conformity of their purely intentional state of affairs to an independent (objective) one is affirmed. We speak of an assertion when the state of affairs that is affirmed is meant to be provably identical with an objective state of affairs. An affirmation, as I am using the term, intends to make a genuine claim to truth even if the affirmed judgment should ultimately turn out to be erroneous. The *sense* of a genuine affirmative sentence is thus derived from a serious claim to truth, and not from the available proof that the two states of affairs are identical. Therefore we are not going to be concerned here with assertions, but with variously affirmed claims to truth. Since any affirmation is expressed in a declarative sentence, we must recall that the pure declarative sentence does not mean to make any claim to truth even though it appears in its wording to be an affirmation. It is therefore reasonable to ask if there are indices that may help us to recognize the difference between a declarative sentence that is the vehicle of a genuine affirmation and one that is not. What, then, is the sense of a pure declarative sentence and of declarative sentences that become vehicles of various types of affirmations?

As we know, the correlate of every sentence is purely intentional. We also know that a sentence is not an independent formation and that normally it stands in a context of other sentences, or that when it appears to be isolated from such a context, it is at least relevant to the situation in which it is uttered. However, when we form a *pure* declarative sentence, we do so without regard to any referential purpose. It has no function other than that of exemplifying the functions of its meaning-units within its sense-unit, and the purely intentional nature of its correlate. Further, we noted the difference between the function of the verb when it occurs in a pure declarative sentence and its function in a declarative sentence that is meant to be at the same time the vehicle of an affirmation in some context. The difference is one in *sense*, which, as we can see, depends on the sense we intend to confer on the sentence in the light of the purpose that it is meant to serve. Finally, we know that the intentional directional factor of a nominal word-meaning points at all times to the purely intentional correlate projected by it. If, however, in a given situation, a declarative sentence ("My fountain pen is lying on the desk.") is used to affirm an objective state of affairs, then we *mean* the intentional directional factor of "my fountain pen" to go beyond the purely intentional correlate and to reach the *also intentional* independent object. That is one moment of the sense of a genuine affirmation. Now what happens when, because of this extended range of the directional factor, the nominal expression is made to refer to the independent referential object?

If we consider only the purely intentional state of affairs of the correlate of a declarative sentence, we know that the correlate as a whole remains purely intentional even though the existential character of the object and of the state of affairs is *of the type of real objects and independent states of affairs*. However, when the intentional directional factor of "my fountain pen" is meant to reach the independent referential real object, then the capacity of the *entire* state of affairs, which within the sentence-correlate pertains to the purely intentional projection of the expression "my fountain pen," is thereby *transposed* into the independent existential sphere of the real referential object and is thus *meant to be identified* with the state of affairs pertaining to this object. If we wish to assess this transposition (*Hinausversetzung*), we should bear in mind several points. The existential characterization does not bring about a transposition, because it merely assigns to objects or states of affairs the character of being of the *type* of real objects or independent states of affairs. The intentional act of transposition means (intends) that the purely intentional object-correlate of the nominal word-meaning (which is the subject of the sentence) shall become, together with the state of affairs pertaining to it, a revealing *presentation* of the referential independent object and that it shall *be identified* with it, because the intentional directional factor means to reach at the same time the presented purely intentional object and the independent referential object. The constituents and the other determinants within the capacity of the presented purely intentional object are thus meant to be essentially identifiable with those of the independent object. Consequently the capacity of the presented purely intentional state of affairs of the sentence-correlate, which pertains to the purely intentional object, is also meant to be essentially identical with the independent state of affairs pertaining to the independent object. Obviously the state of affairs of the sentence-correlate does not cease to remain purely intentional in the course of the transposition, but its capacity is meant to conform to the independent state of affairs to such an extent that the presented purely intentional state of affairs and the referential independent one shall be considered to be essentially identical, and should therefore be *identified*. Because of this identification, the purely intentional state of affairs of the sentence-correlate becomes, as it were, transparent. Our attention is riveted to the independent, referential state of affairs while the purely intentional one disappears from sight, for we tend to ignore the intermediary presentation by which an object or state of affairs is revealed. We must repeat, however, that the state of affairs of the sentence-correlate does persist in its pure intentionality in spite of its conformity to the independent referential state of affairs with which it is identified. Should further proof be called for, it may be mentioned that the pure intentionality of a sentence-correlate may be readily seen if we consider affirmative sentences such as "Every body is extended" or "My (this, that) pen is on the desk." In an objective state of affairs there is no body that is "every" and no pen that is "my," "this," "that," etc. It is only our purely intentional turning to an object that produces such distinctions, but these disappear from sight because the directional factors of any of these words and that of "body," "pen," etc., converge in the correlate of the nominal word-meaning. To what extent, then, can we speak of conformity and essential identity between the presented purely intentional state of affairs and the objective referential one? We can do so, as we have already noted, with regard to the formal and material constituents and determinants *within the capacity* of objects and states of affairs that may be transposed, but we must exclude the purely intentional existence and characteristics that cannot be transposed into independent reality.

Clearly, a genuine affirmation could not fulfill its function of transposition without the function fulfilled by the intentional directional factor that means to reach the objective target, and without the conformity, based on essential identity, of the capacity of the purely intentional state of affairs with the referential objective state of affairs. Now, we know that there is no essential identity of any two entities unless both fall under the same general idea. Consequently, transposition can occur only if the general idea of a state of affairs is individuated in the capacity of the purely intentional sentence-correlate and in objective reality; or, to put it differently, if the constant qualitative moment of that general idea is concretized in the former and realized in the latter. When this essential identity is apprehended and the transposition is thus carried out, the affirmative sentence has fulfilled a requirement for its claim to truth. However, for the sentence to be apprehended as affirmative, the function of the intentional directional factor must induce our identifying the purely intentional with the objective state of affairs.

In every declarative sentence the predicate fulfills the function of the verbal unfolding of a state of affairs. It continues to fulfill the same function even when the declarative sentence is meant to be the vehicle of a genuine affirmation, except that as a result of the intended affirmation the predicate is meant to fulfill yet another function. Because of its claim to truth, the genuine affirmation confers on the predicate the function of what we called *existential setting*; the predicate means that the transposed state of affairs exists *as a fact*. A genuine affirmation's claim to truth rests on its intention of transposing the capacity of a purely intentional state of affairs into the independent existential sphere, on the transposition's being effected by the intentional directional factor, and on the existential setting established by the predicate. We shall now consider *modified affirmative sentences* (as they occur in a literary text) whose modification is the effect of the affirmation's being merely a *quasi-affirmation*, a *quasi-judgment*. We should emphasize that a genuine transposition and setting must be present in a genuine affirmation; we shall see, however, instances where a certain kind of transposition does not entail a genuine existential setting.

Ingarden distinguishes different types of quasi-affirmative sentences according to the manner in which they approximate pure declarative sentences at one end of the scale and genuine affirmations at the other. The correlate of a pure declarative sentence lacks, as we know, the derived intentionality which means to make an affirmation with a claim to truth about an independent state of affairs. The intentional directional factor of the nominal word which is the subject of the sentence is not meant to point to an independent object. Consequently the state of affairs that pertains to the purely intentional object (which is the subject of the sentence) is not meant to be transposed into the independent sphere of existence, and its conformity with an independent state of affairs is not intended. Even though the projected state of affairs is existentially characterized as of the type of independent states of affairs, the pure declarative sentence lays no claim to truth and its predicate does not have the function of existential setting.

There are literary texts of the type that we may call "purely fictional," which make no pretense that their projections have reference to reality. Nevertheless, quasi-affirmative sentences do create here an illusion of reality. This is achieved by a simulated transposition that is not effected by intentional directional factors but by certain *material indices*, such as the placing of the states of affairs in some specific site. But even that illusion is kept faint because the states of affairs in these works do not aim to achieve conformity with those of the real world; they thus retain their purely intentional character and only barely conceal the fact that they are projections of pure intentionality. Consequently, they are not transposed into an independent sphere of existence, but into a world of their own, a world of illusory reality into which they are *set as they are*, as purely intentional, and where they remain, so to speak, suspended.

A simulated transposition and setting are also found in texts in which the correlates of quasi-affirmative sentences are meant to *adapt*, in general, to the social and environmental characteristics of certain periods in history. Here, too, conformity to individuals and states of affairs is not achieved, because the transposition, such as it is, is not brought about by intentional directional factors. Nevertheless, there is here at least a noticeable adaptation to *typical features of a period* with which the otherwise purely intentional characters and situations are endowed. Individual details, such as names of persons or places, are often introduced to lend verisimilitude to this simulated transposition into illusory reality. This "reality," produced by the intended *adaptation* to typical, general, features can in no way be equated with the reality of individual states of affairs to which the states of affairs of correlates of genuine affirmative sentences mean to *conform* and with which they can be identified.

It is fairly simple to recognize the quasi-affirmative character of sentences in literary texts of the two types we have just mentioned and to see that transposition and setting are merely simulated in these instances. How do we distinguish, however, the sense of quasi-affirmative sentences in literary texts which purport to be "historical" from that of genuine affirmative sentences, for instance, in scholarly works, inasmuch as the former seem to claim that they deal faithfully with individuals and states of affairs drawn from history? I shall have to touch here on a closely related subject discussed by Ingarden within the framework of the subsequent stratum of presented objects in the literary work of art. Let us first retrace some of the steps we have taken so far and amplify our findings at the same time. We know that the sense-unit of a declarative sentence projects a purely intentional state of affairs in whose unfolding we find a *presentation* (*Darstellung*) revealing constituents or other determinants of an object which is the subject of that sentence. When we mean that sentence to be genuinely affirmative, we mean that the intentional directional factor of the nominal word-meaning (which is the subject of the sentence) shall reach not only the purely intentional correlate of that word but also a referential object which is in the sphere of reality. We thereby transpose into this sphere the capacity of the purely intentional object and of the state of affairs that pertains to it. In the course of our affirmation, we also mean that the predicate shall perform its function of setting the transposed capacity of the state of affairs into reality as a fact. We may say that the purpose of the unfolding of a state of affairs projected by a declarative sentence is a *presentation* that reveals a purely intentional object *by means of that state of affairs*. If we mean the declarative sentence to be a genuine affirmation, we transpose and set its purely intentional object and state of affairs into the independent sphere of reality in the manner already described; we mean that the capacity of the transposed state of affairs is essentially identical with an independent state of affairs; and as we apprehend that identity we *identify* the two states of affairs. By this *identification* the purely intentional state of affairs and the independent state of affairs itself are *both directly presented*. In fact, because of the function of the intentional directional factor in a genuine affirmation, the independent state of affairs moves, so to speak, into the foreground and conceals the capacity of the purely intentional state of affairs together with the pure intentionality that projects it. This means that because of that identification *the presentation* of the purely intentional state of affairs in a genuine affirmation is *not apprehended as a reproduction of an independent individual model, nor is it therefore apprehended as a representation of the independent state of affairs pertaining to it.*

In a literary text declarative sentences are, as we know, not meant to be genuine affirmations, and as in all declarative sentences, their correlates are *presentations* of purely intentional objects and states of affairs. At the same time, however, depending on the type of the literary work, we note variously implied claims to truth. In those works that we mentioned first and called "purely fictional," the presentation of the purely intentional states of affairs is only loosely related by certain vague material indices to a simulated reality into which they are transposed and set, though only in appearance. The quasi-affirmative character of these sentences clearly preserves the pure intentionality of their correlates, for here there is certainly no pretense that the created world is a simultaneous presentation of the real world. Similarly, in works of the second type the purely intentional presentations are certainly not meant to be simultaneous presentations of independent individual objects and of their states of affairs, but they do mean to be *representative* of general types of objects and situations of a certain period. Thus, here too, quasi-affirmative sentences project a purely intentional world whose "transposition" is one only in appearance and is a result of its mere similarity to some general features of objective reality. We may conclude that in neither of these two types do we find a transposition effected by intentional directional factors; nor do we note therefore the simultaneous presentation of purely intentional states of affairs with independent states of affairs; nor, finally, do the purely intentional states of affairs recede from sight, for they do not become transparent by means of the identification described. Consequently, the characteristics of genuine affirmations are missing and the sentences are therefore only quasi-affirmative.

Let us now turn to literary works that claim to be "historical," where the quasi-affirmative sentences may therefore appear to be genuinely affirmative. In the text of works of this type *some* of the individual objects and states of affairs projected by some of the sentences are meant to be matched with *some* but not with all independent individual objects and states of affairs (usually of the past) in such a way as to achieve faithful conformity to them. We saw that a *presentation* of a state of affairs may, by achieving faithful conformity (of its capacity) to an independent state of affairs, become essentially identical with it, and that this is *one* of the conditions under which a declarative sentence becomes affirmative. The other condition is that on the basis of their essential identity the two states of affairs shall be *identified through the extended range of the intentional directional factor*. Because the first of these conditions is in many sentences fulfilled, all the quasi-affirmative sentences in literary texts that claim to be "historical" give the appearance of being genuine affirmations. However, only some of the intentional directional factors are meant to reach individual independent objects, and there is therefore no transposition of all projected states of affairs. Consequently there is no identification in every instance. Here, then, *some* of the correlates of quasi-affirmative sentences do *present* purely intentional states of affairs that are essentially identical with *some* corresponding independent states of affairs, but the context *as a whole* precludes a simultaneous presentation of *all* the states of affairs projected by the text. For this reason, the world presented by the text can be only a *representation* of the independent world. To sum up, we may now say that in genuine affirmations the essentially identical purely intentional and referential independent states of affairs become *identified* with each other because of that crucial function of all the intentional directional factors, and the states of affairs in the correlates become transparent, while the independent states of affairs move conspicuously into the presentation. In quasi-affirmations, on the other hand, the purely intentional states of affairs are prominently presented, and they are not meant to be identified with the independent states of affairs, because the *context* does not justify our assumption that *all* the intentional directional factors are meant to reach beyond the purely intentional correlates of the nominal word-meanings. The presentations of the correlates of quasi-affirmative sentences in "historical" works are, then, merely *reproductions* of some individual independent models and *representations* of their independent states of affairs found in reality. Because of the lack of consistent identification, and in spite of the simulated reality, the correlates of quasi-affirmative sentences create a world of their own, separate from independent reality. Ingarden credits the quasi-affirmations of a literary text mainly, though not exclusively, with the effect of creating for us the illusion of reality.

I have been careful to place quasi-affirmative sentences in the literary *text* rather than in the literary *work*. I shall now introduce further distinctions that should help to elucidate this point. Ingarden calls "text" the complex of sentences that *present* the purely intentional world of a literary work. When this distinction becomes useful, I shall call this text the *presentative text*. In the case of an impersonal ("objective") narration the narrator is anonymous and the narrated presentative text presents a world by what we may call a *single projection* through the intermediary of quasi-affirmative sentences. In this presentative text the narrator is not given, he is not projected into the presented world and he is therefore not presented, though we shall later see that he is not entirely absent. Let us suppose, however, that the narrator is given, even if only as a narrator without any specific identity. In this case the narrator projects a presented world, but he himself needs to be projected by some presentative text (which we shall have to identify) so that he may become an element of the presented world. This narrator may be compared to, and may in fact be one of, the presented characters in the world of a novel, i.e., a character who in all seriousness makes affirmations, asks questions, and utters commands. His various utterances may be taken seriously by other characters presented in the same world. We should ask, then, whether the affirmative, interrogative, or imperative sentences spoken by the presented narrator or by any presented character within the presented world are also quasi-affirmative, quasi-interrogative, etc.

Let us assume, then, that an impersonal brief presentative text, which is *frequently only implied*, introduces and presents a narrator. The same presentative text also projects the narrator's *act* of narration; in other words, the narrator and the *state of narration* (throughout its duration) constitute the "first" presented world projected by that presentative text. All presentative sentences that explicitly or implicitly affirm the presence of the presented narrator and the presented state of narration are quasi-affirmative. Within that "first" presented world the presented narrator projects and presents the narrative matter, the "theme." Consequently, we have on one level the original (possibly only implied) presentative text presenting the world of the narrator and the state of narration. Within that "first" presented world, the narrator projects and presents objects, states of affairs, problems, commands, etc., which constitute on the next level the "second" presented world. What we have just described is a *double projection* resulting in nesting structures. The narrative matter presented by the narrator is nested within the state of narration, which in turn is nested within the larger frame of the original presentative text.

The importance of the double projection lies in that a *presented* state of narration is at the same time projecting a different, a nested, *presented world* through the intermediary of affirmative, interrogative, etc., sentences. Whenever a text fulfills the function of projecting a presented world—on whatever level of the nesting structure—it thereby fulfills the function of a presentative text, and the sentences which constitute it undergo that "quasi-modification" whereby an affirmative sentence becomes quasi-affirmative, an interrogative sentence becomes quasi-interrogative, etc. Whenever sentences (of whatever kind) are not regarded in their presentative function but as belonging to a presented world where affirmations, questions, etc., are formulated and taken in all seriousness, the so-called "quasi-modification" does not occur *within the presented world*. For the sake of clear distinctions we may call those sentences "*fictively* affirmative, interrogative, etc.," whose seemingly genuine affirmations, questions, and commands are taken seriously *within* a presented world. Many examples of the same double projections, nesting structures, and modifications of sentences may be observed in a play that we read, as distinct from one that is staged. The problem that we still need to solve pertains to the manner in which a presentative text projects presented sentences.

D. Presentative functions of sentences

1. THE PROJECTION OF PRESENTED SENTENCES BY THE PRESENTATIVE TEXT

So far we have dealt with quasi-modifications of sentences that pertain to only one of their functions: to the function of affirmation of an affirmative sentence, to the interrogatory function of an interrogative sentence, etc. We shall now consider the modifications that pertain to the manifestative functions of sentences. We stated before that speech as indicator performs manifestative functions and that the resulting manifestative characteristics cease when the speaker has ceased speaking. However, manifestative characteristics are detectable in all literary texts and not only in utterances of presented speakers. When a text is impersonal, it lacks these manifestative characteristics, but when it is related by a given narrator, manifestative characteristics are presented, because the narrator then belongs to the presented world. When fictively affirmative, interrogative, etc., sentences are "uttered" by presented characters, manifestative characteristics are even more obviously present, although they are usually apprehended only peripherally. Interrogative sentences do not occur in an impersonal presentative text, for the questioner is always manifestly and manifestatively co-given. For this reason we shall use an interrogative sentence to illustrate how both functions of a presented interrogative sentence, the interrogatory and the manifestative, are presented by the presentative text. Every interrogative sentence is characterized by the interrogatory function, i.e., by the function of projecting a problem as its correlate. The interrogative sentence is also characterized by its manifestative function, by which the questioner manifests a state of mind that is revealed by his desire to know something. When an interrogative sentence is "uttered" by a presented speaker, the sentence becomes part of the presented world. A presentative sentence explicitly or implicitly presents the speaker and his act of asking a question as part of the presented world, but we need to know how his question is presented. Suppose a presented speaker asks another: "Why have you left your house?" This sentence in quotation marks (though of course not the quotation marks themselves) is part of the presented world and is therefore a quasi-interrogative sentence. However, a presented (and, in this instance, a quasi-interrogative) sentence must be projected by a presentative text if it is to fulfill its *interrogatory* and consequently also its *manifestative* functions in the presented world. Where, then, shall we find the presentative sentence? The main thrust of Ingarden's argument is that there is "no materially determined state of affairs or object in the stratum of presented objects that does not ultimately originate in one of the two layers of the literary work which together constitute in it the element of language—that of sound-formation and that of meaning-units."[4] The interrogatory function of the question (the projection of a problem) and the manifestative characteristics pertaining to it are materially determined in the presented world, and we shall now see how they originate in a presentative text. The presented uttered question "Why have you left your house?" is in quotation marks, though in some works the quotation marks may be omitted as long as the sentence is understood to be uttered by a speaker in the presented world. According to Ingarden, the function of these quotation marks (regardless of whether they are given explicitly or only meant implicitly) is to stand for a missing presentative sense-unit. The quotation marks indicate that the quoted sentence is a verbatim record of the suppressed presentative sentence which has presented the sentence as "actually uttered" by a speaker in the presented world. *As a record of the suppressed sentence*, the sentence in quotation marks is integrated into the implied presentative text and thus projects the presented interrogative sentence *in its interrogatory function.* At the same time, this suppressed sentence projects the fictively interrogative sentence as "actually uttered" in the presented world and therefore as one that does fulfill its manifestative function. Ingarden's explanation, which I have applied to both functions, is coupled with the recognition that this is indeed an *indirect* projection, but one which presents

4. *LK*, p. 195; trans., p. 184.

the interrogatory as well as the manifestative functions of fictively interrogative (or affirmative, etc.) sentences as "ultimately" originating in a presentative text. When we read a play we note that all the utterances of the characters are implicitly in quotation marks. This means that the presentative text in which those utterances originate is itself, as it were, suppressed, although the utterances record it. (There are, however, elements of the presentative text of a play which are not recorded by the presented text of utterances, and these elements are the various stage directions and the implicit quotation marks which indicate the suppression of the presentative text that projects the presented utterances.)

2. THE PRESENTATIVE FUNCTIONS OF
PURELY INTENTIONAL STATES OF AFFAIRS

We shall soon explore the layer of presented objects (trans. "represented objects"), but we must first conclude our observations on the presentative functions of declarative sentences. We know that the nominal word-meaning (in this case the subject of the sentence) projects a purely intentional object that is meant to have a certain formal structure and constitutive nature, and that the sense-unit as a whole projects an unfolding purely intentional state of affairs which reveals in a potential-actual manner one or more determinants of which that object is the carrier. This type of state of affairs, which reveals a constitutive property or some of its traits, is called a *state of existential qualification* (*Soseinsverhalt*; trans. "state of essence"). The state of affairs projected by a sense-unit is of a different type when it reveals an object's relation to other objects in the course of some occurrence; such a state of affairs is called a *state of occurrence* (*Geschehensverhalt*). The projected object and the state of affairs (of whichever type) both confront the derived intentionality of the sense-unit by which they are projected. In that the state of affairs as a whole confronts the sense-unit of the sentence, it may seem to belong to the layer of presented objects, but the object itself to which the state of affairs pertains becomes a *presented object* only on account of the presentative function of the unfolding state of affairs that *reveals* it—*presents* it—as the carrier of a determinant. Without that revelatory function of a state of affairs the object by itself, as projected only by an isolated nominal word-meaning, is meant simply as the carrier of its formal structure and of an as yet not particularized essential configuration. For an object to be *constituted* and *presented*, it is enough for one or more of its constituents or other determinants to be revealed by a state of affairs in its unfolding. It is the function of the capacity of *connected* sense-units to present an object that is constituted with regard to a number of its existential qualifications and frequently also with regard to its relations to other objects. What, then, is the process by which states of affairs, projected by connected sense-units, constitute and thereby present a purely intentional object? In an original direct apprehension, as we have noted, we perceive a real object as the carrier of its constitutive nature and of those determinants which we single out at a given time. As we glide from one state of affairs to another, we simultaneously apperceive the concrete object as a whole in which the perceived states of affairs that constitute it are embedded. Our apprehension of a purely intentional object presented by projected states of affairs is very different, because in the course of our reading we proceed from sentence to sentence and we apprehend only those determinants that are revealed by the succession of a necessarily finite number of unfolding states of affairs. Of course, the first sentence which projects a state of affairs also projects (by its subject) the object to which the state of affairs pertains. This object, in its simple projection by the nominal word-meaning, is the foundation on which its constitution by the first unfolding state of affairs is based. Any subsequent declarative sentence pertaining to the thus constituted object projects a new state of affairs which has its constitutive foundation in the already partly constituted object. By virtue of subsequent states of affairs the object thus undergoes further constitutions by additional determinants, with the result that it is presented with accrued existential and other qualifications, depending on the types of states of affairs. This process of consecutive constitutions leads to ever more complex presentations of the object through a variety of unfolding states of affairs. It is clear that the sense-units of connected sentences project as their correlates states of affairs that constitute by stages various purely intentional objects and their destinies, and that through their constitutive functions the states of affairs also fulfill their presentative functions. Because the process of constitution occurs necessarily by stages in which one discrete state of affairs is connected to another, the presented objects are marked by what may be called "cleavages" in the layer of presented objects. These cleavages are veiled by the connection of sentences, but only to a certain extent. Here again, the presentative function of states of affairs usually recedes from our vision, because we direct our attention primarily to the presented objects themselves, and we think of them as if they were concrete and connected.

We can see, then, that the capacity of sense-units of connected declarative sentences projects a succession of seemingly connected unfolding states of affairs which have the twofold function of constituting and of presenting various objects (such as characters, things, actions, occurrences) in a cohesive presented world. Presentation, as we know, is the specific function of the unfolding of states of affairs, which open up and constitute the objects and thereby reveal their determinants. Different types of states of affairs present objects in different ways. We have already distinguished the state of affairs which is a state of existential qualification from that which is a state of occurrence, and we shall now add a third type, which I shall call the *state of phenomenal qualification* (*Soaussehensverhalt*, trans. "state of thus-appearance") because it reveals a phenomenal, i.e., a directly perceptible determinant. If we say, "Wood is a bad conductor of heat," we recognize here only a state of existential qualification, because the revealed determinant is not directly perceptible. The determinant is a phenomenal qualification when a state of affairs reveals it as directly perceptible on the basis of any kind of sensory data gained under appropriate objective conditions. (Ingarden lists the following examples: "In the faint candlelight the room looked dreary." "My wool jacket is soft to the touch." "This pear tastes sweet." "This load is heavy to carry." "This rose smells sweet.") What distinguishes a state of phenomenal qualification is that it must be directly perceptible *and its quality must be intuited*. In every instance of a state of phenomenal qualification we also gain indirectly a notion of the object's corresponding state of existential qualification. On the other hand, only those states of existential qualification that reveal a directly perceptible determinant, point to a corresponding state of phenomenal qualification. Thus, because this rose is red, it also appears red phenomenally. We may say, then, that the phenomenal appearance of determinants may be intuited on the basis of states of phenomenal qualification or indirectly perceived on that of *potentially self-presenting* states of existential qualification or occurrence.

All these projected states of affairs present objects in that they unlock their self-enclosed givenness, in that they unfold and reveal some of their determinants, but each of these types of states of affairs fulfills the function of presentation in a different manner and with different results. Through each presentation we are enabled to *know* what those determinants *are*, although the manner in which their unveiling occurs is different in each instance. We shall call the presentation of phenomenal qualifications *exhibition*, regardless of whether the exhibition is the direct function of states of phenomenal qualification or the indirect function of potentially self-presenting states of occurrence or existential qualification.

Strictly speaking, states of affairs that exhibit the features of any object can be apprehended only in the direct perception of an originally intentional material object's self-presenting qualitative moments. In purely intentional states of affairs that are projected by sense-units this self-presenting quality of features is, of course, a mere semblance; it is we, the readers, who must achieve in our imagination the phenomenal appearance of these determinants by certain acts, which we shall discuss later. After all, the sentence-correlates merely predetermine, by their exhibiting function, what we shall call the "aspects" of presented objects. The states of affairs projected by sense-units are mere analogues of, for instance, the visual sensory data we experience as we perceive a material object. Consequently, for a text to prepare the ground for our intuition of a phenomenally appearing determinant, the presentation must fulfill the function of exhibiting phenomenal qualifications. This means that the states of affairs must be appropriately selected.

A few remarks on *presentation as exhibition* are now in order. From what has been said it is clear that the prevalence of this type of presentation affects the character of a text. Any analysis of exhibition must therefore take into account on the one hand the differences in material moments by which determinants are exhibited and on the other hand the degree of "plasticity" that renders those determinants "striking" and "conspicuous." Connected states of occurrences may be particularly suited, for instance, to making a character's existential qualifications phenomenally perceptible by displaying them through actions in occurrences in which the character participates and by contrasting them with those of other characters.

We should note in this connection that a prevalence of so-called "abstract" words limits the functions of states of affairs to mere presentation, whereas a prevalence of "concrete" words may lead to an exhibition of phenomenal qualifications. A similar effect is achieved by words whose sound-configurations endow their word-meanings with mood-setting "emotional colorations" (or with certain manifestative characteristics), whose prevalence may even affect the kind (genre) of a literary work.

Two additional comments about presentative functions of states of affairs need to be made. States of affairs projected by sense-units necessarily actualize and present only *some* of the multitude of potential states of affairs embedded in an object, so that a selection of states of affairs is therefore unavoidable. Thus one and the same object may be presented and exhibited by different sets of states of affairs, depending on the perspective that dictates a special combination of the presented object's determinants. Also, one and the same determinant may perform different roles, depending on the selected determinants with which it is combined. Consequently, the appearance of an object presented through a certain selection of connected states of affairs, on the basis of which it is constituted, may turn out to be considerably different from what it might be if it were presented by a different set of states of affairs. This consideration leads Ingarden to point out a problem in literary scholarship which has not lost its relevance. The problem pertains to the variations in presentation of one and the same "material" (*Stoff*). If the material is, for instance, a historical personage or event that is known to us, we may have no difficulty identifying it as "one and the same" in spite of the different perspectives from which the variations in its representation stem, because we are acquainted with the manifold states of affairs embedded in it and can supply the omitted or implied states of affairs that are not made explicit in the particular states of affairs selected for the representation. If, however, the material of, for instance, a "plot" is known to us only from the presented world of a certain work, then that material may be treated as "one and the same" in a new version only insofar as this variation conforms to the type of material presented in the original work; the new or modified determinants must appear as if they had been left in a state of potentiality by the previous version. Even so, however, the new variation does entail a new configuration which may be the result of, for instance, the prevalence of states of affairs of types different from those in the original version.

Finally, in reference to Ingarden's discussion of the structure and connections of sentences, we should at least point out that a sequence of simple and clear states of affairs, projected by brief connected sense-units, presents a world by means of "patchlike juxtapositions" that lead us to gradual apprehensions which evolve in the course of our reading. In contrast, an intricate web of involuted states of affairs within a sentence may favor our intuitive apperception of a situation in what may appear to be its original complexity. These instances confirm again that types of presentation are determined by the choice of the nature, structure, and connections of states of affairs.

Chapter 3

1. The layer of presented objects

A. *Introduction*

Throughout the preceding chapter our attention was increasingly directed toward presented objects, and we dealt with them directly when we explored the projection of presented sentences by the presentative text, and the presentative functions of purely intentional states of affairs. We should mention again that when we speak of a presented object, we mean first of all any object (such as a person, a thing, a property, a trait, an act, an occurrence, a circumstance) which is projected by a nominal word-meaning and presented by states of affairs. At times, objects may not be presented in their objectified givenness; they may be suggested through vague or ethereal impressions of personal or emotionally tinged characteristics. Also, as already mentioned, many elements found in this layer are presented only implicitly by states of affairs, and objects that are directly named need not be presented also by a state of affairs. Because the reader's attention is often focused on this layer, i.e., because he often grasps this layer "thematically" to the point of disregarding the others, and because he transfers his experiences of real life to the capacity of the presented objects, he may fail to recognize that these are purely intentional projections. He may thus ignore the particularity of their structure as presentations and fail to recognize them in the role they play in the polyphony of the work as a whole.

The mode of existence of presented objects which are instrumental in generating occurrences, in determining interrelationships of various kinds, or in affecting presented destinies, determines the existential connections between the presented objects. Thus there emerges from the literary work a unified, but by no means always homogeneously determinate, existential sphere. The existential sphere within a literary work is determined, first of all, by everything that constitutes the explicit presentation. Because what is explicitly presented is only a segment of a world, a segment that is revealed so to speak under "a beam of light," the remainder of the work's existential sphere remains shrouded in the obscurity of indeterminateness which forms the explicit presentation's implicit background. To sum up, we may state that the presented existential sphere consists of events and occurrences in which interrelated variously determinate objects participate and also of a pertinent indeterminate spatial and temporal background to which we shall now turn our attention. We should, however, first remind ourselves that the quasi-modifications of all sentences in a literary work result in a corresponding modification of the capacity of all presented objects, and that objects of the type of real objects appear merely "in the garb of reality," for they are not rooted in the real world and have therefore no independent existence within real space and time. Therefore the problem we face is: If the semblance of reality of presented objects is to be preserved, how can they be presented and imagined as existing in space and time?

B. Presented space and imaginational space

It is an essential characteristic of space, of any space, that it can have no discontinuity; presented space therefore has this essential feature too. The walls of a presented room within which certain occurrences take place are spatial and they are in space: they mark off a segment of space. However indeterminate the space outside the walls may be, we still assume that that outer world belongs to the presented world in which the room is located and that it is—although only implicitly—also presented, copresented. This copresented space cannot possibly be the real space of the real world even if the presented space is made to appear "convincingly real" by being "transposed" and "set" in some building or city, i.e., into a space that has a counterpart in reality. Since the presented segment of space together with its indeterminate spatial extension cannot be fitted into real space, from what point of our real spatial experience do we, as readers, nevertheless succeed in bridging the gap between our real space and presented space? To answer this important question we shall have to return to some earlier findings and develop new ones.

We stated that when we *mean* an originally intentional object, we do not necessarily imagine it. Likewise, the meaning-fulfilling acts by which we grasp a presented object are not necessarily accompanied by our imaginational intuitions of its phenomenal givenness. We must therefore make a distinction between, on the one hand, acts of meaning (acts of "categorial formation"), *categorially formed perceptions*, by which we project (or grasp) an intentional object in so-called simple acts of meaning, and, on the other hand, acts by which we imagine it in its phenomenal givenness. In brief, we must distinguish between meaning an object, and imagining it as phenomenally given. What is meant by imagining an object, and what is meant by an "imaginational object" (*Vorstellungsgegenstand*)? When I imagine some distant object (e.g., a person whom I cannot see) that is existentially independent, or even a fictitious object (a centaur), I perform an act of *imagining*, an act of *imaginational intending* (*Vorstellungsmeinen*). The imagined object (the absent person or the centaur) is my originally intentional object, because it is the direct target of my *act of meaning*. It is to this originally intentional object that my act of imagining, and not only my act of meaning, is directed. As my originally[1] intentional object, it confronts, "transcends," both my act of meaning and my act of imagining. This *imagined* originally intentional object is of course *not* the imaginational object that results from my act of imagining. The imaginational object does not confront my act of imagining; it is, in fact, strictly immanent in my imaginational experience.

Here we shall limit our considerations to acts of visual imagining, and our description of the imaginational experience will therefore focus on acts of visual perception. When an individual real thing is given in visual perception, we directly see (in an act of perceptional experience) its surface, color, volume, depth, etc., and its extension *within perceived real space*. The *distinctness* of these perceptions based on visual data is lost in imaginational experience, but visual imagination does have the intuitiveness which is characteristic of perceptional experience. The "flowing and ever changing" imaginational color data that are under the "directive" of the intentional act of imagining (and should not be confused with discrete acts of purely categorial meaning) are intuited within a usually unnoticed "nebulous medium" (which has nothing to do with the so-called visual grayness), a spatial medium that occurs exclusively as the space from which imaginational data, including those of imagined space, emerge and by which they are enveloped. This is what is called *imaginational space* (*Vorstellungsraum*), which must be carefully distinguished from the imagined intentional space and in particular from presented space. Like the imagined intentional object, the imagined intentional space confronts (transcends) our acts of meaning and imagining, but the imaginational object and the imaginational space are both immanent in imaginational experi-

1. Ingarden mistakenly calls this transcendent object "purely intentional" (*LK*, p. 242; trans., p. 229). Obviously, the originally intentional object can be purely intentional or independent, i.e., "also intentional," and Ingarden could not have meant to single out the former.

ence. Obviously, the term "imaginational" has different meanings when applied to an object and when applied to space as the medium within which all imaginational objects emerge.

It follows, from what we have said, that the act of imaginational intending consists of a fusion of acts of intending and acts of imagining (imaginational acts). When we mean to imagine a real originally intentional object, the emergence and the sequence of imaginational data conform to our acts of imaginational *intending*, while the particularity of the details of these data may follow the *directive* of our acts of imagining, which may be affected by a great variety of factors. Depending on the focus and the extent of our imaginational act, its directives may be restricted to only some data of the intentional object when we do not seek to imagine that object in its phenomenal givenness. These data may evolve into imaginational actualizations of some of the intentional object's aspects, whereby an imaginational phenomenal presence of the intentional imagined object may emerge within our imaginational space. This happens if we mean to imagine it phenomenally; then the directives of our imaginational act direct the flowing, mingling, and changing data in such a way as to constitute our imaginational object into an objectified unity within our imaginational space. Because of its similarity to the imagined real object, our imaginational object may become an imaginational "representation" of the intentional object. Obviously, our imaginational object within our imaginational space does not have the "corporeal self-givenness" of a real object in real space perceived on the basis of visual sensory data. What, then, is the relation between our imaginational objects and the derived purely intentional objects presented in a literary text?

We stated earlier that we may gain phenomenal perceptions of objects when sentence-correlates exhibit their phenomenally qualified aspects. Phenomenally perceived presented objects are exhibited by derived intentional correlates of sense-units, and as intentional correlates they confront the sense-units by which they are projected. They confront our acts of meaning and then also those of imagining, but only through the intermediary of the sense-units. It is to these intentional exhibited objects that our acts of imagining are directed, and we imagine them just as—*mutatis mutandis*—we direct our acts of imagining towards originally intentional objects that we imagine. Consequently, we must preclude any possibility of equating our imaginational objects, immanent in imaginational experience, with the derived purely intentional exhibited objects. This means that our imaginational objects, though derived from imagining the imagined presented objects in presented space, must be distinguished from them. To put it more generally, the objects as presented by sense-corre- lates and imagined by us cannot be equated with our imaginational "con- cretizations" based on them.

We may now be able to answer the question we raised initially and iden- tify that spatial experience of ours through which we can, as it were, pass from our real space into presented space. Because of the mode of presenta- tion by which objects within presented space are *exhibited* and *intuited* by us as phenomenally given, they become *imagined* intentional objects in *imagined* space, corresponding to our imaginational objects in the medium of our imaginational space. By way of our imaginational experience we can relinquish our real space, move into *imagined* presented space, and accept from the perspective of our imaginational intending the quasi-reality of imagined presented objects in presented space on so to speak *the same ground* as we experience imaginationally imagined reality itself. This, no doubt, also accounts in part for the appearance of reality of presented ob- jects in spite of the radically different circumstances under which derived intentional and originally intentional objects are imaginationally experi- enced. From within our imaginational experience imagined presented space and imagined real space become, then, each in its own way, inten- tional objects which can be the targets of our acts of imaginational intend- ing that result in the imaginational objects. In each instance, we must em- phasize, our imaginational space envelops the imaginational spatial object.

Whenever we perceive an originally intentional real object (including space), we do so from the perspective of our location, from our so-called *orientational space*, from our *orientational center*—from the *zero point of ori- entation*, in Husserl's terminology. Orientational space presupposes a spa- tially situated subject perceiving objects on the basis of sensory data from a point of his subjective perspective that is located in real space. Likewise, presented objects and presented space must be exhibited *from a presented subject's orientational space*, from which, obviously, the presented space must be located in the presented world. The orientational center may be that of a given narrator, or of one or more presented characters, and it may shift as their orientational space changes. If the orientational center is that of a consistently "invisible" (objective) narrator, the center is constant in that the presentation is always offered from his point of view even if he himself changes his location. Even though the invisible narrator is never explicitly presented, he is, by virtue of his orientational center, at least to that extent copresented. We encounter a somewhat related situation when we read a play. Not only the explicit stage directions, but the stage ar- rangements implied by the text, and in fact all "effects" implied by it in view of a performance also imply an invisible spectator *within* the presented world of the play, a spectator who witnesses the action that is offered to him, performed for him; the real spectators merely shift their orientational center to his, just as the reader of a play or of any presented world must relinquish his real orientational center and enter into the presented world by transposing himself imaginationally into the presented orientational center within presented space. We have shown how this is achieved on the basis of our imaginational experience that makes the transposition possible.

C. Presented time

I shall limit my observations to a few remarks that may prove useful as a basic introduction to what Ingarden calls "presented time." Following Husserl,[2] we need to recognize here that temporal objects (*Zeitobjekte*) not only exist in time but contain within themselves a temporal extension. When we perceive an object we constitute it in its continuing (enduring) sameness or in its continual change (e.g., occurrences). Thus we apprehend that an object has duration and also existence within time; i.e., we apprehend the object as a temporal one. Our apprehension of a temporal object would be inconceivable if our perception itself were not temporal in the sense of being endowed with the continuity which we derive from our experience of lived continuity. Lived continuity is what, according to Bergson, duration essentially is.[3] It is the experienced fluidity of transitions by which our memory prolongs the before into the now, transitions that constitute our experience of duration itself without regard to the temporal extension of any intentional object or of any passing state of occurrence. This *inner time*, this lived time, cannot be measured, and the points in time or phases of time (*Zeitpunkt, Zeitphase*) are, again according to Husserl, mere abstractions and cannot be separated from the continuum of our experience, from our sense of continuity. Bergson conceives of our bridging the gap between our inner time to the duration of things in time by our associating with each moment of our inner life a corresponding moment of time of our body and thus also a simultaneous moment of all surrounding matter. Husserl's term *seiende Zeit*, inner time, designat-

2. "Vorlesungen zur Phänomenologie des inneren Zeitbewusstseins." This paper was reprinted in book form (Halle: Max Niemeyer Verlag, 1928) under the editorship of Martin Heidegger.

3. Henri Bergson, *Durée et simultanéité*, 4th ed. (Paris: Librairie Félix Alcan, 1929), chapter 3.

ing what Bergson calls the "time of inner life," has to be understood as distinct from our concrete subjective time in the empirical world, because that inner time is *immanent* in the stream of consciousness.

We stated that objects are apprehended as temporal when we perceive them in their temporal extension or when we perceive them in their extension in time. Our perceptional intending being itself temporal, our acts of perceiving objects also fulfill the function of constituting the temporality of perceived objects. Because it is important to distinguish the temporal constitutive process of perception from an intuition, I should like to add that when we seek to intuit the timeless essential identity of an object, we bracket its temporality, and when the intuition is accomplished, we integrate the object's identity into the constitutive process of our perception, and that identity thereby assumes the structures of its duration and of its existence in time.

We also noted earlier that if the semblance of the reality of presented objects is to be preserved, they must be presented as existing in space and time. By the very fact that purely intentional occurrences of the type of real occurrences are necessarily presented as taking place in succession or simultaneously, a temporal order is established in the presented world. *Within* this world they are perceived as existing in (presented) time and in their temporal extension (duration), producing a semblance of temporal phases. These projected phases constitute a presented temporal frame within the presented world in which the presented occurrences are placed.

We have seen that it is impossible to equate presented space with real space, but that we can move from real space into presented space by way of our imaginational experience. From our imaginational perspective the presented objects in presented space become imaginational, and we can, within our imaginational experience, cross over into the presented world of presented objects in presented space without a sense of the barrier separating us from them because of their different mode of existence. It is likewise impossible to equate the phases of presented time with concretely experienced time or with "objective" time.

To show the distinctions let us first note that objective time, the duration of the universe, is in its objective determination homogeneous, empty duration as long as it remains unfilled by subjective perceptional constitutions of temporal objects. Obviously, objective time has no place in the realm of the presented world. Subjective time, the time of our concrete experience of duration in the empirical world, and "intersubjective" concretely experienced time, within which we share the experience of collective living, are both experiences of time that are *colored* by the occurrences we perceive in either of these streams of concrete temporal experience. This coloration affects not only every present moment ("now-phase") but also every preceding and succeeding moment in an intricate web of reciprocities whereby the coloration of the present affects and is affected by that of the present that is receding and by that which has receded into the past, and also by that of the future, though only in anticipation. In this connection, Ingarden cites Bergson's distinctions between the various phases of concrete time that are characterized (colored) by the pace determined by the nature of the occurrences and by the perceptional experiences they elicit. Even more important in our context is the zero point of orientation in time; it is the present of concrete time experience, the zero point from which we experience the past as it continuously absorbs the present. It is from this present alone that the past, which is the previous present, can accrue and the future, the potentially future present, can beckon. No wonder the present takes precedence over the past, and the latter, having encompassed the actuality of a previous present, takes precedence over the future, which can be itself only when it eventually becomes actualized present. It is, then, actuality (*in actu esse*) that characterizes the present of concrete time, and it is an existential moment of reality itself. But, as we have already noted, a moment in time or a phase of time are mere abstractions. Time is a continuum and, like space, cannot be discontinuous. Hence all zero points of orientation recede of necessity, and the "farther" they recede from our actual present, the more the past, together with the occurrences that colored it, seems to shrink in our recollection. This *perspectival foreshortening of time* can be temporarily suspended if in spite of our inevitably actual present, we manage to put ourselves back onto a past zero point of orientation and thence perceive the intervening events. This relived zero point, however vivid, can never have the characteristics of the actuality of the present, of present reality, and of the evanescent colorations of the present. The present, we must repeat, is a mere abstraction from a continuum that excludes discontinuity.

Presented (subjective or intersubjective) time derives its colorations from the occurrences of the presented world and from the experiences of presented characters. This is an important reason for excluding any possibility of identifying phases of presented time with those of the author's private life at the time of writing or with those of the reader. Because of the existential heteronomy of purely intentional presented objects, the latter, though they may be of the type of real objects, can never be characterized by the actuality of the present, which as we noted, is an existential moment of reality. Presented present, past, and future result from the *order* in which occurrences are presented as if they were sequentially interrelated. Thus no genuine actuality of the present that characterizes reality can ever be presented, but a simulated present can (and in plays does) have the effect of heightening the *appearance* of reality for as long as we endow *the imagined presented occurrences with the stream of the present* (and hence of other phases) *pertaining to our imaginational objects*.

We may wish to note another effect of the impossibility of genuine actuality of the present in presented occurrences: the presented present has no distinct preeminence over the presented past or future. In the concrete past the previousness of occurrences results to some extent in a leveling of the past phases of time in that they do not seem to surpass each other in any significant respect, whereas the differences between any past phase and the actuality of the concrete present are striking. All phases of presented time, including the presented present, are subject to a reciprocal leveling, although the leveling is relatively less obvious when the presented world is exhibited in the presented present.

Concrete time can have no discontinuity and can, for that reason, never be presented. When we constitute a temporal object, we do so within the continuum that characterizes the constitutive functions of our perceptional experience. However, when occurrences are presented by states of affairs, these cannot, in spite of being connected, fill out all the phases of the continuum of presented occurrences as they are filled out in our experienced time, because presented states of affairs reveal the aspects of occurrences singly or in discontinuous complexes of separate units. Consequently, whenever an object is presented by states of affairs projected by meaning-units, there must always remain unfilled phases within the continuum of our imaginational perceptions. Because we experience concrete time and space in unbreakable continuity, we fill out those temporal gaps and complement the merely implied spatial extensions, in part on the basis of immanent spatiotemporal experiences that cause the unfilled gaps to recede into mere indeterminateness. These are essentially pertinent features of our imaginational perception of presentations.

In the light of these distinctive features of presented time, we can now resume and complement our considerations of the differences between the zero point of orientation in concrete time and that in presented time. Our zero point of concrete temporal orientation is preeminent in relation to the past because of the actuality of the concrete present, but it is also a fleeting point in the stream of our experienced continuity. The present of a character is, however, so to speak congealed in the correlates of sense-units and has thus no particular preeminence over the presented past into which the character can easily step in an act of recollection. In fact, the presented past into which he steps acquires, because of the reciprocal adaptation and leveling of all phases of presented time, some characteristics of the present. In the presented world it is, then, possible to present one and the same occurrence in the light of different points of temporal orientation (perspective) without the sharp contrast that separates any concrete past, and especially a relatively distant past, from the actuality of the experienced concrete present. In spite of the inevitable succession in the course of a narration, presented time need not proceed along a simple linear order of occurrences; it can follow several parallel tracks and the simultaneous phases can be filled out by different occurrences, all of which can be followed at the same time from their respective orientational perspectives. Finally, we must distinguish—again in the narrative—(a) the skeletal presentation of time which is filled out by brief accounts of occurrences that took place within relatively long periods of time and (b) other phases within the same narrative that are colored by detailed presentations. The first of these types of presentation is always apprehended in retrospect and as distant from an implied present. It primarily serves as an orientational device by which the order of events can be established. The second type is apprehended as close to an implied present, because we are made to follow the progression of the zero point of orientation from the beginning to the end of a phase that is richly colored by presentations and exhibitions of intuitively perceptible occurrences. Here, we pass, as it were, through the present of each stretch of that phase, and we witness the explicitly past events in their present unfolding. Of course, the events may be presented in the "present," especially in a play. None of these features of presented time can really be duplicated in concrete time.

D. Points of indeterminateness of presented objects

We have already discussed the perception of a real material object on the basis of visual data, and we spoke of our ability to glide from one of the object's aspects to another while keeping the object's concreteness before us at all times. We saw the difference between these perceptions and those based on the presentations of objects projected by discrete purely intentional sentence-correlates. The number of determinants constituting a real object is, as we know, infinite, and so is the number of states of affairs embedded in it. A chain of consecutive original acts of cognition is, however, necessarily finite, and in such a succession of cognitive acts our apprehension of a particular real object's manifold determinants is therefore inadequate, for most of the object's determinants are bound to remain concealed from us. Concerning this epistemological inadequacy, it may be useful to restate the differences between perceptions of originally intentional real objects and those of derived intentional objects. The particular constitutive nature of an individual real object is a concrete unity of its constituent (absolute) properties and of the *particular* determinants of these properties. For instance, a real object cannot be merely colored: at any given time, it must have a color of a particular hue, shade, value, and density. Every one of a real object's determinants is in that sense particularized, because such an object is in all its existential qualifications absolutely and unequivocally determinate and can have no point of indeterminateness. This means that from an ontological standpoint a real object consists of a concrete unity of particularized determinants. From an epistemological point of view we apprehend a particular real object as a concrete unity, even while we temporarily ignore its unity as we set about differentiating some of its determinants from its other determinants, i.e., when some of its determinants become our originally intentional objects in one act or in a chain of successive acts of cognition. The fact that we ignore most of those determinants in consecutive individual acts of cognition does not at all imply that a real object could at any point be indeterminate; the problem of a real object's points of indeterminateness is epistemological.

Let us now consider the purely intentional state of affairs of the sentence-correlate. As we know, the object is projected by the nominal word-meaning (the subject of the sentence) and also by the unfolding state of affairs. One of the functions of the nominal word-meaning is to project (by its formal content) the formal structure of the purely intentional object. However, this object is, as we also know, meant only as a schema, i.e., a schematic configuration of unspecified determinants: for instance, "a table." Consequently, this object is formally projected as if it were a concrete unity, but the limited number of the projected discrete states of affairs pertaining to it can never establish more than some of the determinants of its particular constitutive nature. Its actualized determinants are only those that are projected, and all its other determinants remain indeterminate and potential. Furthermore, most of the actualized determinants of an object in a literary work are general, and they are hardly ever the particularized traits which characterize the constitutive nature of an individual real object. Consequently the presented object is never determinate in every respect and unequivocally; it is only a schema. This fact accounts for the points of its indeterminateness and for the impossibility of basing our concretization of the presented world exclusively on what is textually actualized.

While we read we are usually not aware of points of indeterminateness. First of all, the projections by nominal word-meanings contribute significantly to the semblance of concrete reality of the presented objects exactly because these are projected in their formal structure as if they were concretely unified. This causes us to assume, on the basis of our experience of reality, that they are in every respect and in all specificity materially determinate. Secondly, the explicitly and implicitly presented determinants and the copresented spatiotemporal dimensions of the presented objects (which are not real, but are only of the type of real objects) are made conspicuous by the text, so that we become aware of points of indeterminateness only in retrospect, when we attempt to account for certain of the object's traits and realize that they have been left, as it were, empty. We often unknowingly fill in some of these gaps by complementing presented determinants of an object with determinants that were left out, and we may not always do so in compliance with textually admissible actualizations. In some works ambiguity may be intended, so that definitive complementations may not be meant to be feasible; or inconsistencies in the presented existential sphere may be purposely introduced, so that consistencies corresponding to our empirical world shall not guide our reading. We should remind ourselves here that the purposeful ambiguity of the purely intentional sentence-correlate cannot be made unambiguous by "interpretations" based on our experience with states of affairs embedded in a real object which, as we know, cannot be ambiguous exactly because such an object is absolutely determinate. The purposely ambiguous purely intentional object is meant to be opalescent, and our resolution of the ambiguity is meant to be left in a state of suspension.

2. The layer of schematized aspects

A. *Introduction*

We have dealt repeatedly with the differences between originally intentional and derived intentional objects and with the different modes of presentation by purely intentional states of affairs. We shall now have to expand our explorations and establish the nature and functions of *aspects* (or *adumbrations*) without which an intuitive grasp of presented objects in their phenomenal appearance cannot be achieved. We should also point out that we shall deal here only with presented objects of the type of real objects and we repeat that such objects can never be fully determinate, that they are not concrete unities but mere *schematic structures* characterized by various kinds of indeterminateness. The conditions under which the phenomenal appearance of objects of that type can be exhibited and intuited must be understood in the light of the phenomenal givenness (and intuition) of originally intentional real objects. However, we shall first turn our attention to some basic considerations that will provide useful background information.

Ingarden refers his reader to an article that he wrote in 1918.[4] I consider this article to be fundamental for our understanding of his treatment of schematized aspects, but I shall limit my exposition to what is indispensable for our purposes. To begin with, we are dealing with the perception of material objects which exist independently of our bodily existence. When they confront our acts of perception (of perceiving), we call such acts of consciousness acts of *external perception*. Although an act of perception is inseparable from whatever object is perceived, the act of that perception is different from the object perceived. If proof is needed, we may recall that a material object's existential qualifications may be such that they *themselves* may or may not cause the appearance of phenomenal qualifications by becoming targets of acts of perception. Also, when we perceive an object, our acts of perception may *themselves*, regardless of the object, differ according to the degree of our attentiveness or the keenness of our eyesight. What, then, does it mean when we say that we perceive an object? When we perceive an object, we *mean* it (our consciousness is directed at it) *and* we *apprehend* it. By apprehending it we get to know it in its primary self-givenness, as it is, and we constitute it in its particular configuration, in its formal structure for what it is and in its existential qualifications for what it is like. If the degree of our attentiveness or open-mindedness is low, we may fail to apprehend the object fully and exclusively in its primary self-givenness, as it presents itself, but we do still perceive it, except that our apprehension of it is then dictated largely by previous "experiences" of like objects or at least of previously encountered objects in terms of which we now apprehend the new object. In fact, we *mean* it, rather than apprehend it, as relating (by habit) to our *empirical* self. Experience, in this sense, is to various degrees present in every act of perception, but we may

4. "Über die Gefahr einer Petitio Principii in der Erkenntnistheorie," *Jahrbuch für Philosophie und phänomenologische Forschung* 4 (1921): 546–68.

free our acts of perception of that experience to some extent by focusing on the primary givenness of the perceived object.

What do we mean when we say that we perceive a material object in its phenomenal givenness, i.e., that we apprehend it in its formal and material structure, in its phenomenal configuration? It may be useful to consider very briefly a treatment of that question in Husserl's *Logical Investigations*.[5] If I see an object such as a box, I see that same object whichever way I turn it or tilt it. With each turn, however, I *experience* a new "content of consciousness," i.e., I experience only a new facet, a new *aspect*, of one and the same object. With each new aspect, I experience a different content of consciousness, but I still perceive one and the same phenomenally given object, that self-same identity; I *perceive* the object which I *mean*. In other words, at every turn of that object, I *experience* new *sensory contents* but I apperceive all these contents "in the same sense," i.e., as my perceptional experiences of one and the same *intended* object; and this is how "the being of an object is first constituted for me." We may conclude, then, that our so-called sensations, experiences of sensory contents based on sensory data, are not perceptions, for what we perceive is the object, the box, in its phenomenal givenness, whereas sensations are experiences of the sensory contents, experiences that *accompany* and found—form the substratum of—our acts of perception. For the sake of clear distinctions, I should add here that we may experience sensory contents without at the same time perceiving the object (the box). For instance, I may see only a section of one side of that box, and that part may be insufficient to allow me to see the object, to recognize it for what it is, and thus to intuit it in its phenomenal givenness. Only if the sensory contents that I experience are sufficient to constitute an aspect of the box, can I through the aspect intuit the box as objectified. We can, therefore, speak of an aspect only when through it the object appears in its phenomenal givenness.

Just as there are differences in acts of perception that affect the sense and the scope of the perceived object, there are also different degrees of "being in consciousness" (*Bewusstseinsgrad*) as we experience sensory contents or aspects during our acts of external perception. Normally, we only experience sensory contents or aspects but do not apprehend the sensory data, for our consciousness is directed toward the perceived object. If at the height of our awareness we do become conscious of the sensory data or the aspects, we may, even while perceiving the object, *apprehend* them, but we do not apprehend them in any objectified givenness, and usually

5. Investigation V, no. 14.

only marginally. There are, then, degrees of consciousness in our state of experiencing sensory contents or aspects.

Insofar as we are conscious of our perceptions we say that we *live through* them. As I live through my act of perceiving an object, my so-called pure self apprehends that *act* as one of intending—of meaning—that object and possibly also of apprehending it. My pure self acquires a cognition of my act of perceiving, and this cognition differs from perceptional cognition in that the latter is based on sensory data. Living through and perceiving are both acts of consciousness, but the act of perceiving need not be accompanied by the act of living through it. On the other hand, the act of living through cannot occur without some intentional object that we perceive or, for that matter, wish, love, hate, etc. Likewise, we can live through our experiences of sensory contents. These contents (i.e., that which is experienced in the course of an external perception) are heterogeneous in respect to the pure self, "strange to the ego" (*ichfremd*, trans. "extra-personal"), just like any intentional object at which the lived-through perception (or wishing) is directed.

We are now ready to present Ingarden's discussion of the *phenomenal givenness of originally intentional real objects*, and we shall first turn our attention to aspects experienced in the course of external perception, aspects that are the means by which that givenness is achieved.

B. Aspects based on sensory data

In the course of an external perception of a real object, I experience on the basis of sensory data a continuous flux of ever-changing sensory contents which make up a recognizable aspect of that object. From the point of view of our goal in this discussion, it is important to realize that such aspects are experienced during acts of external perception, and that we experience sensory contents as aspects only when we perceive (i.e., when we mean, and when we apprehend to a certain extent) a real object at the same time. Consequently, every act of external perception of a real object contains experiences of various sensory contents and of aspects (regardless of the degree to which we may live through these experiences).

When I perceive a red sphere, for instance a billiard ball, i.e., when I do not merely look at it but see it, I apprehend it as a concrete unity although I know that I can never see the whole surface of that solid body at any one time, not to mention its inside. Whether I turn the sphere, raise it, lower it, bring it closer to me, or move it some distance from me, all that I can at any one time look at, see, and experience is an aspect of that sphere. Regardless of what my orientational center may be, there always remain sides of any visually perceived material object that I cannot see during any one act of perception. We have repeatedly pointed out that what is given in our perceptional experiences is not static and that we constantly shift back and forth between experiences of aspects and perceptions of the concrete object itself. We never quite apprehend a single aspect, but rather a continuum of flowing and merging aspects, and we experience any one concretely given aspect as a complex of flowing and merging adumbrational elements that constitute it. We may see, then, that (1) we experience any one concrete aspect in its complexity and as one of innumerable aspects of one and the same object; and (2) we intuit through each experience of an aspect the phenomenal givenness of the perceived object. Aspects in external perception are thus highly complex perceptional experiences of sensory contents that are based on sensory data which in the course of our perceptional acts are in an even greater flux than the aspects. The sensory data thus constitute only the substratum of a concrete aspect. While we experience the aspect, we are hardly aware of the sensory data, for we are more concerned with the aspect and especially with the object that appears through the aspect as phenomenally given.

It should be useful to remind ourselves that the perceived object appearing in its phenomenal givenness is not given only in its formal structure (of, for instance, a certain thing), but also with some of its qualitative determinants. Thus in the case of the red billiard ball, any of its aspects is experienced as *referring to* the object perceived as a sphere and also, for instance, to the uniformity of its coloration and to its phenomenal solidity and phenomenal smoothness. It is fairly obvious that if we did not know the object or any object of that sort at all, we could not perceive it through its aspect, for we would be incapable of an objectifying interpretation. The fact that we do perceive the object through the experience of any one of its concrete aspects is nevertheless remarkable because of the considerable differences between an aspect and the object that appears through it in its phenomenal givenness.

> (1) First of all, the sphere and the aspect through which we intuit it differ in that the sphere is independent and self-sufficient, whereas the aspect is clearly marked by dependence and connectivity, for it exists only when we experience it as an aspect. The billiard ball with its existential qualifications continues to be what it is regardless of our acts of perception. By contrast, only potentially self-presenting existential qualifications (which be-

come phenomenal) and phenomenal qualifications constitute the evanescent concrete external aspects. The aspect itself is thus experienced directly, immediately and ever so briefly. Consequently, we cannot speak of a concrete external aspect without recognizing that it depends, at the same time, on (a) the object's phenomenal and actualized potentially phenomenal qualifications intuited on the basis of experiences of sensory contents of various kinds; and (b) on an intuiting subject's experiencing the aspects as referring to the object's phenomenal givenness.

(2) Another difference lies in that the sphere is enclosed and in every respect determinate, whereas the capacity of any of its aspects reveals only that side of the sphere that we happen to face from the orientational center of our perception.

(3) Furthermore, none of the aspects is spherical, whereas the object (the billiard ball) is. Depending on our center of orientation, its aspect may appear to have an elliptical surface as distinct from anything existing objectively in the capacity of the sphere.

(4) Also, within the aspect we experience sensory contents of different kinds and particularly a flux of different shades of red and of other colors, too, yet the perceived object is meant to be uniformly red.

In spite of all these differences, the aspect does refer to the phenomenal givenness of the object and also to all its hidden aspects, aspects that we do not actually face at any present moment, but which may have been actual before, or which may be merely anticipated on the basis of previous perceptions of a similar object.

What we experience within the capacity of an aspect may be considered to be its "fulfilled" formal and qualitative data—the *fulfilled qualities* of the aspect. Because we perceive an object through its aspect although the object is constituted by various qualifications that are different from those that we experience in the aspect, there must be some *unfulfilled qualities* in the aspect that make that perception possible. These unfulfilled qualities are always present in any aspect, and they refer to the object, its properties, and its other aspects. The extent to which and the accuracy with which we can anticipate the hidden qualifications of an object on the basis of previous experiences determine the effective range of the referring function of the unfulfilled qualities of the experienced aspect. There are also unfulfilled qualities that refer to hidden adumbrational *elements* that are within the range of that very aspect. For instance, the uniform redness of an aspect of the red sphere has as its substratum a flux of different color data, and on the basis of these data we experience the sensory contents of merging shades of red. These are the qualitatively fulfilled elements of this aspect. However, this aspect also contains the unfulfilled quality which refers to and thus brings about the phenomenal appearance of the uniform redness of the aspect. Once this uniform redness is experienced as a fulfilled quality of the aspect, the aspect acquires the unfulfilled quality that refers to the uniformity of redness in the anticipated other aspects of the sphere. Ingarden is right when he says that without the unfulfilled quality in the aspect the uniformity itself of that shade of red within that aspect cannot be made to appear phenomenally; but we should remember that the effectiveness of the referring function is in this instance to be ascribed to our perceiving all the elements of one aspect and ultimately all the aspects that are of a given shade of red to be identical in respect to the idea of that coloration. (To be more precise, we can speak here only of essential identity, because in each experience of the concrete aspects, the uniformity is based on various shades of red.)

Among the relations between aspects we find also *functional dependences*. We discussed features of such dependences in other contexts and noted the colorations of various units that result from the functional effects of previous or of anticipated units. In a static situation the proximity of units determines the effectiveness of reciprocal colorations. In a succession of adumbrational experiences it is the functional dependence of any present experience on the previously present one that becomes conspicuous. Perceptions of uniformity, similarity, or contrast are some of the effects of functional dependences between sequentially experienced aspects of one and the same object, or between aspects of different contiguous objects.

It might seem as if all moments within an aspect were based exclusively on visual data. In any present perception of a concrete aspect there is always some synthesis of different sensory experiences: for instance, we see the smoothness of paper or the softness of silk. Another feature of the relationship between aspects is that which we experience between an aspect of a material object and aspects of objects on its *periphery* (as perceived from a given orientational center). In these perceptional experiences the different aspects also show a reciprocal functional dependence, but the objects that appear on the periphery do remain "background" objects, unless of course we should focus on them in the course of our perceptional transitions.

Let us sum up our findings pertaining to objects given in external perception. We have noted that during the act of perceiving we experience an aspect (strictly speaking, we never experience a single aspect but merging aspects) of the perceived object which appears to us in its phenomenal givenness through that aspect; that the experience of the aspect consists of a flux of various sensory contents, i.e., of variously blended sensations (visual, tactile, acoustic, olfactory, gustatory), based on external sensory data, such as color, sound, odor, etc.; and that the external sensory data *appear* to us not as they are, but as sensory contents which we experience: e.g., as the color or the sound of a certain quality, or as a surface of a certain roughness, etc.[6] This means that the capacity of an experienced aspect must be distinguished from its stratified "structural moments," i.e., that sensory data must be distinguished from the experienced sensory contents which found the external aspects. The capacity of an external aspect must, however, also be distinguished from the capacity of the object phenomenally appearing through it. We also established that because of the referring function (unfulfilled quality) that is present in every aspect, a phenomenally given object is made to appear through the aspect; and, finally, that in the course of an external perception the aspect is not given to us in objectified givenness, but only as experienced. Before discussing so-called "internal aspects," we should determine what is meant by "schematized aspects."

C. *General observations on schematized aspects*

We stated that we experience sensory data as a continuous flux of ever-changing sensory contents and that what is given in our perceptional experiences is, therefore, never static and can never be the same in repeated experiences. Furthermore, our acts of perceiving are never the same, not only because of changing external circumstances during which they may recur, but also because of our varying dispositions which necessarily affect our repeated perception of one and the same object. And yet we say, on "repeating" the experience, that we experience the "same" aspect and intuit the "same" phenomenal object. Objects, as we know, are considered essentially identical if because of their essential constitutive nature—their essential schematic configuration—they fall under a general idea in whose constant qualitative moment their schematic configuration is reflected. We may say, then, that the essential identity of objects rests on the identity of the absolute schemata that constitute their nature.

On this basis, we may say that every concrete aspect consists of an abso-

6. Edmund Husserl, *Ideas*, trans. W. R. Boyce Gibson (New York: Collier Books, 1962), no. 85.

lute skeletal—schematic—structure and of variable moments which vary according to each experience. These variable moments of an aspect are subject to, for instance, the effects of functional dependences, whereas the elements of its absolute schematic structure are not, and it is therefore this schematic structure of the aspect that allows us to recognize an aspect as "the same" during recurring perceptional experiences. Consequently, the concrete aspects that we consider to be the same in repeated experiences are through their unchanging schematic structure essentially identical. Likewise, an object can appear to us in its primary self-givenness repeatedly as essentially the same only by virtue of those of its aspects which we experience as identical because we *schematize* them and do not take into account their variable moments. Thus the concrete aspects of one and the same uniformly red sphere must be schematized, i.e., conceived of in their absolute skeletal structure, to be recognized in repeated experiences as essentially identical and serving as the immediate foundation for our repeated intuitions of the phenomenal appearances of that uniformly red sphere.

D. Internal aspects

When we deliberately turn our attention inward and perceive, for instance, one of our character traits or a psychic state, we find that it appears through what figuratively may be called internal aspects. An internal aspect is, then, experienced during an act of internal perception, which is a reflective act of consciousness, on the basis of which we may also experience an internal aspect of some other subject. If we perceive psychic states (for instance, joy or sadness) or character traits (for instance, brutality or irresoluteness), what are the internal aspects through which these objects appear to us and what is the substratum of these aspects?

Using Husserl's terms drawn from the *Ideas* (no. 85), we may state that, in external aspects, sensory data (color, sound, etc.) are "the concrete data of experience." We also established that these data are experienced as sensory contents and that the latter may be experienced as external aspects during an act of external perception. What, then, are the analogous data in the case of internal perception?

I shall draw on Husserl's *Logical Investigations* (V) as well as on his *Ideas* (no. 85) and I shall choose and adapt terms that I hope may clarify, at least for our purposes, the relation between term and correlate. First, we should note that not every internal aspect has in its substratum an analogue of the sensory contents that found external aspects. When an internal aspect does have analogues of sensory contents, we shall call them *sensile data* (*Empfindungsdaten*, trans. "sensory data"). For instance, the sensile datum of the *pain* of a burn is derived from a sensile *impression* originating in a tactile sensory datum. Similarly, the sensile datum of the *pleasure* of smelling the fragrance of a rose is derived from a sensile *impression* originating in an olfactory sensory datum. Any one of these sensile data is a *blend* of sensory datum with sensile impression. Just like sensations that are experiences of sensory contents, these sensile data of the feelings of pain or pleasure have no intentional character. We shall call sensile data of this type *feeling-sensations* (*Gefühlsempfindungen*, trans. "emotional sensations"). Feeling-sensations are thus analogous to sensations that are experiences of sensory contents, and they too may constitute aspects, i.e., internal aspects through which we intuit the phenomenal appearance of such *psychic states* as sadness or joy. These feeling-sensations contain elements that pertain to certain bodily functions. Not all internal aspects are, however, founded in sensile data of this type. There are, for instance, sensile data that pertain to the body but which are of the kinesthetic type arising from the movement of joints or the strain of muscles. These sensile data are not blends of sensory data with sensile impressions, as feeling-sensations are. There are still other sensile data, such as feelings of fatigue or freshness, which contain "bodily" elements but do not seem to stem from any clearly identifiable part of the body.

We must repeat here that not every internal aspect has in its substratum sensile data, but we are still dealing with those that do. The highly complex, changeable and constantly changing capacity of these internal aspects depends on (1) the types, and the intensity, of its various founding sensile data and (2) other founding elements which are the psychic or mental *dispositions* of the experiencing subject, dispositions which have no bodily sensile data in their substratum. The capacity of all internal aspects always contains founding elements of the latter kind. Now, what does Ingarden mean when he states that *that which* appears in internal perception *of* (such objects as) psychic states, processes, and character traits depends on the capacity of the internal aspect, but that the *same* character trait (for instance, brutality) or the *same* psychic state (for instance, joy) may be founded by feeling-sensations of different kinds?[7] For instance, let us con-

---

7. "*was* uns in der inneren Wahrnehmung *von* unseren psychischen Zuständen . . . erscheint" (*LK*, p. 292, emphasis added). This is mistranslated as "*which* of our states . . . appear in internal perception" (trans., pp. 273–74, emphasis added).

sider the character trait brutality as the object that is to appear through two internal aspects which differ because one is founded in part in the feeling-sensation of pain and the other in that of pleasure. Since all internal aspects contain as a constant element a psychic (or mental) disposition, we shall consider vehemence as that constant in both aspects. Thus vehemence will affect the feeling-sensation of pain in one aspect, and the feeling-sensation of pleasure in the other. Consequently, one part of the concept brutality will appear through one of the aspects, whereas another part of the concept will appear through the other aspect. Conversely, if the same feeling-sensation (e.g., the same bodily pain) partly founds two internal aspects, through which different psychic states appear, and if one aspect contains a vehement and the other aspect a phlegmatic disposition as its constant, the phenomenally appearing psychic states may accordingly differ and reveal themselves as resentment or anguish through one of the aspects, and as impassive endurance through the other.

We should now mention those internal aspects that are not founded in any sensile data. For instance, the psychic state of indecisiveness may appear through various inner aspects whose elements consist not only of the disposition to delay and to hesitate, but also of inclinations to do so in a particular situation that elicits a decision, or to one's own stand in the matter, or on account of the type of decision that is to be taken. In our context, I believe, one may be justified in considering these nonsensile elements that elicit and blend with the responses derived from our psychic or mental dispositions as performing a function that is analogous to the sensory data, which elicit sensile impressions and blend with them to constitute the sensile data that found the internal aspects.

Finally we should consider the degree of awareness which may affect our internal perceptions. Our awareness may range from unconsciousness, or repression into the subconscious, to a gradually dawning awareness and finally to the fully conscious internal perception of psychic states, processes, or character traits that appear to us phenomenally through variously "lived through" experiences of internal aspects.

E. Schematized aspects in the literary work

We have seen that there are many points which Ingarden's text seems to take for granted but which need clarification if we wish to avoid misconceptions. This is particularly true with respect to schematized aspects and their actualizations. We saw in our seemingly detailed, but in fact cursory, presentation of external and internal aspects:

(1) that we cannot speak of an aspect unless we can intuit through it the phenomenally appearing object;

(2) that the cluster of founding data must be sufficient to constitute an aspect and thus to permit the phenomenal appearance of the object;

(3) that an aspect is founded in a complex structure of various phenomenally given experienced data that form a concrete unity;

(4) that an aspect is not perceived as objectified, but only experienced as a flux of merging data;

(5) that the capacity of an aspect differs from that of the object;

(6) that the aspects of any perceived material object are in principle innumerable;

(7) that the capacity of an aspect contains unfulfilled qualities whose function is to refer to the phenomenally appearing object and, in an anticipatory manner, to its hidden determinants and aspects;

(8) that an external aspect is experienced as colored by contiguous aspects or by aspects of adjacent objects;

(9) that all external aspects are founded in experienced sensory contents elicited by sensory data;

(10) that all internal aspects are founded in psychic or mental dispositions of the experiencing subject and either in sensile data or in nonsensile data that elicit responses derived from our psychic or mental dispositions;

(11) that no single experience of any concrete aspect can be identically repeated by anyone, and that in order to explain the recurrence of essentially identical experiences of aspects, we must postulate schematic aspects, schemata that contain such elements of aspects as are unaffected by functional dependences or by variables in perceptional experience.

We should conclude this summary by a brief comment pertaining to two points mentioned above (3 and 4). Just as we experience a real object in its coalescence, as a concrete unity, we also experience an aspect as a flux of constantly merging concrete founding data. The flux does not contradict the continuum of concreteness: for instance, the flux experienced in the perception of a gentle wave does not disrupt the continuum of that body of water.

The situation in the case of *presented* objects (normally of the type of real objects) is different. The founding data are presented as correlates of sense-units. Let us recall that the correlates may be states of existential or phenomenal qualification, or states of occurrence; that these sense-units project (1) an object which is *meant* as a categorially formed perception— as a schema—and (2) a state of affairs that pertains to the object in that it determines the object through various individual or clustered individual qualifications consisting of direct attributes, or of acts or processes which in their own way also furnish the object's individual determinants; and that any explicitly presented state of affairs is only one of many embedded in the object. We have emphasized the fact that states of affairs can present qualifications only singly, individually, even when they are presented in clusters. This presentation stands in sharp contrast to the qualifications of a real object, all of whose determinants present themselves as forming the concrete unity of the object that is their carrier. This shows, as we know, that the singling out of any determinant is an act of pure intentionality and that for presented determinants, the purely intentional sentence-correlates perform that function. Because of this rigidly individualized presentation of only a limited number of selected determinants, a sequence of states of affairs cannot furnish the concrete unity characteristic of determinants of a real object, and *cleavages* necessarily occur in a presentation. *All determinants not explicitly presented remain therefore potential.* Since most explicitly presented determinants are general and only rarely particularized traits characteristic of a real object, presented determinants lack the specificity (the tones, the shades, the texture, etc.) that we experience when we perceive an object in its primary self-givenness. This fact, we noted, *accounts for the points of indeterminateness in a presented object.* We may sum up our considerations of the potentialities implicit in presented objects by stating that the purely intentional states of affairs present objects in a schematic manner; that determinants are presented as individualized purely intentional data separated from the concrete unity which they form as qualifiers of real objects; and that most determinants are presented without the particularity of determinants of real objects. For all those reasons *the literary work of art is a schematic structure,* which means that any and all objects explicitly presented by correlates of sense-units are *schematic and lack the concreteness of real objects.* We may see, then, that states of affairs projected by sense-units merely present objects and elements of their aspects. They do not account directly for the phenomenal appearance of the objects themselves. And for all the reasons we have just enumerated, the very aspects are schematic, for the states of affairs necessarily schematize them.

Therefore these aspects are properly called *schematized*. It is only by means of the special constitution of the schematized aspects (and certain acts on the part of the reader, which we shall discuss later) that the presented objects can appear phenomenally in our imagination. Consequently, the schematized aspects fulfill a special function with respect to the merely presented objects, and therefore they constitute a distinct layer of the literary work of art, a layer with its own aesthetic qualities which contribute to the work's polyphony.

We must ask, then, which states of affairs are best suited to predetermine schematized aspects and how these states of affairs themselves must be constituted to fulfill that function in such a manner as to enable the reader on his own to constitute the aspects and through them to intuit phenomenally appearing objects. There are, as we have repeatedly stated, different states of affairs. We have singled out, for purposes of our discussion, states of existential qualification, states of occurrence, and states of phenomenal qualification, though we should at least mention the *states of relations*, in which objects are seen in relation to other objects (e.g., the ties that link parent to child) without any specific state of occurrence through which that relation is made to appear in every instance. Because an aspect (actually always a flux of merging aspects) must be so constituted as to elicit our intuition of the phenomenal appearance of an object, it is necessary that the constitutive determinants of the object be *exhibited* as often as possible by states of phenomenal qualification or by potentially "self-presenting" states of affairs.

However, the appropriate selection of states of affairs does not by itself solve the problems inherent in all presented states of affairs, i.e., the problems posed by the inevitably schematic projection of the object, by points of indeterminateness, and by cleavages. These problems can be overcome only by the reader. A prevalence of suitable determinants and a selection of appropriate types of states of affairs are the most important, but never the only, means by which the reader may be helped to overcome the problems of filling the gaps created by the merely schematic outline of the projected objects and by cleavages, and of complementing the various points of indeterminateness with heightened specificity. One of the textual factors that may direct the reader in his manifold acts of complementation—assuming he is sensitive to such directives—is the very schema of the presented object. We noted many times that this schema determines the reader's complementations at least by imposing on them a certain range beyond which the object may lose its projected (even if only schematically predetermined) constitutive nature, i.e., its identity. This complementation may be, of course, also affected by the sound and particular meaning of the word used to project the object.

Phenomenal qualifications, explicit or implied, have the functions of directing the reader in his constitution of aspects through which the presented objects may appear to him and thus come to life in his imagination. It should be useful to spell out as briefly as we can what the reader's constitution of aspects really means, so that we may the better understand and appreciate the textual functions that prepare, direct, and sometimes even impose on the reader the manner and scope of those of his acts that lead to that constitution. The following remarks are intended to prepare us for the examination of the functions of aspects and for the understanding of some acts of actualization which, *inter alia*, constitute the concretization of the literary work. We stated earlier that every type of projected states of affairs fulfills, in its unfolding and in its own way, *the function of presentation*, i.e., of revealing one (or more) of the presented object's determinants and thus enabling us to *know* what that determinant *is*. We also noted that an act of perception is an intentional act whereby we mean and apprehend it as the carrier of its determinants and as qualified by one (or more) of these. Any one determinant, together with others to which our act of perception is momentarily not directed, constitutes one of the object's existential qualifications that may be presented directly or indirectly by one of the states of affairs we mentioned. We may conclude that the intentionality of our acts of perception, whereby we mean and apprehend an object, aims at a percept of one or more of an object's qualifications; that it aims at a cognition of the object; and that the presentative function of a state of affairs, which reflects the intentionality of our original act of perception, is therefore to convey the result of cognition.

From our explorations of external and internal aspects, we know that aspects cannot be perceived, but that we experience them while we constitute them on the basis of founding data. We also observed that strictly we can experience aspects only in the course of external perception, but figuratively we can experience aspects also during acts of internal perception. What, then, do we mean when we say that we constitute and experience aspects presented through the intermediary of projected states of affairs? As we read, we *mean* the objects and apprehend them with their determinants as they are presented to us in the correlates of connected sentences. We are faced with a multiplicity of derived intentional percepts, all of which are, however, only skeletal structures. So to some extent we complement the points of indeterminateness imaginationally with details known to us from past experience but also under the general directives of the explicitly presented skeletal structures, assuming again that we take the directives into account. Helped by the connection of sentences, we also fill in the gaps left by veiled cleavages and link the rigidly separated states of affairs into complexes which we experience in our imagination as if they merged into a continuum that seems analogous to that which characterizes our original perceptional experiences. We no longer apprehend the objects in the skeletal rigidity of their presentation; we imagine them as more or less concretized when we begin to experience their gradually actualized aspects. The unfulfilled qualities of the aspects favor our further acts of complementation and thus intensify our experience of the aspects themselves. This experience enhances our capability of intuiting in our imagination the appearance of the concretized presented objects in their phenomenal givenness. In the course of our concretizations, which imply complementations, we actualize the merely schematic aspects. However, if we were guided only by percepts presented by states of affairs that do not perform exhibiting functions, our actualizations of the schematized aspects and the concretizations of the presented objects might be carried out primarily, *if at all*, on the basis of experiences of our empirical self and might not be justified by the exigencies of the text. In fact, we may not even succeed in actualizing the data into aspects and in imagining the phenomenal appearance of objects. We may be left with what Ingarden calls "described aspects" that are, as I see it, mere elements of potential aspects which do not yield concretizations and phenomenally appearing objects.

To prepare the actualization and constitution of schematized aspects in our imaginational experience, to impose them to a certain extent on the reader, at least some of the founding states of affairs must fulfill the exhibiting function. As a result of that, the schematized aspects are, as it were, "held-in-readiness" for our acts of actualization, on whose basis objects can appear phenomenally. We shall call those schematized aspects *ready aspects*. It must be emphasized that the holding-in-readiness of aspects does not imply that every instance of their actualization will lead to the same concretization of the presented objects, even for the same reader. Many different subjective conditions, some of which we have discussed, affect the actualizations of aspects, and we have noted the reasons why, strictly speaking, no actualization of external or internal aspects can ever be identically repeated. The holding-in-readiness of aspects has the function of only indicating or sometimes of prescribing the *direction* which their actualization should take. This means that the holding-in-readiness of aspects has the effect of making them less schematic and that the suggested direction of complementations may result in actualizations on the basis of which we can, in our imagination, experience the aspects themselves and the corresponding objects as if they were concrete.

Let us now enumerate some of the devices on the strength of which schematized aspects may be made into ready aspects. We have already noted that the *selection* of artistically effective determinants and consequently of types of states of affairs is important for the projection of the presented world. States of phenomenal qualification or states of potentially self-presenting qualifications are indispensable to our being able to constitute aspects of phenomenally appearing objects at all. All these states of affairs do not merely found aspects; they also fulfill the function of readying them. However, additional devices may be used for readying aspects. We have already mentioned the difference between "concrete" and "abstract" words and the exhibiting effects of the former. Various *images*, by which existential qualifications are purposely exhibited, or *comparisons*, which cause the capacity of one presented state of affairs to exhibit the capacity of another that has not been explicitly presented, are established devices whereby aspects may be amply readied. The layer of sound-formations plays a most important role in this respect: melody, rhythm, manifestative characteristics, or, for instance, onomatopoeic formations contribute, all in their own way, to the exhibition of particularly intriguing elements of aspects, some of which we shall soon mention. Obviously these devices are used selectively to exhibit at least some of the elements of ready aspects, and not all schematized aspects are thus held-in-readiness. This helps to explain why some of our imaginational perceptions of phenomenal appearances occur in separate sudden illuminations, and why—purely textually—neither the continuum of aspects nor the mobility of their flux, as they are known from direct perceptional experiences of real objects, may be experienced throughout the presented world. However, while ready aspects may conceal the cleavages between them and the points of indeterminateness within them, these gaps may, at least to a certain extent, be complemented by imaginational acts during our concretization.

F. Functions of schematized aspects

We shall present here only an explanatory sketch of the conditions pertaining to the *determinative functions* of aspects. The presentations of objects by sense-units vary in accordance with the types of projected states of affairs, but all presentations reveal the object's constitution. The constitution is modified if the object is not only presented but also exhibited by ready schematized aspects and on that basis intuited in its phenomenal appearance. This means that the constitution of an object is *primarily determined* by the capacity of states of affairs as that capacity is projected by sense-units; that it is *secondarily determined*, but only in the sense that its constitution is *modified*, by schematized aspects readied by states of phenomenal qualification or by states of potentially self-presenting qualifications. This modification of the constitution of an object is one of the determinative functions of aspects, and the effect of this modification is that it brings about a phenomenal appearance of the object.

If, in addition to phenomenal qualifications, a special device contributes to the readying of an aspect, the determinative function of that aspect may not be limited to the mere modification which we have just described. Let us assume that there are two nominal expressions that have the same intentional object-correlate, and that we use one of these in a sentence projecting a state of phenomenal qualification and the other in another sentence projecting the same state of phenomenal qualification. The *sense* of both sentences is the same, and they therefore predetermine the aspect in the same manner. If one of the two expressions has a special sound-configuration and the other does not, then that special sound-quality enriches and enhances the readiness of the aspect and thereby endows the phenomenally appearing object's constitution with a quality which that object would not have if it were determined only by the sense of the other sentence. Because of that special sound-configuration, the determinative function of the aspect—readied in this manner—does not merely contribute to the possibility of the object's expected phenomenal appearance; it actually determines the constitution of the object in such a way as to cause it to appear in a modified phenomenal appearance. Where the aspect readied by a special sound-quality thus alters the constitution of an object— but only in its phenomenal appearance—we can speak even more justifiably of the determinative function of ready aspects. We should point out that the new qualification which the object thus acquires is certainly not a projection of a meaning-unit; it has only a semblance of existence. These considerations lead us to the conclusion that the modes of appearance of intuited objects depend on the types of aspects that determine them.

What, then, is meant by "types of aspects" that determine the modes of appearance of objects? To avoid misunderstandings, let us repeat that we are speaking of various phenomenal appearances of objects, and not of objects as they are meant and merely presented by correlates of sense-units. We saw that the mode of appearance of an object, i.e., the way an object appears in our imagination, depends first of all on whether we see it through external aspects (e.g., predominantly visual, or simultaneously of different kinds) or whether we see it through aspects selected and arranged according to certain chosen purposes. The means of readying determine the type of the aspect and affect the mode of the object's appearance. We showed the determinative effect of one special readying device, drawn from the layer of sound-formations, but there are, as we shall see, other readying devices that have a similar functional effect on the appearance of objects.

In this brief discussion of some types of aspects we shall take for granted the presence of states of phenomenal and of potentially self-presenting qualifications in the capacity of any schematized aspect. Therefore we shall focus on other elements by which schematized aspects are readied, their capacity modified, and the mode of appearance of objects to an extent predetermined.

We know that one and the same object (character, situation, process, thing, etc.) can be presented through various types of schematized aspects, and that the manner of readying them results in different modes of appearance of the objects. We stated that the capacity of the schematized aspects of an object may contain simultaneously visual, acoustic, and other phenomenal data. For instance, a character may sometimes be exhibited primarily by acoustic data without our being able to "see" him in our imagination. Furthermore, when he appears to us visually, we may see him in our imagination only from one point of view, or he may appear from various points of view. These readying devices, which affect the capacity of aspects and determine their type, are frequently ignored by the reader, and yet if one and the same situation appears, for instance, at one time predominantly through visually experienced aspects and at another predominantly through acoustically experienced aspects, that situation contains in each instance different points of indeterminateness and elicits different concretizations. Likewise, the appearance of an object presented from one point of view differs greatly from the appearance of the same object presented from several points of view. Frequently, we pass over these distinctions, although they alter the modes of appearance of presented objects. We assume on the basis of transpositions and settings that the objects are real, and we concretize them without regard to their modes of presentation and appearance. Thus when we give an account of them in what is called a "plot summary," we usually divest them of those modes and other artistic means by which they are aesthetically exhibited. The same crippling effects result frequently from translations of a literary work of *art*, and especially of poetry, where in addition to all other readying elements in the capacity of aspects, the sound-configurations of words play a most significant role.

The principles governing the selection and arrangement of adumbrational elements play an even more important role in readying the capacity of aspects and in codetermining their type. There is a type of aspects whose function is to bring about a novel and quite unexpected phenomenal appearance of objects which we have become accustomed to seeing and recognizing in a traditional and everyday appearance. The introduction of aspects capable of such effects marks many major departures from established currents not only in literature, but also in the other arts. We find comfort and security in what is familiar, and we resist the recognition of seeing familiar objects in a new light. The capacity of this type of aspects may, for instance, be readied by a prevalence of previously unnoticed or purposely ignored (sometimes socially disapproved) tactile, olfactory, or gustatory data.

We encounter a similar, though in one respect significantly different, situation when for a number of personal or social reasons we develop the habit of perceiving familiar objects through traditional aspects which exhibit only surface traits that are incidental, average, and shared by most objects of the same type. There is, then, a type of aspects which is readied by data that lead to a new appearance of familiar objects, an appearance which exhibits the characteristic traits that single out the objects in their essential identity. The selection of devices for the readying of this type of aspects depends entirely on the writer's ability to apprehend the essential configuration of objects, characters, processes, or situations. It may be very difficult to make a general statement about the nature of such devices, some of which are also used in combination with other types of aspects, so that what characterizes the resulting type of aspects is primarily a point of view that governs the selection of readying adumbrational elements. In this case, though of course not in this case only, the writer's center of orientation, the perspective from which he sees objects in their essential nature, is a determining factor in the disposition of the selected elements.

Another type of aspects is characterized primarily by the manner in which connections between the states of affairs that found the aspects are arranged. We know that in the presented world it is impossible to connect states of affairs in such a way as to produce a continuum of presented aspects. Because the resulting cleavages are inevitable, the question is how their existence may be veiled or exploited and with what effects on the modes of appearance of the objects. This type of aspects may be characterized by at least two clearly distinguishable patterns of connections between states of affairs, which, we may add, need not be mutually exclusive in one and the same literary work. One of these patterns emerges through a close connection of consecutive features of a situation. For instance, by means of a detailed description of aspects of contiguous objects within a presented space the narrator can give the reader the impression that the gaps between the aspects and the objects have been filled in. Thus we are not only guided in our concretizations; they are imposed on us, for there seem to be no gaps left for us to fill in. The other pattern of connections exploits the necessary discontinuity of aspects of the presented world. Here we find relatively small clusters of connected states of affairs that form aspects through which the objects appear like "snapshots," in separate flashes of illumination.

We shall now conclude our explorations of schematized aspects by a consideration of the *aesthetic qualities*, i.e., *qualities that elicit our seeing, our intuiting*, that are contained in ready aspects, which in turn constitute the aesthetic qualities that characterize the appearance of the objects. Ingarden's description of the artistic work of a photographer provides a valid analogy for the exploration of aesthetic qualities in aspects. A photographer cannot limit himself to a mere representation of an object, i.e., to a presentation of similarities between his picture and his model. If he aims at a certain mode of appearance of the object in his picture, he must select the aspects, assess their capacity, and determine the aesthetic effects of light, color, and lines. We may, I believe, on the basis of our previous findings, and without present reference to other sources in Ingarden's work, consider the photographer's model as his *imagined* intentional object, and the object presented in his picture as an exhibition of his corresponding lived-through *imaginational* object. An object in a literary work may likewise be considered a presentation of its imagined intentional counterpart. We may assume that the writer must select states of affairs capable of *presenting* the imagined object. His selection of states of affairs serves first the immediate purpose of presenting a likeness between the imagined and the presented object. Beyond that, somewhat like the photographer, he must also select the types of aspects through which his presented object should be *exhibited* so that we may intuit it in its appropriately predetermined phenomenal appearance. For that purpose he must select states of affairs that contain various phenomenal qualifications. This selection already introduces a certain variety of adumbrational elements which contribute to the readying of the aspects and carry with them aesthetic qualities that predetermine to some extent the mode in which the object may then phenomenally appear as, for instance, predominantly seen or heard from one point of view or from several. Thus the capacity of the aspects is constituted. Under the general directives of one or another organizational principle—for instance, with an eye to essential characteristics or to closely connected states of affairs—appropriate "decorative" elements (e.g., from the layer of sound-formations) are also made to ready the capacity of the selected types of aspects even further. Each adumbrational element and each adumbrational type brings its own aesthetic quality into an evolving system of the mutually complementary aesthetic qualities of the manifold aspects within a work of art. This system may be called *the style of the aspects* of that work. This fact leads to an important conclusion not only with respect to our aesthetic grasp of the work of art, but also to our proper assessment of the constitutive and aesthetic functions of the layer of schematized aspects. To develop the conclusion it will be useful to compare the style of the aspects, the *adumbrational style*, in real material objects with that in a literary work of art.

Among the various aesthetic qualities of an aspect of a real material object we may mention at least those that are derived from the interplay of colors, light, shadows, and lines, from which there may emerge a harmonious configuration of aesthetic qualities of that aspect. We have just noted that the configuration of aesthetic qualities of all the aspects of an object may be called the adumbrational style of that object. Consequently, the aesthetic qualities of each aspect as well as the configuration of these qualities of all the aspects of that object *are all adumbrational*. Yet in an external perception we do not apprehend the aesthetic qualities as adumbrational; they impress us as the style of the object itself. We noted the difference between external sensory data as they are and as we experience them: that we experience them not as they are, but as they appear to us. This means that the experienced phenomenal qualifications that are constitutive of an aspect cannot be equated with the founding existential qualifications that we apprehend in the object. An aspect is never a real constituent part of a real object, for an aspect exists only as constituted by us when we experience certain sensory data during the perception of a material object. Consequently, the intuited aesthetic qualities are not constituent parts of the object but of its aspects that we constitute on the basis, to be sure, of the real existential qualifications of the object itself. This does not mean that the aesthetic qualities are not objectively accessible; but they are subjective in that their constitution depends on our sensitive intuition of sensory data.

The aesthetic qualities of the ready aspects of a literary work of art have even greater significance than the concrete aspects of a material object.

First of all, ready aspects have, as we saw, the function of determining the mode of appearance of presented objects and thus of endowing them with aesthetic qualities which they would not have if they were predetermined only by the capacity of projected states of affairs. Furthermore, a literary work of *art* is intended to be apprehended primarily as a carrier of a configuration of aesthetic qualities that is all its own. Because a literary work of *art* (1) depends on the phenomenal appearance of the presented objects, and this appearance can be brought about only through schematized aspects founded in various states of phenomenal qualifications, and (2) because its style consists to a large extent of a system of adumbrational aesthetic qualities determined by the readying of schematized aspects, it follows that without ready aspects there is no literary work of *art*. It also follows that the aesthetic qualities of the layer of presented objects pertain distinctly to ready aspects, that they are *properly* adumbrational. However, through the intermediary of ready aspects they do pertain to the objects, but only as the latter appear in various modes of phenomenal appearance.

3. Functions of presented objects

A. *Introduction*

So far we have dealt with the formative functions of the layers of sound-configurations and meaning-units in the constitution of schematized aspects. We also saw the effective range of the functions of all three layers with respect to the projection, presentation, exhibition, and phenomenal appearance of objects. On the basis of all these functions the presented objects may finally be intuited in the process of our concretizations. It may seem that with the achievement of this purpose the layer of presented objects may have no functions to fulfill *within* the structural range of the literary work.

Since we often ignore the pure intentionality of the presented world, we may not be aware that we are assigning to presented objects functions that are normally associated with practical purposes, functions fulfilled by real persons, actions, and occurrences in the world we live in. There are readers who ignore the functions of the layers within the literary work, and their interest is riveted to the presented characters, their actions, and destinies. For some of these readers literature has the function of providing entertaining distraction. On a more sophisticated level, readers assign to presented objects the functions of providing edifying insights through pleasing instructiveness, of awakening moods or emotions that may have beneficent and sometimes inspiring effects on their mental states or on their personal or social commitments. Some works are seen to have the cultural function of enlightening readers lulled in complacent ignorance, of broadening their perspective, and of revealing to them past or contemporary views and conditions through the intermediary of a perceptive witness, the "author," whose personality may sometimes become the focus of attention. These functions are assigned to literature when it is viewed as a "civilizing" agent.

It should be abundantly clear that in *The Literary Work of Art* Ingarden does not seek to explore such practical uses of literature, but its nature, which means that he is seeking to determine the intrinsic functions of the elements of an "organic" unity, functions founded in the structure of the literary work of art. Here we find Ingarden in search of the specific function of the layer of presented objects, that is fulfilled *within* the work. Our grasp of this function can occur, however, only in the light of the formative functions of the other layers which produce the predetermined appearance of the presented world and found its function.

Sometimes it is claimed that the function of the presented world lies in setting forth a truth or an idea. Ingarden is only too obviously right in stating that if that were indeed the main purpose of a literary work of art, one might reasonably argue that it could be achieved directly and more appropriately by a different mode of writing. This argument implies that the *proper* function of a literary work of *art* is different. We shall see that Ingarden considers this function to be the revelation of a sense of life that usually remains concealed in the whirling current of living, and that this function is fulfilled by the presented world. Before we can deal with this function, we should, I believe, turn our attention to what is often meant by truth or ideas. I am therefore again disregarding Ingarden's sequence of topics, and I trust that the reader of his work will find this step justified. I shall discuss now various concepts of "truth" and "idea" and I shall do so with due regard to his article "Des différentes conceptions de la vérité dans l'œuvre d'art."[8]

B. Truth and idea in a literary work of art

Truth is the name of the intended relation of identity between a purely

8. *Revue d'esthétique* 2 (1949): 162–80.

intentional state of affairs projected by a genuine affirmative statement (as it is meant by a genuine judgmental act) and a corresponding objective state of affairs. Truth is thus based on a proposition whereby we *mean* to assert the *conformity* of the proposition to an objective state of affairs. By extending the meaning of the word "truth," one sometimes considers the statement itself or its projected intentional state of affairs to be a truth. Finally, and rather inappropriately, even the referential objective state of affairs is called a truth. These meanings of truth cannot apply to a literary work of art because of its fundamental characteristics: every affirmative statement contained in it is only a quasi-affirmation, for no affirmation in a literary work of art is meant to refer to an objective state of affairs. Any affirmative statement in a literary work is at most fictively affirmative and therefore valid only in the presented world. Here there are no genuine transpositions.

Sometimes one speaks of "historical" literary works as especially suited to capture the "true idea" of a period, of its heroes, social types and situations, and of its mentality. I believe it may be appropriate to point out that what is meant by the "true idea" in this context is not the truth in terms of the definition mentioned above, but rather a designation of a felicitous simulated transposition whereby a successful *adaptation* only to some typical features of a real model is achieved and a simulated reality produced. Consequently this so-called true idea is true only because of the mere adaptation of some of a work's presentations to some typical features of reality. Reality, however, does not consist of only those features; it is multifaceted, intricately involved, and above all concrete. The schematic structure of a literary work with its cleavages and points of indeterminateness can draw only certain features from reality, and furthermore, its intention is not to induce *identification* through the conformity of all its projected purely intentional states of affairs with independent ones: at most it seeks to reproduce and represent a model. There is no attempt here to deny or belittle the presence of those so-called true ideas in literary works; all that needs to be stressed is that they are not genuinely judgmental. Even if we were to concede that certain "historical" works contain some genuine truths, we would still have to note that those instances are exceptional and that they do not apply to all literary works—to the literary work of art as such. Secondly, we would have to recognize that in a literary work the representation of some incidents is part of a presented world fashioned by characteristics of literary exigencies and that the literary modes of appearance of exhibited objects force us to focus our attention on the representation of the independent models, and not on the individual objects to which they are supposed to refer. Their representation is not transparent, as it is when we mean to affirm the identity of a presentation with an independent state of affairs. Therefore, in our imagination, the represented objects displace the independent objects. And yet we keep alive the illusion of their identity, for we fail to recognize the pure intentionality of presented objects and we focus on their capacity alone. Let us suppose, however, that in certain instances the resemblance between the presented and the real objects is so great that we do believe we see the latter in their primary self-givenness. Even then we have no assurance that what we apprehend as truth is not merely its semblance, because of the rather frequent concern of many authors for our receptivity as readers. Whether the adaptation of the presented to the objective world is based on the resemblance of a great number of features or on that of especially characteristic traits, our illusion of their identity is enhanced by *our* notion of what that objective world is like. When we discussed the different principles that may govern the readying of types of aspects, we noted the special modes of appearance which result from the selection of elements of aspects through which one and the same familiar object may appear in such an unconventional mode that we may not recognize it as the object that is familiar to us, i.e., that we may not perceive any resemblance between the presented and the real object. Although the aspects selected for representation do in fact resemble those of the real object, we still fail to recognize the resemblance because we are not familiar with the presented aspects of the original model. Our image of reality may be so personal, or so dependent on conventionalized notions adopted by particular groups of people at certain periods, that we expect representations through familiar types of aspects, or, more generally, in a light that corresponds to our views of reality, views that may not conform to reality. These conditions, which affect individual concretizations even of "historical" works of literature, are bound at least to call in question the veracity of any literary representation and the authenticity of the "idea" of the mentality of a period that emerges from it.

We have noted that in works with representational intent the reader's recognition of resemblance may be based primarily on either the similarity of a great number of features or that of characteristic traits, and on a selection of aspects that anticipates the expectations of the reader. In works that do not aim to be representational we may still recognize a special adaptation to reality which we need to consider. Our apprehension of the identity of a real object is based on our recognition that all the properties of which it is a carrier are appropriate to its nature in that they qualify the object as a concrete unity. Obviously, a presentation that has a representational intent must observe this principle of cohesion; but presentations without representational intent also follow this principle, for there is no conflict between cohesion and fiction, not even when the presentation is drawn from the realm of the fantastic. Any cohesive presentation must be based on consistency throughout the phases of the work. This means that any modifications or changes that occur, for instance in the personalities of presented characters, must be consistent with their originally projected identity. Presentations characterized by cohesion and consistency are considered to contain "internal truth." This truth may be yet another means whereby our illusion of reality may be enhanced. Sometimes the "sincerity" of the "author," who is copresented in the presented world, may impress us with the veracity of what we are told, and our illusion of the truth in the presentation may thereby also be enhanced.

All these considerations may suffice to show that we seek in vain to grasp the *truth* in a literary work on the basis of adaptations of the presented world to the real world. When we recognize the fundamental characteristics of literary presentations, we realize that the presented world has its own reality, its quasi-reality, in which to various extents and on the basis of various presentational means we may perceive a "quasi-incarnation" of independent reality. The presented world has its own life, its own truth, and its own idea, governed by "organic" structural functions and aesthetic interdependencies that can indeed endow the presented world with the semblance of autonomy that is all its own. This "autonomy" does not depend on resemblances to the real world but on its own structural principles of formation. In fact, as long as this autonomy derives from literary structural principles, it remains unaffected even when the presented reality is a distortion of independent reality.

Before we turn to the discussion of ideas which Ingarden calls *metaphysical qualities*, it is advisable that I introduce one other "idea" contained in the literary work: the idea as *view of life*.[9] A brief discussion of this idea should help to set off the idea as metaphysical quality. A literary work may be seen as a configuration projected from the ground of a view of life on which, figuratively speaking, it is based. Regardless of how veiled the belief of a character may be, it can be determined, rationally conceived, and formulated, for its direct ontic source is in the layer of meaning-units. By view of life, however, I do not mean the beliefs of presented characters,

---

9. Although Ingarden does not deal with what I call the idea as view of life, I believe that this expansion does not contradict his views.

but the spirit that actuates their thought, attitudes, and feeling. Thus, for instance, in Sophocles' *Antigone* we find, among others, two sharply conflicting beliefs embodied in Antigone and Creon. Each character sets forth a belief that is based on allegiance to a specific value, whereas the work as a whole is based on a view of life that endows the beliefs and actions of these characters with the *qualities* of absolute commitment to values and of renunciation of vital personal interests. The beliefs of these characters are not tragic, but the view of life, in which the qualities informing these beliefs are grounded, constitutes a center of crystallization from which the metaphysical quality of the tragic can emerge. We shall later see that Ingarden distinguishes the idea that emerges *within* the presented world from that which emerges *through* it. It is the idea as view of life, I believe, which emerges in this play within the presented world, whereas the metaphysical quality of the tragic is intuited through this phenomenally appearing presented world.

C. *Metaphysical qualities*

A metaphysical quality such as the tragic, the sublime, the dreadful, the sorrowful, the grotesque, the holy, the sinful, is an essence; a so-called *derived essence*. Metaphysical qualities, we should stress, are not objective and perceptible qualities of an individual carrier, such as the sadness of a character or the sinfulness of an act. A metaphysical quality hovers over certain *situations*. Since it is not a determinant of an object, it is not revealed explicitly; it is, however, founded in the exhibited world.

To understand why Ingarden considers metaphysical qualities to be *derived essences*, it may be useful to recall some of our earliest explorations and to explain this term together with that of *simple essence*. Squareness is a derived essence, whereas rectangularity, equilaterality, and parallelogramness are simple essences. Whenever these simple essences are concretized at the same time in an object's right angles, sides of equal length, and parallel opposite sides, we derive from that combination the constituents of a square, whose constitutive nature is a concretization of squareness. Our intuition of the essence squareness *through* an individual square implies our rising from a perception of its constituents and of its particular constitutive nature to the contemplation of its "idea," a contemplation that affords the intuition of that essence. During this intuition we ignore the various determinants of the object, but the intuition is *based* on our perception of them. We thus intuit the essence squareness and apprehend the determinants of the square almost simultaneously, in that we move back and forth from perception to contemplation and intuition. Consequently, we may state that while the essence squareness does not derive from the simple essences of rectangularity, equilaterality, and parallelogramness, our intuition of squareness does ultimately derive from our perception of the concretions of these simple essences in an individual square.

We have just stated that when we intuit squareness through an individual square, we also perceive the constituents of the nature of the square together with its actualized variable (lateral dimension). This means that for this quality (essence) to reveal itself through an individual square, our intuition must be founded in our perception of a harmonious structure of elements constitutive of that object's nature, a structure that is a prerequisite for the emergence of that quality. Perceptible constituents and traits can be rationally apprehended and their nature can be formulated: they are describable. The derived essence squareness can be only intuited.

These ideal conditions for our intuition of a derived essence cannot be duplicated in empirical reality or in the presented world, because the situations and occurrences through which metaphysical qualities may be intuited are complex and richly variable. As I see it, what we have just said about the determinants of the square and the essence squareness, also applies to the equally apprehensible determinants (e.g., beliefs, actions, etc.) of a presented world through which, for instance, the tragic may emerge. Like all other metaphysical qualities (derived essences), the tragic too can be only intuited. Like all derived essences, a metaphysical quality needs an appropriate medium (a configuration of beliefs, actions, attitudes, occurrences, etc.) through which we may intuit it. In real life it is impossible to predict the nature and composition of occurrences from which a metaphysical quality will emerge, and this is why it always reveals itself unexpectedly. Also, because metaphysical qualities cannot be rationally apprehended, they reveal themselves to us in real life only through situations in which we live and which affect us. The affective impact of these experiences is usually too strong for us to be able to reflect on our experience and savor the metaphysical quality itself. Its effect is in real life a lasting one, but for the reasons just mentioned we cannot recapture it in retrospect and we therefore associate it with the situation in which we experienced it. Intuitions of metaphysical qualities in real life are rare, but when they do occur we experience the discovery of a sense which life usually keeps concealed, but which makes life worth living, regardless of the pain or joy, horror or ecstasy which the discovery of that sense may bring with it.

As we now turn to the function whereby presented objects reveal metaphysical qualities in a literary work of art, I believe that it is worth recalling (1) that the determination of a layer as a structural entity rests on the functions the layer fulfills within the literary work of art; (2) that the function of sentences is to project states of affairs of various types; (3) that the function of appropriately selected states of affairs is to present objects and to found their aspects; and (4) that the function of aspects is to predetermine the modes of the phenomenal appearance of presented objects. Now, it is only when the presented world does appear phenomenally in the process of our concretization that a metaphysical quality can reveal itself through it. This obviously means that a metaphysical quality is not presented directly and explicitly in the work; that it is founded directly in the layer of presented objects in their phenomenal appearance and indirectly in the other layers; and that the presented objects must themselves be projected, exhibited, and predetermined by the joint operation of the functions of the other layers. This "organic" interaction of functions culminates within the presented world and founds our intuition of a metaphysical quality. The metaphysical quality is of course not a layer. Our intuition of it is a function of the layer of presented objects in their phenomenal appearance. Similarly, our intuition of squareness is the function of the constituted square. Like all derived essences, a metaphysical quality is concretized in a configuration of concretized simple qualities (essences). These must be appropriately selected and exhibited to satisfy the prerequisites for the emergence of any metaphysical quality.

When we consider some of the differences between the intuition of a metaphysical quality in real life and that which we experience through a presented world, we note that in the latter instance we usually have a foreboding of that quality already in some of the preparatory phases of the presentation, although it reveals itself only during the phase of culmination. Because that essence is not realized in real life but concretized in a presented situation, it does not stir us as deeply as the experience we might know from real life, nor does it have the same lasting effect. To some extent we always remain distanced, in the sense of not belonging to the presented world, and we can therefore savor the metaphysical quality as we intuit its revealed appearance in our *aesthetic stance*. For instance, we can endure the tension of a tragic situation that we witness in a stage play, and we can even savor its tragic quality, because cushioned as we are by that distance from the shock and the crushing pain of lived reality, we are relieved (purged) of pain and left free to contemplate the *quality* of events calmly with an aesthetic attitude and thus *see* the tragic in its concretion.

Ingarden thought that it was this relief and calm that Aristotle may have meant by catharsis.

Here we do not extract an idea from the literary work in order to gain some rational insight that we may possibly relate to a concrete situation in everyday life; here we have an intuition of a quality concretized in an exhibited situation whose features may or may not be adapted to reality. We see what the situation essentially is, and we intuit the metaphysical quality through it while we also apprehend the congruity between the quality and the essential configuration of that situation. For that reason we can intuit the metaphysical quality not only through its concretion, but also in and by itself. In this intuition of the metaphysical quality in conjunction with its concretion we discover an extraordinary sense of life and thereby also a sense of living that is wrested from the presented world in the privileged moment of that exceptional conjunction. According to Ingarden, it is the accomplishment of the congruity between a metaphysical quality and the essential configuration of a situation that characterizes the creative act of a writer. Finally, it is the metaphysical quality that allows us to grasp the cohesion of the various phases of a work, for it is the metaphysical quality that welds the work of art into an essential unity.

D. Metaphysical qualities and aesthetic qualities

We have seen throughout our explorations that the literary work consists first of all of a stratified schematic structure that is organic in the sense that the reciprocal functions of the layers form an intricate web of relations. It is the conjunction of these functions that constitutes the organic unity of the literary work as an *anatomical* structure. Secondly, each layer has its own complex of aesthetic qualities that furnish their particular voice to the polyphony of the aesthetic qualities of the whole work of art. By virtue of this polyphony the presented world is readied and to a certain extent predetermined for a special mode of phenomenal appearance that may be imaginationally perceived and intuited if the concretization is undertaken from an aesthetic stance, which is characterized by a sensitive response to aesthetic qualities. Therefore we must differentiate between, on the one hand, the anatomical schematic structure of the work and, on the other hand, the work as "aesthetic object" constituted by the polyphony of aesthetic qualities. The aesthetic object is thus not a mere sum of aesthetic qualities but a new entity founded in the aesthetic qualities of each layer and produced by the conjunction of the aesthetic qualities of all layers in the unfolding stratified structure as a whole. Clearly, aesthetic qualities are not properties of a carrier; they are characteristics of its phenomenally exhibited properties, and they may be actualized in the process of concretization. The harmony of the polyphony depends, of course, on the congruity of the aesthetic qualities that constitute it.

For a metaphysical quality to reveal itself in the concretization of a work, it is necessary (1) that the polyphony of the aesthetic qualities of all layers produce a harmony, a harmony that aims at and requires as its complement our intuition of a revealed metaphysical quality, and (2) that the reciprocal functions of the anatomical structure achieve a conjunction, i.e., that they form increasingly larger harmoniously welded complexes of functions that are capable of founding the polyphony of aesthetic qualities. Because this last point needs further elucidation, and especially because it explains the emergence of the polyphony of aesthetic qualities, I shall add here some relevant material drawn from a treatise by Ingarden on the problem of form and content in the literary work of art.[10]

E. Form and content in the stratified structure of the literary work

When we analyzed isolated nominal word-meanings we distinguished within their capacity the following intentional moments: the formal content, the material content, the intentional directional factor, and the existential moments of characterization and setting which are functions of the formal and material contents. Thus the derived intentionality of a nominal word-meaning means that an intentional object shall have a certain formal structure, a constitutive nature qualified in a certain manner, and an existential character and setting, and that its directional factor shall be sensitive to whatever syntactic shifts may occur in the projection of sense-units. One and the same nominal word-meaning contains, then, variable, but at any given moment stabilized, intentions. As soon as we modify the material content, for instance, by attributing to one and the same intentional object one set of its determinants rather than another, the function of the material content necessarily affects the formal content and the intentional directional factor, and it may affect the existential moments also. A modification of the formal content also entails far-reaching effects on all other moments.

10. "Das Form-Inhalt-Problem im literarischen Kunstwerk," in *Erlebnis, Kunstwerk und Wert* (Tübingen: Max Niemeyer Verlag, 1969), pp. 31–50; translated as "The General Question of the Essence of Form and Content," *Journal of Philosophy* 56, no. 7 (1960): 222–33.

According to Ingarden, the *content* of the nominal word-meaning is the totality of its stabilized intentional moments, and its *form* is determined by the reciprocal functional relations of these moments, i.e., by the manner in which the reciprocal functions of intentional moments are "arranged" at any given time of their stabilization. At the point when a nominal word-meaning is about to become an element of a sentence, it has a stabilized content and form, i.e., it has its *formed content*, which is its "full meaning." As an element of the sentence, it fulfills its functions in relation to the other elements of the sense-unit, but it is also affected by their functions, and especially by their syntactic functions. As a result of these reciprocal functions every element in the sentence acquires a new formed content, and the elements thus modified now constitute the content of the sense-unit (i.e., the sense of the sentence as a unified whole). The form of the sense-unit is determined by the manner in which the reciprocal functional relations of its elements are established. Again, when a sentence becomes an element of a complex of connected sentences, it brings with it its *formed sense*, which is its "full sense." Its functions affect the other sense-units, which are the elements of the complex of connected sentences, but it is at the same time affected by their functions. Each of these sense-units is formed by the reciprocal functions of the other sense-units within that same complex, and therefore the content of the complex of connected sentences consists of all these formed sense-units. The form of the complex of connected sentences is determined by the manner in which the reciprocal functional relations of the sense-units constituting its content are arranged.

We began this description of the hierarchy of increasingly complex sense-units with the nominal word because it holds a key position in a sense-unit, as the finite verb does, but it exemplifies more fully, at that basic level of the hierarchy, the relation between content and form of a meaning-unit. Thus we considered as *content* first the totality of the functionally stabilized (formed) intentional moments of a basic meaning-unit. Then we called content the totality of the (formed) elements of a sense-unit. Finally, we called content the totality of the (formed) sense-units within a complex of connected sense-units. The term "content" has thus been applied first to a meaning-unit and then to sense-units of increasing complexity.

As long as we focus only on the anatomical stratified structure of the literary work (without regard to the aesthetic functions of any one of its layers), we may say that the *content* of the literary work consists of the *sense of the entire layer of meaning-units* as formed by the reciprocal functions of all complexes of connected sense-units. The *form* of the literary work is determined by the manner in which the reciprocal functions that contribute to the founding of all layers are arranged. This is what Ingarden means by the content and the form of the anatomical stratified structure of the literary work.

Obviously, the form of the anatomical structure of the literary work is only a framework, but an indispensable one, within which the formal structure of its aesthetic qualities evolves. In other words, the polyphony of the aesthetic qualities of a work is grounded in the reciprocal functions of all the layers and the structural order of sequence. Consequently, the gradually emerging revelation of a metaphysical quality depends (1) on the harmony between the reciprocal functions that constitute the formed content of the literary work as anatomical structure and (2) on the evolving polyphony of aesthetic qualities grounded in it.

F. The symbolizing functions of presented objects

The representational function of presented objects in some literary works has already been mentioned. We shall now conclude our explorations of the functions of presented objects by a brief comment on their symbolizing function.

The revelation of a metaphysical quality is the *proper* function of the layer of presented objects in any literary work of art. This function must be distinguished from the symbolizing function of that layer. To appreciate the difference between these functions, we must bear in mind that the revelation of a metaphysical quality occurs through the phenomenal appearance of the presented world, and that we intuit the phenomenal appearance of the presented objects and the revelation of a metaphysical quality together and separately at the same time *from within* the presented world. Objects which fulfill a symbolizing function refer to what is symbolized. This means that the presented objects belonging to the presented world refer to objects that do not achieve phenomenal appearance in that same world—that in fact do not achieve any phenomenal appearance at all. It is an essential trait of what is symbolized that it does not reveal itself, and it is symbolized for only as long as it remains mysteriously inaccessible and unrevealed. Furthermore, when objects fulfill the symbolizing function they become subordinate to what they symbolize, and if they are perceived only in the light of that function, they are means to an end. By contrast, the presented objects, in which a metaphysical quality is concretized and through which it is revealed, come into prominence exactly because we intuit the metaphysical quality through them.

4. The structural order of sequence in a literary work

The stratified structure, which we have explored so far, does not by itself account for the organic cohesion of the literary work of art, for every work has also an extension from a beginning to an end, a structural order of sequence. Normally we associate a sequence of events with concrete time, but what sort of sequence do we have in mind when we consider a completed literary work in which every sentence is an element of a complex of connected sentences all of which are in their places *at the same time?* Obviously, the structural order of sequence of the work cannot be equated with the sequence in which we read a work. After all, our reading and concretizations follow the already established structural order of sequence, and it would be absurd to assume that this order might be derived from sequential acts of reading. We also know that the sequence of the events that constitute a story need not be presented in the order of plausible succession, that it may, but need not, be congruent with the structural order of the sequence in which the parts—*the phases*—of the work are arranged from beginning to end. For instance, it is possible to present various events of the story in flashbacks without affecting the structural order of sequence. This means that one may introduce into the structural order of sequence an event which in terms of presented time precedes the point already reached in the account of the presented events. We should note here that the primary purpose of flashbacks of various sorts (for instance, of events, experiences, characterizations) is to present complementary material that was left indeterminate in the linear presentation. Our previous explorations have also shown how presented time differs from the sequence of concrete time and why there is no now-phase in the presented world.

What is the order that constitutes the sequence of the phases of the stratified work? We have seen that the principle of *founding* governs the succession of sentences within a complex of connected sentences, that each sentence founds the following sentence, and that founding accounts for their connection. Likewise, the complex of connected sentences constitutive of one phase of the work founds the complex of sentences of the following phase. Because we are focusing on the founding *within* the structure of the work, we ignore the founding in any external agent, including the author. The following sketch of the system of founding that underlies the structural order of sequence of the phases in a literary work needs some preliminary explanation.

First, by a phase we mean here a stage in the simultaneous development of all the layers of the work. This means that every phase contains within its range the corresponding phase of each layer (a) with its reciprocal functions and those it fulfills with respect to the other layers and (b) with all its aesthetic qualities and their manifold functions. Thus a phase contains all these elements and not only states of occurrences by which the sequence of the events of the story is constituted. (We should add here that the phenomenal appearance of the exhibited world *in its unfolding* necessarily depends on the order that prescribes for each phase its place in the structural order of sequence.)

Secondly, a phase has a recognizable identity in that it is distinguishable from other phases, but it is only relatively self-sufficient because it is at the same time a part of the work as a whole. Thirdly, it is constituted by various elements and by their moments. Finally, we must distinguish founding elements (or moments) from founded elements, although one and the same element may be founded and founding at the same time.

Every phase must contain elements that do not need to be founded in elements of another phase. These are the elements that furnish a phase with its relative self-sufficiency and with its distinctiveness as a phase. Every phase—with the exception of the initial one—contains some elements that are founded in elements which in the structural order of sequence belong to an antecedent phase. This founding of elements accounts in part for the connection of phases in the structural order of sequence; "in part," since the connection may also be established (a) by moments in a given phase that are founded in moments of an antecedent phase, or (b) by other moments of the same given phase that found moments of a subsequent phase. The founding moments mentioned under (b) may themselves be founded in the phase to which they belong in elements that require no founding or in elements of an antecedent phase.

All founding within one and the same phase is reciprocal, whereas the founding between different phases is one-directional: from a structurally antecedent phase to a subsequent one. We should note that elements that require no founding in an antecedent phase provide the *basis* for the *ontic foundation* of all elements and moments of the phase in which they occur. Consequently, all elements and moments of a given phase that are founded in an antecedent phase have the basis of their ontic foundation in elements which belong to that same given phase and which require no founding.

We may conclude that every work thus displays a line of unfolding from which its "internal dynamics" can be determined. There are preparatory phases that lead to a culminating phase, which may, in some works, occur only at the conclusion, whereas in others there may be a series of culminating phases. Among the many possible variations there may be a sequence of phases that may be compared, for instance, to the flow and ebb of occurrences with concomitant tensions that may rise, abate, or be suspended. What we need to stress is that *each layer* has its own inner dynamics and that, for instance, the phases of culmination of one layer need not be congruous with those of all the other layers. It should be obvious that analyses of founding in the structural order of sequence of literary works are crucial for any investigation of compositional patterns.

5. The ontic position of the literary work

We have seen throughout these explorations that the thrust of Ingarden's argument has been to determine the identity of the literary work as an object that exists in its own existential sphere, a sphere distinct from that of ideal objects, of real objects, and particularly of mental experiences. He has shown that what constitutes the identity of the literary work is its schematic structure, which cannot be equated with any of its inevitably varied concretizations that occur in different readings even by the same reader. We saw that this schematic structure was constituted primarily and fundamentally by heteronomous sense-units of complexes of connected sentences. It is the heteronomy of the sense-units and of their correlates that accounts for the heteronomous existence of the literary work as schematic structure. We discussed the heteronomy of purely intentional objects, but we did so primarily from the point of view of their heteronomous existence, i.e., of their coming into being, and not from the point of view of their heteronomous subsistence. There we saw that purely intentional sense-units and their correlates originate in acts of consciousness, that they confront (transcend) them, and that they are heterogeneous with respect to them. Thus we saw the identity of sense-units (and their correlates) secured by that transcendence and heterogeneity. At the same time we saw that the heteronomous existence of these purely intentional objects was founded in autonomous acts of consciousness from which they originate.

Since sentences are neither ideal nor real, how do they—not being autonomous—subsist when they are not being read? Their identity and subsistence are both of the utmost importance, for without them all sentences, even those in scientific writing, would lose their intersubjective identity. Therefore, we would have no access to them, and we could not reactualize them in an identical manner. Since sense-units are not moments of the acts of consciousness by which they are projected, since they consequently cannot be moments of the state of mind of the author, whose death obviously does not affect their subsistence, they cannot, for analogous reasons, be moments of the reader's acts of apprehension either. Furthermore, every reader concretizes in his own manner the correlates projected by the sense-units of a work, which means that no single concretization can possibly be equated with the unique identity of a work in respect to which we find certain so-called "readings" more adequate than others, just as we judge different performances of one and the same identical musical composition. Finally, sense-units obviously cannot be equated with the system of written or printed letters that serve as indicators for the apprehension of sentences, nor with the concrete phonic material of recitation. Since sense-units are not identifiable with moments of the author's or reader's autonomous consciousness, or with the real printed (written) patches of ink on a page, or with the concrete sounds of an oral delivery, how do they subsist, or rather, how are their heteronomous existence and subsistence founded? Heteronomous existence must be founded in autonomous existence, and heteronomous subsistence must be founded in autonomous subsistence. We know that their heteronomous existence is founded by autonomous acts of consciousness from which they originate. However, these acts cease the moment the sense-units have come into existence and they can therefore not found the subsistence, i.e., the continuing existence, of sentences while these are not read, uttered, or thought. We must find the autonomous ontic foundation of the subsistence of sentences because their intersubjectively reactualizable identity rests on it. If sense-units did not subsist, they might indeed have to be moments of the acts of consciousness in which they originate, lose their identity, and become intersubjectively inaccessible, regardless of whether they are truly judgmental or quasi-affirmative.

What, from an ontological point of view, is brought into being by those acts of consciousness that project sentences, i.e., sense-units, and their correlates? What is "created" by those acts, and by means of what characteristics can this "creation" subsist? Without a satisfactory solution to these problems, the intersubjective accessibility of the literary work is open to question. After all, sentences provide the structural framework of the whole literary work, for they are its fundamental constitutive element on which all layers depend existentially, except the layer of sound-formations and those elements of the other layers that are constituted by it. This does not mean that the layer of sound-formations itself is independent of sentences; there is reciprocal existential connectivity in their coexistence, but the particularity of the layer of sound-formations as it may emerge, for instance, in one language rather than in another, is not founded in sentence-forming operations.

The immediate ontic foundation of the existence of sentences is the creative sentence-forming operation which is the culmination of complex subjective operations of autonomous consciousness. What is "created" is obviously not an autonomous object, for if it were autonomous, its subsistence would not present a problem. In the sentence "The rose is red" the projected object is only meant to be a rose which is only meant to be red. The entire projected state of affairs is purely intentional. Here, redness is not embodied in that rose; it is not a *realized* ideal quality, i.e., it is not a realization of the essence redness as it would be in a real rose; here, we have only an *actualization* of that quality by a word-meaning. Even the existential character of reality of that purely intentional rose is merely meant to be assigned to it.

At this point, it may be necessary to recall that purely intentional sense-units are the immediate ontic foundation of presented objects, which are also purely intentional. We also noted that presented characters are the immediate ontic foundation of the sentences they utter, sentences that present objects, and so on in progressive nesting structures. It appears, then, that heteronomous objects may be founded directly in other heteronomous objects, but we must not forget that presented objects and utterances of presented characters are all founded in sentences of a presentative text, which is a projection of autonomous acts of consciousness.[11]

So far we have established that sense-units are heteronomous creations which depend for their existence on originating acts of consciousness and that they must subsist if they are to be accessible intersubjectively as they were meant when they were projected. What is the autonomous ontic foundation of their heteronomous subsistent identity? This ontic foundation is twofold. We find, on the one hand, concepts and essences (ideal qualities), which are ideal objects and therefore autonomous; and, on the other hand, real word-signs. Let us now consider these ontic foundations.

11. *Der Streit um die Existenz der Welt*, 1:86–87.

Early in our explorations we noted that the meaning-intention of a word parallels our direct (original) intending of an intentional object, and that we can fulfill the meaning-intention of the word because it is essentially identical with the manner in which we mean the object. This means that the formal and material contents of the meaning-intention and the content of *our* meaning are essentially identical in respect to the *general idea of the object*. Thus in the correlate of the nominal expression "this table" the word-meaning "table" projects a skeletal structure of the (essential) configurational cluster of properties which is reflected in the constant qualitative moment of the general idea "the table." On the other hand, my intentional real object "table," which I see, is not only the carrier of its (essential) constitutive nature consisting of a characteristic configurational cluster of properties, but also of all its particular features. Consequently, the content of the meaning-intention of the word "table" actualizes only the essential constitutive nature of the perceived object, and the nominal expression "this table" may thus refer to any table which I happen to perceive. To sum up, the correlate of "table" and my directly intended object "this table" are essentially identical in respect to the general idea of the object "table."

The general idea of "table" must, however, be distinguished from the *concept—the particular idea—*of any intentional individual table, because the concept contains in addition to the object's (essential) constitutive nature all its determinants, including those it may acquire from its relations to other objects. A concept is thus the *ideal* (and, consequently, autonomous) sense of an intentional object. This sense confronts our meaning-forming operation and the word-meaning itself. The concept provides the ideal model in the light of which the specific meaning of any word is actualized in the course of a sentence-forming operation. Similarly, the word-meanings whose correlates are properties of a purely intentional object are actualizations of *ideal qualities* (essences) which are intentionally assigned to it. Every word-meaning is an actualization of a part of a concept or of an ideal quality. It is with a view to these ideal models that the elements of sentences are actualized and arranged into the unity of a sense-unit. This is the productive effect of a sentence-forming operation. This means that the sense-unit of a sentence derives its existent identity from subjective actualizations of sense-contents of ideal concepts, and that its heteronomous subsistent identity depends on these concepts (and ideal qualities) in view of which it can be reactualized. But for this reactualization to be feasible the heteronomously subsistent identity of a sense-unit must be accessible by way of the sound-formation which is its carrier. Before we turn to the ontic foundation of the layer of sound-formations, which is a part of the identity of the literary work, we should remind ourselves that meaning-intentions of words are subject to semantic changes in the course of the development of a language and that we may lose cognizance of the original ideal concepts of which they are actualizations. When that is so, the literary work may undergo modifications unless our reactualizations are guided by insights derived from the history of the language.

What, then, is the ontic foundation of sound-formations that safeguards—in spite of all the variations of their (pronounced) concretizations—the subsistent identity of these formations as constituents of the subsistent identity of the literary work? The resolution of this problem is necessary for the establishment of the heteronomous subsistence of the whole stratified structure of the literary work, because the layer of sound-formations carries that of the meaning-units with their projections of presented objects and schematized aspects.

We must first recall that word-sounds are relatively constant typical sound-configurations on which *we confer* the function of being carriers of word-meanings; that no one concrete sound-formation is ever the same in all utterances and that we nevertheless recognize it as the carrier of its word-meaning because it is in every instance a concretization of one and the same word-sound as we mean it; and that for these reasons the concrete sound-formation cannot be part of the identity of a literary work, whereas the word-sound as a relatively constant typical configuration is a part of that identity. When we say that the word-sound is only relatively constant, we do not mean at all that it is modifiable once it is a part of a literary structure, for it is normally *meant to be and to remain* the very configuration which it is at the time of its inclusion in the work, regardless of the modification it may incur because of the phonetic development of the language. The word-sounds of a living language are intersubjectively identical and, at least for long periods, constant configurations that may be recovered even after phonetic changes have occurred. They are intentionally incorporated by an author into a literary work with the assumption that it is they—as he means them—that are going to be concretized in oral delivery or through conventionally established intersubjectively identical word-signs. However varied the concrete utterances of the same word-sound may be, we recognize them, as we have shown, as essentially identical. They are essentially identical because each is a concretization of the one intentional identical configuration of the word-sound. Although this identity is not timeless like that of ideal objects, it is at least relatively constant. What is thus incorporated into the literary work is this intended identity of the word-sound with its admissible range of variable concretizations. The question is how this heteronomously *existing* word-sound is founded in order to *subsist* in its identity and as part of the identical structure of the stratified literary work. Graphic signs of letters perform that function, but they themselves must be *founded materially* if they are to be apprehensible (for instance, visually in print, auditorily in a recording). Their material foundation is thus the indirect ontic foundation of the work.

It may be appropriate to point out that the graphic signs that fix the word-sound by indicating it are not the ink spots on the printed or written page.[12] Similarly, we cannot equate the word-meaning with the concrete phonic material that is its external carrier. No purely material thing can by itself perform a nonmaterial function such as the indicatory function. It must be endowed with such a function; i.e., we must intend that it shall have the function of meaning the indicated object. This function is intentional, and the ink spots become signs by the intentionality we confer on them. Furthermore, the individual particular type in which letters are set (or the particular kind of handwriting on the written page) may differ, but the indicatory function remains unaffected as long as we can recognize the same typical configuration of the letters, just as we recognize the same word-sound concretized in variations of the phonic material by which it is uttered. Here, too, it is on this typical configuration that the indicatory function is conferred. The printed letters—as typical configurations—are formations of intentional acts of consciousness. These configurations are relatively constant, and as long as their conventional indicatory functions subsist, they can be intersubjectively apprehended as identical. Thus the printed (written) word-signs are conventionally established regulative indicators by which intended word-sounds, with an intended range of concretizations, are incorporated in the literary work and intersubjectively recognized in their subsistent identity. Thus the heteronomous sense-units and the sound-formations consisting of word-sounds are ontically founded in their existence in autonomous subjective operations; and in their subsistence in ideal concepts, essences, and ideas, and indirectly in the material basis of word-signs.

12. *Untersuchungen zur Ontologie der Kunst* (Tübingen: Max Niemeyer Verlag, 1962), pp. 23–27.

Chapter 4

1. The concretization of the literary work and its life

We shall now turn our attention to Ingarden's analysis of the process of cognition of the literary work of art. By way of introduction, we shall consider the chapter of *The Literary Work of Art* dealing with the "life" of the literary work and its concretizations.

As we read a literary work of art, we may not be aware of its skeletal structure which we concretize: the points of indeterminateness we complement, the gaps we fill in, and the potentialities (e.g., ready aspects) we actualize. Of necessity, we fulfill these functions only to a certain extent in repeated readings. As we concretize its skeletal structure, we constitute the work in one of its concretions. As a skeletal structure, the work always retains its identity, but no two concretizations can ever be identical, because our mental and emotional attitudes change from one reading to another and because the cultural and social conditions under which readers live differ with time and place and produce differing expectations.

We have seen again and again that the intentional object—here, the literary work in its concretion—must be distinguished from the acts of consciousness by which it is constituted. These acts, by which a concretization takes place and a particular literary work is constituted as an aesthetic object, are different in every instance. Thus a literary work of art, as a schematic structure, becomes an aesthetic object as it is set off, projected, so to speak, in its concretion from the ground of its skeletal structure. The aesthetic object is not an element of the acts of consciousness by which it is constituted, but it has its ontic, and in many respects also its material, foundation in these acts and in some of the experiences concurrent with these acts. Just like the work of art, it confronts those acts and experiences. We do, in fact, apprehend the aesthetic object in its transcendence; if it did not confront those acts and experiences, i.e., if it were a component element of them, we should be able to apprehend it in the only manner in which those acts and experiences can be apprehended, namely through reflexive inner perceptions. Obviously, that is never so, and we must therefore recognize that the aesthetic object's heteronomous existence is founded in our constitutive acts and in the schematic structure of the literary work of art.

Although we shall deal with the acts and experiences by which we apprehend and constitute the literary work of art when we expound *The Cognition of the Literary Work of Art*, we may at least mention at this point what these acts and experiences consist of. The *cognitive acts* consist of:

(1) perceptions of word-signs, of sound-formations (word-sounds and sound-formations of higher rank), and of representations of presented objects in a stage play;
(2) apprehensions of meanings, founded in (1);
(3) imaginational intuitions of presented objects in their phenomenal appearance, founded in (1) and (2);
(4) possibly also intuitions of metaphysical qualities, based on (3).

Among the *experiences* we should mention:

(1) the experience of aspects readied by the work;
(2) experiences of aesthetic enjoyment;
(3) experiences of various feelings and emotions aroused in the course of our reading. Although these experiences affect us during our apprehension of the work, they are not of the same kind as those listed under (1), which are instrumental in the concretization, and those under (2), within which the concretization occurs.

Because these acts and concomitant experiences are brought to bear in most varied combinations on the highly complex structure of the heterogeneous elements of the literary work, it stands to reason that every reading should result in a differently structured concretion. First, in any given instance we focus on a text with only some of our cognitive functions, in some of their possible combinations, while other cognitive functions and experiences are involved peripherally (although not without effect on the central cognitive process). Secondly, in different readings we do not always focus on the same components of a layer or on the same layer of the work. Finally, although the exigencies of the text demand that we focus our cognitive functions and experiences on certain components of its structure rather than on others, we do not always follow those directives. Even concretions therefore remain schematic. Consequently, we do not do justice to all components of every layer and we therefore apprehend the work, as it were, only in a perspectival foreshortening. Clearly, every concretization is different from any other and cannot, for that very reason, be equated with the structure of the work which subsists in its identity.

We may perhaps be tempted to ask whether we can gain access to the schematic structure of the literary work if we have to pass through a concretization that seems to cast a veil over it. In the first place, the preceding investigations have established in a theoretical, purely cognitive, procedure the constants of the general idea of the literary work. On this basis we can reconstruct the schematic structure of an individual work if we adhere to the strict apprehension of meaning-units and refrain from complementing points of indeterminateness, filling in gaps, and actualizing various potentialities. Of course, a reconstruction does not lead to an aesthetic grasp of the literary work of art; only a concretization does that. Our concern over safeguarding the identity of the literary work throughout the acts and the experiences through which the work is concretized demands that we assume an aesthetic stance and that we bracket to a considerable degree the reality of the world we live in. Only thus can we pay attention to the exigencies of the text and carry out the complementations within the range of variability determined by the work. Thus alone can we increase the potential adequacy of our concretizations, apprehend the world as it is presented, and savor with appropriate feelings and emotions its aesthetic qualities. We noted several times that only real objects are fully determinate and that presented objects are necessarily schematic projections. Regardless of the number of our complementations, we can never complement in any concretization all the cleavages and points of indeterminateness. Consequently, no concretion can ever equal the concreteness of real objects. Nevertheless, since presented objects are in general of the type of real objects and our complementations cause their skeletal structure to recede, we are, for this reason as much as for any other, tempted to lend credence to their reality, forget that they are purely intentional, and deal with them as if they belonged to *our* reality. We are likely to endow them with traits drawn from our real world into which we have integrated them. If, however, we assume an aesthetic stance, we focus on the presented world, observe its schematic nature, recognize its range of potential concretions, and complement the various gaps and points of indeterminateness with appropriate concretizations admissible within that range. Only thus can we select those elements that fit the range of admissible complementations prescribed by the work itself and avoid impairing its identity. Moreover, it is the aesthetic attitude that prevents us from yielding completely to the delusion of experiencing the presented world as real, in spite of the alluring experience induced by quasi-affirmations and our concretizations. It is true that without suspending our disbelief we could not intuit the vital phenomenal appearance of the presented world, but without the aesthetic attitude and the attendant distance we could not savor the aesthetic and metaphysical qualities.

As shown by all the foregoing findings, no concretion can be equated with the schematic structure of the literary work, but it may be useful to single out at least some pronounced differences between them and to show that we can remove the veil which concretizations seem to cast over the schematic structure to the point of making it appear to be irretrievable in a reading. For instance, the word-sounds, which are mere configurations in the work itself, on the one hand prescribe, and on the other hand tolerate, a certain range of possible concretizations in a recital. The concrete sound-formations have their own aesthetic qualities which may or may not fit this range. In every instance these qualities are different while the word-sounds remain identical. If these qualities do not accord with the prescribed or at least admissible range, they are found to be unsuitable. The aesthetic qualities of the concrete sound-formations may, in an appropriate recitation, enhance the mode of appearance of certain presented objects, whereas in an inappropriate recitation the latter may be deformed. It is clear that whatever the actualizations of the potentialities of word-sounds may be, their effect brings into view the difference between the concretized work and its schematic base.

Another example that reveals the difference between the potentialities of the schematic base and the concretized work may be seen in the layer of meaning-units. For instance, when regionally (or politically) determined connotations of various words are woven into the apprehension of sense-units, connotations that are objectively absent from the meaning-intentions of these sense-units, they may affect the phenomenal appearance of the presented objects. We may thus impose a complementation on some of the text's points of indeterminateness and alter the sense of the units to various extents. One would wish to assume that this is an exception to the rule, and that we normally do actualize the conferred intentionality of the sense-units of the schematic structure. However, even the actualization which adheres to the projected sense is different from the mere potentiality of the sense-units of the text, because the reader means that sense to be actual. We may add that the reader's grasp of the actuality, which he acquires in the process of his concretization, is yet another reason why the pure intentionality of the sense-units becomes veiled for him.

The most striking difference between the skeletal literary work and its concretions is due to the aesthetic qualities of readied aspects which determine the style in which the presented world appears to us. In our concretizations, we experience, on the basis of the merely readied skeletal aspects of the work itself, the imaginational appearance of the exhibited objects (or their perceptual appearance, in a stage play). The range of possible complementations and actualizations in the process of our concretization is considerable. Moreover, every aspect of a presented object is experienced as a mere segment of the capacity of the object and is therefore functionally dependent on that capacity as a whole. This fact widens the range of possible complementations and may lead to actualizations of *types* of aspects—and consequently to appearances of objects—that are not founded in the ready aspects of the work. Thus the concretized work may acquire a style that is not predetermined by the schematized aspects themselves. Only if the phenomenal appearance of the exhibited objects permits such stylistic complementations, may we claim to have safeguarded the identity of the literary work. The determination of the range of possible actualizations of ready aspects is the task of practical criticism and of stage-directing in the theater.

Finally, we should mention the difference between the structural order of sequence, as it exists in the schematic structure of the literary work, and its transformation into a chronological sequence on account of the actual duration of the sequential acts of reading and concretization. Without this transformation we would not fathom the unfolding of the "internal dynamics" of the work and of the aesthetic qualities carried by the system of founding on which the structural sequence of phases depends.

Thus the schematic literary work of art subsists in its identity regardless of the different concretizations through which it attains a variety of concretions. Although every concretization is in some respects distinct from every other, it is a common experience that in repeated readings we carry over some elements from previous to subsequent concretions. At the same time we discover new facets whereby our increasingly complex view of the work is enriched, and previous remembered or recorded concretions are modified. However, we should recognize that in principle certain modifications may be carried out even within the skeletal structure itself without radically affecting its identity. The author may change the wording, omit and rearrange certain parts; a translator must change the layer of sound-formations, and he may also have to introduce modifications in accord with the language into which the work is translated. These modifications or changes, which pertain to the skeletal structure, do not testify to the life of the literary work; it is only through its concretions that a work may undergo changes which reveal its life.

When we speak of the life of a work of art, we mean that it is created, that its popularity endures for a certain time before it declines, and that it may ultimately recede into oblivion. Obviously, not every work follows quite this pattern of life, but it is in the light of some such pattern that we may reasonably speak of the life of a work. For those phases of life to occur, certain changes in the concretizations must occur. We have noted several reasons why concretizations differ from one reader to another and from one reading to another even by the same reader. Moreover, as we have also noted, no concretization can ever be fully adequate for all the potentialities prescribed by the work, even if a critical reader is conscious of the differences between the work's skeletal structure and his own acts of concretization. The naive reader, however, is inclined to believe that his concretization is identical with the work itself, for he perceives the work only in its concretion—he "absolutizes" his concretization. As a result of his unawareness, he may go so far as to actualize parts of concepts which are contextually not indicated, or he may even endow word-sounds with meanings they are not intended to carry. As a consequence of that absolutization the work itself is violated, it vanishes, and "lives" solely in its absolutized concretions. In this interpretation it may be transmitted from reader to reader and survive for a time. Certain absolutizations often occur when a work is transmitted in writing in a so-called "dead" language. Some of its manifestative characteristics and ready aspects may be lost, some of the predetermined modes of appearance of its presented objects may fail to be recognized, and the original work may die unless it is saved by historical literary scholarship.

We may speak more appropriately of the life of a literary work when we follow those stages in the sequence of a work's concretizations that coincide with cultural periods. We can speak of such periods only in the sense that we associate with them a prevalence of a certain mode of inquiry, of certain values and aesthetic predilections. The reciprocal functions of the cultural and literary atmosphere of a period have a determining effect on cultivated readers' concretizations, and each temporal phase of critical concretizations affects subsequent phases in various ways. Certain phases may establish models of concretization, and critical traditions may thus emerge, but they may be superseded by countercurrents of a later period. The phases of concretizations, marked by the "spirit of the times," reveal clear distinctions, even though they may be carried out in the light of the prescriptive exigencies of a text; the distinctions are based primarily on the changing assessments of the work's range of admissible concretizations. To trace the life of works through phases of their concretizations is, as we shall see, the task of the history of literary criticism.

2. The relation between the literary object and acts of cognition

In *The Cognition of the Literary Work of Art*, Ingarden seeks to lay the foundation for the methodology of criticism. He traces the process of cognition whereby we get to know a literary work and are enabled to apprehend its artistic and aesthetic values objectively.

We have already discussed various cognitive operations and made distinctions between, for instance, mere understanding of sense-units and imaginational apprehension of presented objects in their phenomenal appearance, i.e., between preaesthetic cognition and cognition based on aesthetic experience. We also distinguished cognition of objects through external perceptions from the cognition of other objects that can be gained only through internal perceptions, and we noted the different degrees of "being in consciousness" during these acts of perception. Throughout our explorations we emphasized the difference between our intuitive apprehension of essential configurations and the step-by-step constitution of an object's individual qualitative determinants. Thus there is a considerable variety of acts of cognition; there is also in the process of cognition a range which may extend from a passively receptive experience to a reflective knowledge of objects. Moreover, the process of cognition does not depend only on subjective acts, but also on the nature of the object of cognition that prescribes an appropriate cognitive approach and appropriate cognitive operations.

Clearly, we are not dealing with the course and functions of cognitive processes as they may apply to specific works of literature. What Ingarden aims to expound is the cognitive process in its essential course and with its essential interrelated functions, and it is to be expected that this process must correspond to the exigencies of the essential structure of the literary work. Once this process is established in the light of the essential structure of the literary work as the object of cognition, we are enabled to distinguish this process from what takes place in an individual reading of a specific work. We learn to separate essential functions—corresponding to essential literary structures—from those that occur in our complex experiences of a specific work, and thus to penetrate to the schematic structure of the specific work that we seek to apprehend. Further, as we separate those essential functions, we gain a better grasp and a fuller appreciation of those other functions of our cognition that are elicited by and correspond to the features of the specific work which we are reading.

3. The basic process of cognition

As we are about to trace the cognitive functions performed during the reading of a work, we should begin by stating that we assume certain optimal conditions: the work is completed in a printed format; the language in which it is written is in a relatively stable phase of development; the reader has a native knowledge of the language; the reader is not introduced to the work by a previous commentary on it. Finally, and only provisionally, we assume that the work is of a type that may be apprehended in a single reading without interruptions.

Since the cognitive functions correspond to the heterogeneous and interrelated layers of the structure of the work, the functions themselves are heterogeneous and interrelated. Also, one facet of the cognitive process has a temporal extension whose course makes the dynamic unfolding of the structural order of sequence of the work apprehensible.

A. Apprehension of the printed signs and word-sounds

We discussed the indirect founding function of printed signs and we noted that these spatial, physical signs become indicators by our conferring that function on their typical configurations. We have found that the printed word-signs are only the material regulative indicators whereby intended word-sounds are incorporated in the literary work. Although it is the function of the printed signs to incorporate the word-sounds into the work, they do not form a unity with them, and therefore they do not belong to the literary work itself.

How do we apprehend the printed signs? Our perception is, of course, directed at the spatial word-signs, but the particular traits of the letters recede—though without vanishing—from our awareness. Actually we focus only on the typical configurations of the letters, unless the special traits of the letters attract—and may even be meant to attract—our attention. We apprehend simultaneously the configuration of the printed word-sign as the indicator of the configuration of the word-sound, and the word-sound as the carrier of a word-meaning. We should point out in this connection that even in silent reading we hear, though only peripherally, the intended word-sounds and the melodic formations which they constitute. Thus the correlate of our visual perception of a printed (or written) word-sign, which is apprehended as a typical configuration, and the correlate of the simultaneous auditory apprehension of the typical phonic configuration of the word-sound, appear as two distinct, but closely connected, facets of the same "body of a word." This body of the word becomes the "expression" that carries the meaning of the word.

With the apprehension of the configuration of the printed word-sign, the word-sound, and the meaning it carries, we apprehend simultaneously various manifestative characteristics, some of which are carried by the word-sound. We have discussed the manifestative characteristics of communicative expressions, and we have ascribed manifestative ("emotional") characteristics of this particular kind to the presented speaker (and also to the presentative text in which the narrator is given). These manifestative characteristics are related to psychic or mental states, such as joy, fear, or anger. They are not the effects of the word-sounds themselves, but of the *tone* in which the words are uttered. There are, however, also different manifestative characteristics carried by certain word-sounds on account of the shades of meaning which the respective words or phrases acquire in a given language. We apprehend these characteristics with the shades of meaning and the melody of the words even in silent reading when we master the original language in which the text is written. These characteristics may be modified or lost in translation into a language that has no equivalents.

We should emphasize again that the apprehension of the word-sound and of its meaning is simultaneous, for they form the unity of the word. This means that normally, if we master the language, we do not separate these apprehensions in our experience, and we apprehend word-sounds only peripherally as fleeting transitions to the understanding of words and sentences. However, sound-formations of higher rank, such as rhyme, rhythm, and melody, or such qualities of sound as softness or hardness do elicit our aesthetic perception by the functions they are meant to fulfill in the work—for instance, the function of evoking a special mood that hovers over presented situations, or of affecting the mode of appearance of individual presented objects.

B. *Understanding of words and sentences*

We discussed the derived intentionality of word-meanings, their various moments, and their syntactical and logical functions on the strength of which they enter into reciprocal relations and establish analogous relations between their correlates. Thus we hinted at least at the foundation of our experience of understanding word-meanings and sense-units. We carry out the mental act of understanding—a *signitive act* in Husserl's terminology—in that we actualize the intentionality of word-meanings directed at their correlates. Of course, every word is part of a sense-unit, of some context, which narrows down its potential range of meanings to one (sometimes only relatively) unambiguous meaning. In its lexical form, which is an artificial construct, a word usually has several meanings which point to the broad linguistic system of which the word is a part. Thus our understanding of an expression is governed by the sense-unit and by the linguistic system of which it is a part. Within the linguistic system the word is understandable because it is apprehended in its relation to other word-meanings that are already understood and also in its relation to the part of the concept of an object which it actualizes. Because of the regularities of the linguistic system any word-meaning is apprehended in syntactical, and not only in logical and material, relations to other word-meanings. Consequently, even if we do not grasp the meaning of a given word, the systems and the immediate context often reveal its meaning.

As we read we hardly ever focus on any single word-meaning within a sentence but on the sense-unit as a whole, which means that we apprehend ever so briefly the individual word-meanings of the sentence in their contextual significations and with their manifestative characteristics and melody. We understand the sense-unit in that we actualize the sense of the sentence: its intention becomes our intention, and the two intentions become identical as we reenact the intentionality of the original sentence-forming operation.

Just as a word is not independent of a sentence, a sentence, too, is only an element of a complex of sentences. Thus while the actualized sense of one sentence lingers in the mind, we already expect the following sentence to connect with it in a coherent sequence. As we begin reading the new sentence, we actualize the sense of this sentence as the plausible continuation of the previous one, in that we concretize the connection between the correlates of the two sentences. In rereading a text we become especially aware of the codetermining effects of anticipated sentences on certain sentences that precede them, and we thus realize the manner in which the development of a topic affects the cohesion of connections between sentences. Proceeding in this manner we ascertain the formed content of the entire layer of meaning-units and follow the dynamics of the unfolding sense in its plausible sequential coherence, regardless of the structural order of the work. Without the unfolding of the sense in the layer of meaning-units, the aesthetic qualities of this layer and their effects on the mode of appearance of presented objects would be adversely affected.

If we are not to misunderstand the sentences, and especially the declarative sentences, in a literary work, we must recognize their "quasi-modifications," for otherwise we should fail to focus on the presented world itself and dwell on extraliterary reality. The cognitive process that seeks to fathom the literary work as a work of art presupposes our focusing on the presented world. We discussed the quasi-affirmative character of declarative sentences, but a few complementary remarks are in order at this point because our recognition of literary language is so important to our understanding of a literary work of art and to our aesthetic apprehension of its presented world. In a text which is meant to be an account of independent reality, the language is transparent; i.e., the word-meanings are used in their literal sense, ambiguities are avoided, and the attention of the reader is directed toward the independent objects and states of affairs with the purpose of facilitating their conceptualized apprehension. By contrast, the language of literary art is used to elicit in the reader a grasp of the imaginational appearance of the *presented* objects *as if* they were real. The presented world must have a semblance of reality, because the reader must be able to apprehend it as the carrier of aesthetic qualities. However, this world must have only a semblance of reality because the reader's attention should not stray into his real world, of which the presented world may be at most a representation. The work of art uses artistic language to separate the presented from the real world, to evoke a mood, a pervasive tone, and an emotional atmosphere in which the presented world is steeped and, most importantly, from which it seemingly materializes colored by qualities that enable us to grasp it aesthetically. We must be able to see it in its givenness and experience it intimately in its quasi-*reality*, which is yet distanced because it is a *quasi*-reality, a mere semblance. To achieve this complex effect, artistic language plays its part by various means, such as the cadence of sentences, rhyme, rhythm, melody, and words with a particular phonic (sometimes onomatopoeic) quality. By such sound-formations words attract the sensitive reader's attention to their aesthetic qualities and to the objects they thus present. Also, words with metaphorical meanings, if properly understood, may have a similar effect. By being double-rayed, metaphorical meanings are particularly apt to bring forth certain kinds of opalescence in which quasi-reality may be sometimes suitably steeped. On the one hand, they draw the reader's attention to themselves and thus emphasize the objects their figurative meanings present; on the other hand, they also suggest at the same time, though of course indirectly, other objects which appear, as it were, captive in the mirrorlike objects which metaphorical meanings present within the presented world. Thus the reader is hindered from transposing the suggested objects into independent reality. Of course, he may ignore the figurative meaning the very moment he has recognized the suggested, i.e., the ultimate, the "actual" meaning. When this occurs, the suggested objects cease being apprehended aesthetically through the metaphorical meanings, lose their opalescence, and may end up being dryly conceptualized, the fate of many a poem as soon as its "images" have served their purpose of leading the myopic reader to the no longer equivocal "content" to which the poem has thus been reduced.

Those are some of the devices by which both layers of language, if appropriately grasped, enhance our capability of intuiting and appreciating the aesthetic qualities of presented objects and of recognizing the quasi-reality of their world. Of course, these devices, which are used primarily in poetical works, are not found in every literary work of art, and different linguistic (or other) means help in inducing the reader's aesthetic attitude. We should mention here Ingarden's article on the functions of language in a stage play, which appeared as an appendix to *The Literary Work of Art*. Within the presented world of the stage play the spoken words perform various functions: presentation of objects, experiences, and states of mind; communication between characters; and the influencing of those addressed. Outside of the presented world is the audience, the spectators. In plays that are performed on an "open" stage and clearly elicit the participation of the spectators, all the means we have described—and others—may be used to emphasize the presented world, because here there is no attempt to approximate reality. There are, however, so-called "naturalistic" plays, performed on a "closed" stage with the actors supposedly unaware of the spectators' presence; i.e., the functions of communication and influencing are supposed to be effected without any regard for the audience. These are the plays which in their maximal approximation to reality are intended to cast a veil over the quasi-reality of the presented world and to induce the spectators to identify the presented with the real world. At the same time, however, the closed stage is meant to evoke in the spectator a particularly strong aesthetic experience precisely because of his exclusion and the distancing which it is expected to bring about. Thus the words uttered on stage and addressed to the characters of the presented world, in which those words are taken seriously, are meant to induce in the characters, for instance, fear, whereas the same words, which the spectator, too, is hearing as they are uttered on stage, are not meant to evoke in him the same reaction. Shielded as he is by his exclusion, he is to fathom them in their artistic function and apprehend them in distanced aesthetic reaction with, for instance, pleasure or displeasure. What, we must ask, is the reason for this difference in functional effects, considering that the characters and the spectators hear the same utterances? (There are, of course, spectators who do identify the presented with the real world and do not distinguish, even subliminally, the actor from the character during the performance because they do not understand how and why one and the same utterance may fulfill the functions of communication and influencing with such different effects.)

At this point we must remind ourselves of the distinctions made earlier between what I called the presentative text, which projects the presented world, and the text of uttered statements that are taken in all seriousness in the presented world. There we also discussed the means by which uttered sentences are projected into the presented world. We learned that the presentative text may be only implied, and that the actually uttered sentence within the presented world of a play is a verbatim record of a suppressed sentence belonging to an implied presentative text. Consequently, if we wish to safeguard our aesthetic grasp of a play performed on a closed stage, we must understand the double projection we are witnessing. Although we hear only one uttered statement, we understand that it is actually double. One statement is uttered by the *actor*, and this we apprehend as the presentative text. The other statement, heard simultaneously, is the presented statement, uttered by the presented *character*, and it is this statement that fulfills all its functions in and for the presented world. Thus even in a play of that kind, the layer of sound-formations and that of meaning-units, if properly understood, reveal the quasi-reality of the presented world and support the spectator's distanced aesthetic apprehension of it.

In conclusion, as long as we remain in the sphere of our signitive acts (in what Ingarden calls the passive, receptive, manner of reading), i.e., as long as we merely actualize the sense of the sentences in their linear sequence and simply follow the projected states of affairs, we do not apprehend imaginationally the presented objects, and we therefore fail to recognize their aesthetic qualities. Only when we proceed from passive to active reading can we apprehend the projected objects in a synthesis of their presented properties, features, and interrelations. In this manner alone do we move out of the transitional realm of sense-units into the world of *objectified* presented objects. Only thus can we as readers begin to perform those creative acts whereby our various complementations may lead to concretions, which make it possible for the objects to appear as present in our imagination. The question, then, is how that move from sense-units to presented objects is carried out.

C. Objectification

When we actualize the sense of a sentence in an act of understanding, we apprehend the correlate of the sense-unit. Since declarative sentences are fundamental in the projection of the presented world, we shall limit our discussion to states of affairs. Suppose we consider the categorially projected state of affairs "Wellington defeated Napoleon in the battle of Waterloo." As we reflect on this state of affairs, we may "think of" and have perhaps also an incipient imaginational visualization of an objectified Wellington as the victor, or of Napoleon as the vanquished, or of the battle of Waterloo, or we may carry out all three objectifications. By such objectification the categorial structure of the state of affairs, on which the objectification is based, may recede into the background. But objectification need not occur in conjunction with an imaginational process; it can be mere apprehension, simple knowledge, derived from the sense of the sentence. The conditions that favor the objectification of one object rather than another, or one kind of objectification rather than another, depend on the inclinations or interests of the readers or of the same reader at different times. The range of possible objectifications increases when the same interrelated objects are being presented in changing situations revealing their varying characteristics. With each modification in the evolving characterization of the presented objects, the reader's objectifications are enriched or altered. In some presentations the number of possible and admissible objectifications may be so great that most are bound to remain potential in the course of a single reading. This may be so because of the reader's inclinations or capabilities, or because the text elicits some objectifications rather than others, so that the reader may not even become aware of most of the possible objectifications unless he interrupts his reading or reflects upon the work as a whole, as happens in every critical study of a literary work. In any case, even when the reader is attentive, only some of the potential objectifications are realized in any one uninterrupted reading. Consequently, the formal structure of the objectified presented world is different in every reading, and some states of affairs always remain only on the level of our signitive understanding. The differences in objectification can thus have far-reaching effects on our aesthetic apprehension of the presented world.

While we move from one sentence to the next, we absorb into the flow of our experience the sense of the text and whatever spontaneous or intended objectifications occur. However, by our objectifications the presented objects become, as it were, fixed. In our fleeting acts of distancing, when we synthesize and unify the projected materials scattered in the text and thereby objectify certain objects, we note that these fixed objects emerge from the flow of our experience and finally constitute the presented world as objectified. This world is brought out in relief and we come to witness it as distinct from our own. However, in the very process of our objectifications, our imagination is already being enticed to simultaneous but distinct acts of concretization, because the world that is at first more or less categorially objectified is only skeletal.

When we objectify the correlates of sense-units that pertain, for instance, to one presented object, we do so in a synthesizing and unifying apprehension of as many pertinent states of affairs as possible. Of course, we read the sentences in their linear sequence, but we select for our objectification only those of their correlates that may be unified in a synthesis of the object's properties, traits, relations, etc. Because the pertinent sentence-correlates do not normally follow one another but are scattered in various phases of the work, we cannot locate them in an uninterrupted succession of sentences. Thus we learn to distinguish the order in which presented objects are objectified—the objective order—from the order in which sentences constitute the structural order of sequence. Consequently, in the course of our active reading we also learn to recognize the layer of presented objects as distinct from the layer of meaning-units. Our recognition of this distinction is clearly imposed by the text, and it is a condition for our appropriate apprehension of the presented world.

We know that the quasi-affirmative character of declarative sentences in a literary work and the reader's actualizations of the sense-units conceal their pure intentionality and contribute to the impression that those sentences are genuine affirmations. Furthermore, we know that concretizations veil the skeletal structure of presented objects and lend credibility to their reality. We may now add that objectifications play their own part in endowing the presented world with a semblance of reality because the objectified and, in a sense, "fixed" objects are made to stand apart from the flow of our experienced reality in a sphere of their own, where we can behold them and deal with them almost as if they were imagined real people, actions, and occurrences.

D. The concretization of presented objects and the actualization of ready aspects

Every literary work is a schematic structure, and points of indeterminateness are therefore inevitable. In fact, they are necessary for our aesthetic apprehension of the layer of presented objects, because too many textually explicit details may diffuse that apprehension and blur the salient features of the phenomenally appearing objects. Our concretizations, effected by spontaneous complementations of different kinds, are induced by the semblance of concrete reality of presented objects, and also by our aesthetic attitude as we seek to visualize the merely objectified skeletal presentations of characters, places, actions, and the often barely sketched intervals between stages of presented life. Every work contains, of course, different points of indeterminateness, but certain types of indeterminateness may be found in works of various styles that are characteristic of certain periods and literary kinds. There is great latitude in our concretizations and they vary from one reading to another. They may be knowledgeably adapted to the exigencies of the intended style or they may deviate from it. Some "modernized" concretizations in certain stage plays (Hamlet wearing a tuxedo) may be aesthetically striking, but one may wonder of what aesthetic value such an innovation can be when it affects the intended harmony of the other aesthetic qualities of the play. Our concretizations may sometimes be affected by personal experiences or culturally determined attitudes, and the aesthetic effect of the work as a whole may be distorted, or may be heightened by aesthetically valuable concretizations that accord admirably with the range of textually admissible though not suggested complementations. Appropriate concretizations, based on almost simultaneous objectifications, are a condition for an appropriate aesthetic apprehension of a work, and the reader's own creative activity is indispensable if the presented world is to emerge from its schematic structure. Nevertheless, even our complementations are necessarily incomplete and still leave the phenomenally appearing world largely schematic; but the effect of our concretizations is to cast a veil over the remaining indeterminateness, which is thus left in a state of abeyance.

So far, we have dealt individually with certain cognitive functions, although they occur almost simultaneously. We began with the signitive apprehension of sense-units and moved to the synthesizing grasp of states of affairs relevant to the reconstruction and objectification of presented objects. These objects, thus readied for our concretizations in the course of which they emerge with their aesthetic qualities, can at last be intuited in their phenomenal appearance. The objectification and concretization of presented objects is carried out simultaneously with our actualizations of at least some ready aspects through which the objects may be intuited. Presented objects cannot appear phenomenally if our reading remains on the level of signitive apprehension, i.e., if we do not actualize their aspects. To actualize and concretize these aspects is to perform acts of vivid imagination that are analogous to perceptions founded in concretely experienced aspects. In our discussion of schematized aspects and their role in the literary work of art, we noted that in the work's schematic structure they are only potential. The states of affairs that present the properties and features of objects do not by themselves elicit our experience of aspects, even when these are readied by states of phenomenal qualifications and by certain sound-formations, unless in active reading we assume an aesthetic stance, respond to the textual suggestions, and constitute the aesthetic qualities of potential aspects in our imagination.

We have noted that salient features of a phenomenally appearing object may be blurred if the text contains too many explicit descriptions of its traits. This is particularly true of existential qualifications that are not even potentially self-presenting, so-called "described aspects." When they are presented with exaggerated specificity, the reader, instead of experiencing them, may be induced to objectify them to the detriment of the objects which should appear through their aspects and be endowed by them with aesthetic qualities. It is on the objects that he should be made to focus, for it is they that are meant to be exhibited, whereas their aspects should show them to the reader so that he may intuit them. Therefore it is his function to recognize readied schematized aspects, and to respond to them by appropriately actualizing and concretizing them, so that the objects may receive shape and distinctness and stand out vividly and concretely in his imagination. Obviously, no text can impose an absolutely accurate actualization of aspects, because they are schematic and also because a reader may, for instance, have no direct experience of the objects that are to appear through them. However, if he is attentive and sensitive to the directives of the text, he may achieve a reconstruction of aspects that approximate the creative intention. A quotation from John Ruskin's *The Stones of Venice* may fittingly conclude these remarks and introduce those to follow:

One of the main functions of art in its service to man, is to arouse the imagination from its palsy, like the angel troubling the Bethesda pool; and the art which does not do this is false to its duty, and degraded in its nature. It is not enough that it be well imagined, it must task the beholder also to imagine well; and this so imperatively, that if he does not choose to rouse himself to meet the work, he shall not taste it, nor enjoy it in any wise. Once that he is well awake, the guidance which the artist gives him should be full and authoritative: the beholder's imagination should not be suffered to take its own way, or wander hither and thither; but neither must it be left at rest; and the right point of realization, for any given work of art, is that which will enable the spectator to complete it for himself, in the exact way the artist would have him, but not that which will save him the trouble of effecting the completion. . . . So that the art is wrong, which either realizes its subject completely, or fails in giving such definite aid as shall enable it to be realized by the beholding imagination.[1]

E. The unifying apprehension of all layers and of the idea of the work

As we know, the self-enclosed unity of the literary structure is the function of its interrelated and reciprocally adapted (modulated) heterogeneous layers and of the structural order of sequence of its phases. So far, we have sketched the concretizations of the layers individually; we shall now consider the concretization based on their organic unity.

Here, the term "organic" is not used in its strict sense, for there are considerable differences between a literary work, even as it is apprehended during a concretization, and an organism. An organism fulfills the function of preserving an individual life and thus the continuation and survival of the species. This is its main function and its reason for being: therein lies its "sense." It consists of organs whose different functions are interdependent, complementary, reciprocally adapted, and subordinate to the main function in a hierarchical order. The proper performance of each of these functions in its own sphere and in unison with the other functions is based on the equilibrium of all the functions within the organism. An anomaly in any one function, if it cannot be offset by self-regulatory effects of other organs, may damage the affected organ, interfere with other func-

---

1. This quotation is taken from the conclusion of the third volume of *The Stones of Venice*, in *The Works of John Ruskin*, ed. E. T. Cook and Alexander Wedderburn, 39 vols. (London: George Allen, 1903–1912), 11:213–14.

tions, and endanger the main function, which is performed by the organism as a whole and not by any one organ in particular. In the schematic structure of the completed literary work there is no activity, there are no processes that sustain its life, and no functions are being fulfilled. The layers of this structure are not organs, but they are heterogeneous, interdependent, and the layer of meaning-units is the least dependent in the hierarchy of dependence. Only in our concretization of its layers and in our unfolding of its structural order of sequence does the work have a semblance of organic life, of a process in which the functions of its elements are being fulfilled. Our constitution of only one layer by itself (e.g., the layer of presented objects or that of meaning-units) does not allow us to see the work's organic structure. In fact, that insight escapes us even when we have constituted all the layers separately but have not taken into account their interdependence and the structural order of sequence of the work, without which the dynamic unfolding of the process of functions cannot be experienced. At this point in our discussion of organic unity we shall simply recognize the importance of the structural order of sequence; the cognitive acts directed at its apprehension will be treated later.

Since all the functions of an organic unity culminate in the main function of the organism as a whole, we must ask what the main function is when the organic unity is that of a literary work of art; to be sure, not of any particular literary work, but of the literary work of art as such. We have dealt with various functions that are attributed to the literary work and are based on some misconceptions of the existential character of the presented world. We have also discussed various meanings of "truth" embodied in a literary work, and we recognized that the *idea* of the work should not be based on the "truths" that derive from adaptations of the presented world to the real world, but that it may emerge, for instance, as a view of life, or as a metaphysical quality. The main function of the literary work of art is thus not to "express" that idea, but to afford us the experience of intuiting it through the congruity of the work's aesthetic qualities.

It is a fact that any work of art bears the marks of its author, but tracing them in an effort to ascertain the author's intellectual and psychological makeup does not furnish appropriate means for our apprehension of the main function of the work as art. It is also a fact that certain literary works, even literary works of art, are meant to fulfill social functions, sometimes by a polemical advocacy of various social or ethical views. When this tendency moves into the foreground, the reader may be deflected from an apprehension of the work's aesthetic qualities and consequently from an intuition of the idea of the work which is its main function as an organic structure that founds an aesthetic object.

In my discussion of a metaphysical quality as an idea of a literary work of art, I explained its emergence by referring to our intuition of the derived essence squareness through an individual square, because a metaphysical quality is a derived essence. With that explanation in mind, we shall proceed with our exploration of the literary idea. Here we shall focus on the idea as an aesthetic configuration, i.e., as the synthesis of the aesthetic qualities of the total organic structure of the work. We know that the essential nature of a square consists of three concretized constitutive qualities: parallelogramness, rectangularity, and equilaterality. Its particular constitutive nature is further determined by the length of its sides. We could say that those three *qualities* form the "center of crystallization" of the unity of a square, while their concretizations and a given lateral length are necessary for the square to be constituted so that its "central quality," squareness, in which those congruous qualities culminate, can be intuited *through* it. In that center of crystallization, parallelogramness is the *core* and the other two qualities can be seen as complements of the core when all three qualities are concretized in an individual square. We have used the term "idea" in reference to an object's general or particular idea, and we know the difference between an essence and such an idea. We could say, however, that squareness *as the central quality* of an individual square in which it is concretized, in which it is thus founded, and with which it forms a unique unity, is the "idea" of that individual square. It confers on that object the unity, the wholeness, of its cohesive structure. It is incorrect to speak of organic structure in reference to an individual square, except perhaps, and then only in a figurative sense, when we visualize the process by which that square is constituted and the mere schema of a parallelogram is seen to assume the shape of a square, while rectangularity, equilaterality, and a lateral dimension exercise their formative functions.

This oversimplified model may help us to understand the rather complex configuration of what Ingarden calls the idea of the literary work of art, which can be apprehended only in general terms, because every single literary work creates its own "type" of idea. The literary idea, in general, derives from a displayed and intuited essential cohesion of reciprocally modulated synthesized aesthetic qualities. The idea is the intuitable central quality wherein the congruous and cohesive aesthetic qualities culminate, a quality that forms a unique whole with the founding literary work of art. That cohesion of qualities confers a "visible" organic unity on the schematic structure of the literary work as we concretize it. The qualities stem from all layers and from the structural order of sequence of the work, and they differ accordingly. In truly great works of art these qualities are arranged in an organic hierarchical order. Some qualities form a center of crystallization from which the idea ultimately emerges, while the other qualities within the work complement them. At the *core* of the center of crystallization there is a quality, or a tight cluster of qualities, which affects the reader's emotions: a quality of occurrences which is founded in a particular structural order of the sequence of phases; or a quality that derives from the dynamics of temporal perspectives of presented time; or a quality that derives from sound-configurations or from the melody of verses; etc. We mentioned earlier that the center of crystallization may consist, for instance, of qualities constitutive of a certain view of life, qualities of absolute commitment to values and of renunciation of vital personal interests with which the beliefs and actions of characters may be endowed and which mold intersubjective relations, as in the *Antigone*. At the core of that center of crystallization—of that view of life—we find the quality of the compelling force of ethical values, a quality that may reveal already at the core the ultimate emergence of the metaphysical quality of the tragic.

Ingarden calls the aesthetic quality at the core of the center of crystallization the "idea of the work in the narrower sense of the word." The quality at the core—the idea in the narrower sense—and those congruous qualities which together with it form the center of crystallization emerge, in my view, as the idea *within* the presented world, whereas the idea as a metaphysical quality emerges *through* it.

The center of crystallization is that cluster of qualities which is the focal point around which aesthetic qualities of all layers and of the structural order of sequence gather into a harmonious unity which ultimately constitutes the unified aesthetic object of the concretized work as a whole and culminates in the phenomenal appearance of the presented world. Assuming that our concretization of a true work of art is appropriate, we should discover only one center of crystallization of qualities to which all the complementary qualities are subordinate. All the anatomical elements of the skeletal structure of the work function jointly to found the evolving idea through a conjuncture of aesthetic qualities, a conjuncture that parallels the cohesion of an essential configuration. In a work of art that is not built on such a pattern, the value of unity, the organic cohesion, and the idea as the main function of art are missing even if the work is otherwise rich in aesthetic qualities. It is obvious that a concretization with no regard for the subordinate complementary functions of all layers and of the structural order of sequence may not attain to the vision of the organic structure and of the idea present in a work.

In view of the complexity of the structural functions of a literary work of art, any appropriate concretization presents considerable difficulties, especially if the reader does not possess the guidelines for his actualizations and also if he cannot bracket his personal or "cultural" prepossessions. In the case of great works of art the difficulties are increased, for there are no models to unlock the secrets of their uniqueness. In a single reading certain distortions are inevitable even under conditions that are favorable to an appropriate concretization, because of the many varied acts of apprehension that need to be carried out simultaneously. We may fail to pay equal attention to all the strata, to the order of sequence of the phases, and to their interrelated functions, because of constant variations in our span of attention and also because some features attract our attention to the exclusion of others. We usually focus on the layer of presented objects and ignore the layers of sound-formations and meaning-units. Sometimes, for the many reasons we have discussed, we fail to actualize and experience the layer of schematized aspects. As a result of the richness and complexity of the work of art and of our own limitations, we apprehend certain features of the work and certain phases of its unfolding in what are inevitable perspectival foreshortenings.

F. The concretization of the structural order of sequence and temporal perspectives

We have spoken repeatedly of the functional effects of the structural order of sequence on the mode of appearance of the presented world, and we have just mentioned that the structural order may in some works furnish an aesthetic quality for the very core of the center of crystallization, a quality that may be the principle of the work's structural cohesion, of the polyphony of its aesthetic qualities. Bearing in mind these points as well as the principle of founding of the structural order of sequence of the phases of a literary work, we shall now turn our attention to acts of concretization in which that order is apprehended.

The structural order of sequence is the most obvious determinant of the dynamics of unfolding occurrences and our apprehension of the pace at which the sequence of sense-units is experienced. These artistic values of compositional patterns affect the aesthetic worth of the work in their own way, while the principle of founding governing the order of sequence provides a foundation for the unified sense of the work and for the aesthetic cohesion of its concretion. The structural order of the phases of a completed work is, of course, already in place when our reading begins, but the process of our cognition necessarily follows a line of temporal succession, and for this reason we can get to know the phases only one by one in the order of our reading (which in a short work may occur in a continuum). Consequently, the temporal succession of the phases of our cognition necessarily follows the established structural order of sequence and transforms the order of *founded* sequence into a *temporal* succession of concretized phases of the work.

Even the reading of a compound sentence requires more than a single moment for our signitive apprehension of the sense-unit in its unfolding. During our constitutions of successive sense-units, which are accompanied by our peripheral grasp of various sound-formations and by other acts of cognition appropriate to active reading (objectification, complementations, synthesis), we can keep vividly in our consciousness only what we apprehend in any *present phase of cognition*, which usually coincides with one or more sense-units, depending on the *range of vivid consciousness* (which differs from one reader to another). The already apprehended elements become increasingly foreshortened as they recede from vivid consciousness into memory. In the course of reading, every present phase of cognition is characterized by more or less vague *prospective* apprehensions, which move into our vivid consciousness, and then recede (without, however, disappearing altogether). During a present phase of cognition we actualize and concretize all the layers, though we sometimes pay special attention to certain occurrences which we are just witnessing. As the prospective phase of the work moves into the range of our vivid consciousness, the actual phase of the work recedes but lingers for a while in our *vivid memory*: sound-formations reverberate briefly before they die away; the just actualized sense-units are automatically summarized and subsist as condensed and simplified categorially intended sense; and the presented objects which we have just intuited through experienced aspects become divested of their phenomenal appearance and pass on foreshortened until they are lodged in our memory as objects we "know about"—unless of course they continue to linger in our vivid memory because they have impressed us with their striking aesthetic qualities.

In the light of these observations, we can appreciate the importance of vivid memory, which is, as it were, an extension of our *consciousness of the actual present*; it is the sense of what has just occurred and is still connected with what is passing through our consciousness. The objects in vivid memory linger for awhile in close proximity to our actual present, but yield to the constant flow of new objects, events, occurrences, and their qualifications, and recede into increasingly remote spheres of memory, from which, however, they may be recalled by acts of remembering. Because of the connection of vivid memory with the actual present, objects in vivid memory play an important part in that they color objects we apprehend in the actual present. However, the latter are also colored by anticipated parts of the work. It is important to realize that these colorations affect all layers of the work, for we may fail to experience those elements of ready aspects that are effects of *temporal perspectives*.

The particular founding of the structural order of sequence determines the dynamics of unfolding occurrences. Sometimes it may cause us to anticipate certain developments in the light of which we concretize a given present phase. We may then find that, for instance, a foreboding inevitably leads to a catastrophic ending, or that the founding has been so arranged as to permit an equally plausible but unexpected resolution, which necessitates a recall of already foreshortened concretized phases of the work into vivid memory so that their concretizations may be modified. All these acts of concretization reveal not only the pattern of founding of the structural order of the phases of the work, but also the effects of our temporal perspectives—induced by the founding—on various aspects and therefore on the evolving appearance of the presented objects.

To fathom the importance of these effects we should recall that our concrete experience of time is colored by the occurrences we perceive in it. This means that only those phases of our present and past that are qualitatively determined by perceived occurrences, or by occurrences that we have imaginationally experienced, appear to us as concrete phenomena. We know that phases of time are mere abstractions, which cannot be separated from the continuum of our experience of lived time, and so we fit these phases of time into a *formal temporal schema* and orient ourselves in relation to this schema from those points of time which we called the now-phase. We should note, however, that we fit into that formal temporal schema not only those phases of our present and past that appear to us as concrete phenomena because of perceived or imaginationally experienced occurrences, but also occurrences of the past which we have not experienced, about which we have been only informed. Now, this formal temporal schema, into which we fit temporal phases abstracted from the continuum of lived time, necessarily contains gaps, cleavages, which we veil by establishing dependences and connections. Moreover, we can also fit into that temporal schema phases of the future, which are vaguely determined by anticipated occurrences.

Every now-phase through which we live sinks relentlessly into the past, and so do the occurrences that determine it qualitatively. When we step into the past through recalling previous events, we are usually not aware of the effects of various experiences that fill and color our actual present. Consequently, the recalled events, even though we may remember them with clarity, take on a coloration that is different from the original one and are thus transformed within that temporal perspective.

In spite of considerable differences between spatial and temporal perspectives, we should at least mention that objects appear in various transformations because of spatial distance or because of being perceived from different angles. Consequently, the *spatial aspect* of an object codetermines its mode of appearance. Likewise, the *temporal aspect* of any object, and especially of an occurrence in the actual present—in the fleeting stage of its actuality—codetermines its mode of appearance at that moment; but as soon as this phase moves into vivid memory and then recedes into the past from which it is recalled, the temporal phase and the occurrence which colors it undergo various foreshortenings: i.e., the temporal aspects are foreshortened because of the changed temporal perspective, and the object or occurrence that emerges through those aspects is marked by a new appearance.

There are numerous possible variations in temporal aspects depending on the relation between, on the one hand, a temporal phase of the past and the type of occurrence that has determined it (e.g., perceived, imaginationally experienced, or merely reported occurrences) and, on the other hand, that zero point of orientation at which the act of remembering occurs. For every instance of such a relation there is a corresponding temporal aspect in the temporal perspectival foreshortening of the occurrence. Thus, in some instances, a past occurrence may fade into insignificance when seen from a perspective of subsequent occurrences, or its significance may change because new aspects, e.g., previously unsuspected motivations, have come to light. Sometimes our recollection may expand and we may remember facts that were simultaneous with a past event and may perhaps have gone unnoticed originally. From the perspective of such an expanded recollection the past event acquires modifying aspects by its functional dependence on aspects of objects on its periphery that we now recall. Most of the changes in the content of aspects and in the temporal phases themselves are well known from experience. Depending on whether we remember an occurrence in great detail or in a condensed form, it may appear to us as having lasted a fairly long time or as having been of short duration. Phases of time that seem long because we concentrate on the passage of every moment (e.g., when we feel that our life is threatened) may be recalled as brief. When we witness a scene filled with "action," we experience it as brief, but in our recollection it may seem to have been of much longer duration. We should note here that past phases do not always appear shorter the farther removed in time they are from a present moment of recollection. Thus, regardless of how far back in the past an occurrence may be, it will appear the closer to our present, the greater the number of its aesthetic qualities we can recall in a single act of remembering. Finally, the dynamics of an occurrence which we have observed in its unfolding through its culmination to its conclusion may, in vivid memory or if we remember it in a single act of recollection, appear stabilized and rigid.

An appropriate concretization presupposes our apprehension of textually predetermined temporal perspectives in which presented objects, especially occurrences, appear. Temporal perspectives are built into the structural order of sequence in all layers, and result in temporal aspects of many varieties, some of which are selected in response to the exigencies of literary kinds. While temporal aspects are textually only in a potential state, they are meant to be actualized in the course of our concretization. The tenses of verbs in the layer of meaning-units play an important role, but the use of, for instance, the past tense does not necessarily cause the reader to assume an attitude similar to that he takes in remembering past events, because the tense by itself is not always decisive. If occurrences are presented with considerable specificity, the reader is induced to step into a past which he experiences as if he witnessed the presented time. He may also anticipate the events that are "still to come" with the peripheral knowledge that they "have already taken place," and distinguish them from the stream of events that he is just witnessing. When the reader is to keep the experience of his concrete present, or if he is to remain in the past phase that he is witnessing as if it were his present, a temporal distance may be achieved between that present and other past occurrences if these other occurrences are merely summarized without specific indications of when they took place and without a presentation of their unfolding. All such past occurrences appear relatively equal in their anteriority, and the reader fathoms them in a foreshortened perspective.

A repetitious recurrence of certain only slightly varied situations may purposely disrupt the linear flow of events in order to focus the reader's attention on the situations themselves, which are sometimes seen in the distance, sometimes brought into the foreground through the narrative present, or at times only anticipated, thereby acquiring a temporal three-dimensionality and aesthetic qualities that form the center of crystallization, or its core, from which the idea of that presented world may emerge as the terror of an obsession (as, for instance, in Robbe-Grillet's *Jealousy*), or as the pathos of existence (as in Becket's *Waiting for Godot*), to mention at least some effects of such temporal perspectives.

In plays, every present moment is in a process of actualization. We apprehend each moment without temporal distance, and as we progress from one witnessed moment to the next, we experience each in the light of what has already occurred and what we still anticipate; but there remains a distance interposed by our perceptions, by our apprehension of what is taking place: we remain spectators. By contrast, if our apprehension is limited, let us say, to the presentation *in the present* of a past incident that was experienced by a lyrical subject, not only may the temporal distance be eliminated, but the presented past incident may move into our present because we project ourselves into the present of the presentation: we identify with the quality of the emotion, but not with the particularity of the incident experienced by the lyrical subject. If that same incident were presented in the past, we would experience it as the witnesses of another's memory.

One more point needs to be stressed: in the *course* of our reading, we concretize the work at each step not only from a new temporal perspective and in the light of the temporal aspects that are determined by the text, but also with the range of vivid memory and the power of recall we ourselves may be capable of. Because of the inevitable foreshortenings, we can never apprehend all the phases we have read in their vivid presence, nor can we do so after we have completed the reading. During our reading, we may, if we are attentive, experience the dynamics of the unfolding layers in the structural order of sequence of the work, and we may, at the conclusion of our reading, have the experience of some of the reciprocal functional dependences of the layers and of the phases in the compositional order of their founding. These experiences *of a first reading* provide an indispensable basis for the cognition of the literary work of art.

G. *Different ways of reading a scholarly text and a literary one*

We have just noted the importance of a reading without major interruptions if we are to apprehend the dynamics of the unfolding of a presented world. It is this unfolding that determines in large measure the mode of appearance of that world, reveals aesthetic qualities peculiar to it, and contributes decisively to the work's aesthetic value. By contrast, a scholarly work is often necessarily read with numerous interruptions during which the logical connections between sense-units need to be established and word-meanings verified to avoid ambiguities. The reason for the fundamental difference between these modes of reading is that the function of a scholarly work is to determine results of scientific inquiry and to transmit them so that further investigations may be fruitfully continued. Its purpose is not to create a self-contained presented world culminating in the concretization of an aesthetic value, but to refer to objectively existing states of affairs by means of sense-units that make a genuine claim to truth (even if they should turn out to be erroneous). These affirmative sense-units seek to establish the legitimacy of that claim by their logical factual connections and by verifications that draw the necessary proof of the validity of their claims from experience or from formulated findings that have already established their validity. We have seen that the sense-units of a scholarly work mean to direct the reader to objectively existing states of affairs, and that that is the function of their intentional directional factors. Their purely intentional correlates are transparent, and no aesthetic qualities of, for instance, sound-formations are to hinder the reader from passing right through them to objective reality. All structural features of a scholarly work must serve this end, and aesthetic qualities of the layer of sound-formations or of meaning-units may even impede its proper function. In some domains of scholarship, certain sentence-correlates sometimes exhibit a model of an isomorphic object of objective reality. Such a model is meant to facilitate our visualization of the *referential* object, and not, as in a literary work of art, to exhibit a purely intentional object with its aesthetic qualities so that it may contribute its share to the work's polyphony of aesthetic qualities. In a literary work we are directed to the particularity of the presentation, and we are barely—if at all—concerned with the represented objective world, because the artistic presentation captivates us as if it were represented reality itself. Its primary purpose, as we have so often seen, is to incorporate aesthetic qualities for our intuition, for our aesthetic experience. If this purpose is not achieved, the literary work is not a work of art, regardless of psychological or social insights.

The scientific work is meant to induce our investigation of existing reality, but a literary work of art should not be read as an informative treatise about that reality. Even though objective reality may indeed be reflected in the presented world, the reflection does not constitute the literary value of the work. We must bracket that reality, we must detach ourselves from it, if we wish to apprehend and reconstruct the presented world and its idea through the cohesion of its interdependent and interacting aesthetic qualities. Through its layer of meaning-units the scientific work is apprehended as a reference to an objective world. Ideally, the literary work of art must be apprehended through its entire stratified structure in the structural order of its sequence, if we wish to savor the accomplishment of its aesthetic creation and to intuit its idea, which it alone can reveal, provided we assume the aesthetic attitude and consider the world presented in the literary work of art as an aesthetic object.

Chapter 5

1. The aesthetic experience and the aesthetic object

In the closing remarks of the preceding chapter we said that we have to detach ourselves from reality if we wish to experience the literary work *as art*, and by "reality" we meant that objective reality to which the work's content, i.e., the sense of the layer of meaning-units, may seem to refer. Of course, the raw material, the so-called "subject matter" of the work, is in some respects similar to objective reality, and it is no wonder that the naive reader is tempted to establish referential correlations between the presented world and the extraliterary (and especially the *represented*) world of reality, and that he may be tempted to judge the presented world favorably if it succeeds in keeping alive his illusion that the presented world is meant to be real.

In the following sketch of the aesthetic experience, which is the experience of apprehending a work of art as the foundation of an aesthetic object, we shall see that as soon as we assume an aesthetic stance, we do *to a certain extent* abandon the notion of seeking correlations between presented and objective reality, but we detach ourselves from reality in yet another respect. We have mentioned various attitudes with which readers may approach a literary work, and what they may expect to derive from their reading. At this point, we shall deal only with the competent reader who wishes to actualize an aesthetic concretization.

To illustrate his sketch of the typical characteristics of the aesthetic stance and experience, Ingarden describes an aesthetic apprehension of the Venus of Milo. I should like to preface the exposition of this subject by references to his essay on the work of architecture.[1] Suppose we see a piece of cloth with one half of one color and the other of a different color. To one person the cloth may serve a practical purpose; for instance, it may be used as a bedspread. To another person that same piece of cloth may be a flag evoking feelings of respect. It depends on the attitudes of these two

1. "Das Werk der Architektur," in *Untersuchungen zur Ontologie der Kunst*, pp. 257–315.

persons what the function of that materially identical object is to be. Each means that object from the point of view of his attitude, but the cloth by itself is neither a flag nor a bedspread. Therefore, the piece of cloth is the ontic foundation of an object—other than the cloth—created by an intentional act of consciousness. The heteronomous existence and subsistence of this purely intentional object are founded in the real material (the cloth) and in appropriate acts of consciousness derived from certain attitudes.

Let us now consider another example: a real object, a building made of stone, brick, or concrete. It is constructed according to certain laws that depend in part on the properties of these autonomous materials. The internal dispositions and certain external features are dictated by the purpose the building is intended to serve, though we know that many a building has been made to serve purposes very different from those for which it was originally intended, and to serve the new purposes without significant structural adjustments. Let us assume that the building is meant to be a church and is made to serve that purpose by appropriate acts of consciousness (consecration and services). The church is a purely intentional object, and is different from its real material foundation. Because of certain traditional architectural styles, we may immediately recognize that a given building is a church; the relation between style and building is very close, and we may for that reason fail to realize the difference between the real building and the purely intentional church. We may make this difference clearer by recalling that certain churches or other monuments of architectural art have been destroyed by wars and rebuilt in accordance with preserved documents. In spite of new material foundations, the same purely intentional architectural works of art have been restored.

Of course, the type of material that serves as the foundation is of considerable importance. For instance, a building whose foundation is made of smooth, glossy marble appears through phenomenal qualifications that are different from those of a building made of brick. The aesthetic qualities carried by a brick foundation cannot constitute an aesthetic object whose material base is polished marble. If the foundation is not appropriate to the purposes intended by the artist, the aesthetic object cannot emerge before us with the qualities the artist had imagined before he produced his work of art. In any case, the real building and some of its properties are only the basis on which the viewer may apprehend the building to be a church and also a work of art. On the basis of the aesthetic qualities of that work of art, he may be induced to constitute an aesthetic object. He himself must intuit these qualities on the basis of the perceived self-presenting existential qualifications of the material, because, as we know, the real material by itself has no phenomenal appearance. In other words, neither the quality of reality nor the properties of the material can be the object or the source of our aesthetic experience. The source of that experience is our aesthetic stance and the object we experience in that stance is constituted by certain acts of consciousness which, directed to a statue or a building, are made possible and aided by perceptions of real objects. Thus an aesthetic object is not a real object with certain attributions, and it can therefore not be apprehended as a configuration of sensory data. Clearly, to intuit an aesthetic object, we must go beyond its material base, and, as we shall see, beyond the work of art.

We realize that we may naively identify the aesthetic object with its real carrier. Consequently, if we wish to have aesthetic experiences, we must not entertain the notion that aesthetic objects are real, and we must not assume that we can apprehend an aesthetic object *at a glance*. In particular we must first abandon the practical attitude in which we deal with works of art for a purpose other than that of having an aesthetic experience. We must also abandon the purely cognitive attitude of, for instance, an art historian. The purpose of that kind of cognition is, after all, the determination of the existence and manner of being of objects, whereas the aim and purpose of an aesthetic experience is the apprehension of aesthetic qualities and of that quality which results from a synthesis of the congruous aesthetic qualities of a work of art and stamps the work with its uniqueness. An aesthetic experience can occur only in an aesthetic attitude. It is a complex process, and not a momentary event. We should note that an aesthetic experience does not need to begin with the perception of a particular real carrier, for it can originate and develop in our imagination on the basis of imagined objects that we have never perceived, such as a literary plot.

When we look at the statue of the Venus of Milo, we perceive the marble only peripherally, for if we focused on it and on some of its blemishes (as an art historian should, and many a naive viewer does, though for vastly different reasons), we should be distracted from our aesthetic experience of the qualities of the presented figure.[2] In an aesthetic attitude, we gloss over the material and most of its traits and imperfections. We pay no special attention to these findings of our perceptions; sometimes we go so far as to complement—though not in any detail of course, but rather as a mental sketch—missing parts of the sculptured body. We perform these

2. It is worth mentioning that in nonrepresentational art (architecture, music, and so-called abstract painting) we can move immediately from what is concretely given to what is presented. In representational art (sculpture, painting, and in its own way, literature too) whatever is concretely perceptible is more likely to hold our attention.

acts because we already see the figure called Venus and try to imagine the missing qualities of movements and gestures, because we seek to apprehend the statue as a qualitative whole. We do not perform these complementary acts (as an art historian may) in order to discover the artist's original intention; we do so because we are fascinated by the prospect of seeing the qualities of the whole and the quality that emerges from the synthesis of these qualities: the *Gestalt* of that work. The aesthetic quality of the whole cannot possibly be apprehended on only one side of the statue and from only a single angle. To come anywhere close to an apprehension of the synthesis of qualities, the viewer must see the object through as many of its phenomenal qualifications as possible and with a variety of inevitable perspectival foreshortenings. Clearly, a truly aesthetic apprehension implies many diverse acts, and therefore no aesthetic experience can be reduced to a momentary impression, although aesthetic experiences vary in duration (and in complexity), depending on subjective and objective conditions. It is obvious that the experience of a literary work of art or of a musical composition unfolds in many more phases than that of a painting, but even in the experience of a painting one cannot speak of only one momentary phase.

We shall now continue this general description of the aesthetic experience with a more or less implied reference to some statue (e.g., again the Venus of Milo), and then we shall consider the particularities of the aesthetic experience of a literary work of art. The aesthetic experience of a statue begins with a visual perception of a real object, a perception that may occur, for instance, in our natural attitude while we are still caught up in the practical concerns of our lives, or in an investigative (e.g., scholarly) attitude in which we pursue purely cognitive purposes. If we are at all disposed to an aesthetic experience, which means that initially we are passively receptive, we may suddenly feel affected, momentarily captivated, by a quality (or by several qualities) of a perceived trait of the *presented* object (not of the marble!). At that moment we cannot say what kind of quality it is. As a result of the impact of this *affective quality* the first phase of the aesthetic experience sets in (if we are not diverted), and we find ourselves in a state of excitement. This is the phase of the *original emotion*, in which the affective quality is not apprehended but only experienced. We are pleasantly surprised by what is occurring and we are astonished by this unlooked for and inexplicable appearance and also by the concomitant mounting desire to behold it, to savor it, and to delight in it. The intensity and the duration of the original emotion are different in every instance. The stronger this emotion, and the more willing we are to experience it, the more it impedes our awareness of the burdens of our real world, and the more likely it is that the full aesthetic experience can unfold. Whenever this occurs and we have to resume our everyday tasks after our aesthetic experience has fully evolved, we usually do so with some uneasiness, because our tasks seem to have less significance, at least for a while. However, if the original emotion is not strong enough, the full aesthetic experience may not unfold. We must conclude that a strong, unexpected, original emotion moves into our now-phase with such force that the connections of our present with immediately preceding and anticipated phases of our practical life are blurred. This accounts for the sense of liberation we experience already under the impact of the fleeting original emotion and far more keenly during the full aesthetic experience.

These personal responses are of course very important if a full aesthetic experience is to evolve. From the moment of our initial surprise and during our preoccupation with our experience of the affective quality we are undergoing a brief psychological transformation (provided, at all times, that we are receptive) which modifies our perception long enough for us to bridge the gap between naive practicality and aesthetic insight. What happens is this: in our natural matter-of-fact attitude we focus on the thing, on its states of affairs, and we note its qualities only as they pertain to the thing, i.e., to the carrier of its qualities. As soon as we experience the affective quality, our original emotion incites us to intuit that quality—to possess it in our intuition. Because our intuition fills our now-phase, we feel separated from past and anticipated temporal connections, we "neutralize" the object, in which the affective quality has appeared, to such an extent that we become indifferent to what that object is and to whether it is real or only a semblance. This shows how our intuition of the affective quality modifies our perception, for not only does the focus of our perception move from the object to the quality, it also shifts in another way: in our natural attitude, our perception is based on the reality of the perceived object, whereas during that intuition the reality of the object and its nature become irrelevant. The intuited pure quality stands out in this phase, and we savor it while our desire for that intuition is being satisfied. We behold its presence with joy and we gain a sense of its value, as we do when we experience, for instance, the fragrance of a rose. This very joy and appreciation incite us to seek further satisfactions, and so we return to the object from which the quality emanates. However, because our perception is altered, we do not return to the object in order to perceive it for its own sake, but for the sake of other qualities emanating from its features, qualities that we hope will complement the original affective quality. For instance, we may discover the affective quality in a facial expression and look for its complementations in qualities of other traits of the face and of the posture. (Similarly, we may discover the original affective quality in the façade of a cathedral or in the beginning of a song.) In this phase, we are searching for harmoniously complementary qualities that may lead to the constitution of the cohesive aesthetic object. But we should bear in mind that initially we seek complementations that harmoniously fit the original affective quality (or the harmonious configuration of two or more original affective qualities) and that we only vaguely expect the subsequent complementary qualities to fit harmoniously into an evolving cohesion of aesthetic qualities, because we are not yet able to foresee the ultimate cohesion of the aesthetic object we are thus constituting.

Sometimes the work of art fulfills our expectations as we discover, in stages, those of its details on which we can intuit aesthetic qualities that accord with the original affective quality. Harmoniously complementary qualities are considered *relevant* if by their synthesis a cohesive whole— the aesthetic object—can be constituted. Sometimes our anticipations may cause us to *imagine* complementary qualities so vividly that without realizing it, we endow the work with them even if the structure of the work does not suggest them. We simply create an aesthetic object without proper regard for the directives of the work. Sometimes we may not notice that harmoniously complementary qualities are being suggested by the work, but it may also happen that the qualities suggested do not quite fit the original affective quality, so that we fail to constitute an aesthetic object on the basis of the work.

We have stated that we synthesize complementary aesthetic qualities into a cohesive whole when we constitute the aesthetic object, that we recognize aesthetic qualities as relevant if they are appropriate to the exigencies of the evolving synthesis, and that during our aesthetic experience we do not foresee the ultimate cohesion that will eventually constitute the aesthetic object. All we can do is to approach it with increasingly clearer approximations. During the early phases of our aesthetic experience we would be unable to direct our exploration of relevant complementary qualities without the original affective quality. Consequently, we may say that the relevance of aesthetic qualities is adapted initially to the original affective quality and then simultaneously also to the evolving aesthetic object, and that we select and synthesize aesthetic qualities in the light of this retrospective and anticipatory relevance. We shall now describe the actual process of synthesis, and we shall see that we focus on the work of art in which we apprehend aesthetically relevant qualities, and that during the process of synthesis, we must be guided by the evolving structure of the qualitative harmony of the aesthetic object.

We are on the threshold of an aesthetic experience when we discover, let us say in a statue, the affective quality pertaining, for instance, to the slender shape of the human body. What we have before us is a block of marble, but we *perceive* a human body—we mean it categorially to be that. *To this extent* and in this instance we do preserve the notion of a correlation between presented and referential reality. We construct, as it were, a feigned but appropriate object of various attributes that would pertain to it if it were alive. In other words, we abandon the realm of reality (i.e., of the block of marble) while we perform the act of categorial substitution and mean a new object from which the affective quality could emanate. This feigned object thus becomes the *presented object* and assumes a concrete presence. At the same time we construct that object's psychic and physical properties with which we can sympathize and feel what that object might feel if it were alive. It is with regard to this categorially meant presented object that our acts of synthesis of intuited qualities are carried out, and it is with regard to the qualities emanating from this object that our constitution of their cohesion, and thus of the aesthetic object, takes place.

Now let us consider the structure of the harmony of aesthetic qualities of any, and especially of a literary, aesthetic object. Since all these qualities are proper to the categorially meant presented object, they must be modulated with regard to it, but they must also be reciprocally congruous if they are to be harmoniously cohesive. Moreover, every quality always appears in conjunction with other qualities; consequently, although every quality has its identity, it is colored by the qualities with which it appears. As a result of the harmony of aesthetic qualities pertaining to the presented object and of their reciprocal congruity there emerges a cohesive aesthetic object whose unity reveals a single new quality that is founded in the cohesion of the modulated and synthesized relevant qualities. This new quality of the cohesive whole is the *Gestalt*—the "form" in the sense in which we used the term—of the constituted aesthetic object. If we now consider the structure of that cohesion of aesthetic qualities with the already emerged *Gestalt* in mind, we can see the latter as the ultimate determinant of the cohesion. The *Gestalt* culminates in the presented world but it is grounded in the anatomic structure of the work of art and founded in the congruous aesthetic qualities of the organic concretion of that work of art. It may be appropriate to remind ourselves of what we said earlier of the center of crystallization of the aesthetic qualities of the concretized work: that it was a cluster of qualities around which aesthetic qualities of all layers and of the structural order of sequence gather into a harmonious unity that constitutes the aesthetic object and thus culminates in the phenomenal appearance of the presented world. The *Gestalt* is, then, that form which emerges from the arrangement of aesthetic qualities whose harmonious unity constitutes the aesthetic object.

Before we continue discussing the structure of the aesthetic object and thus of its form, let us briefly note that the original affective aesthetic quality may be discovered in any part of the aesthetic object. Because it is an integral element of the harmonious unity of qualities that make up the aesthetic object, it can fulfill its important function of leading us to the discovery of another aesthetic quality with which it is congruous, and that newly discovered quality can lead us to the following discovery, and so on. It is thus that the aesthetic object is constituted.

Within the cohesive unity of the aesthetic qualities that constitute the aesthetic object we may distinguish segments, *articulations*, that are characterized by a particularly close connection between some of the qualities. The connection between the qualities of any given articulation is closer than that between qualities of different articulations. We may thus distinguish articulations of higher and lower rank within the order of the qualities that constitute the aesthetic object. The system of articulations within the cohesion of the harmonious qualities of an aesthetic object is the *structure* of this cohesion. When we carry out the structuring of articulations, we do not form the structure of the aesthetic object, we merely establish an order of its articulations. Our structuring of articulations may in some instances depend on the course of our individual aesthetic experience, but the work of art does provide guidelines for our determination of the structure of its harmonious qualities.

When the constitution of the aesthetic object is accomplished, we enter the culminating phase of our aesthetic experience, in which we respond in a contemplative attitude to the revealed harmony of qualities that constitute the aesthetic object. On the one hand, our response consists of acts of so-called "intentional feelings," such as delight, pleasure, admiration, or enthusiasm. These are feelings generated by our direct intentional relation to an appropriate object. On the other hand, our response also consists of a "pure feeling," which is our response to our contemplation of the aesthetic object and of its *Gestalt*. This pure feeling is an *appreciative acknowledgment* of the directly apprehensible worth (value) of an aesthetic object that is capable of eliciting our delight and admiration. This pure feeling of esteem is akin to our first response to the value of the affective quality, but our emotional response to the value of the constituted aesthetic object is incomparably fuller and deeper. The difference between an intentional and a pure feeling lies in that the former is generated by the intentional qualities in their evolving harmonious cohesion, whereas the latter is our appreciative acknowledgment of and response to the *value* of those qualities as constitutive of an aesthetic object, which may also reveal its *Gestalt*. However, our esteem is far from being a judgmental act; it is an emotional response to the value which we find directly given in our experience. If we wish to make a valid judgment about a *work of art* and recognize *its artistic value* in that it may lead to the constitution of an aesthetic object, then this judgmental act must be based on an aesthetic experience and substantiated by our feeling of esteem for the value of the aesthetic object.

Assuming that we discover an original affective quality; that we succeed in constituting an aesthetic object which transcends the material foundation and the work of art that guides our constitutive acts; that we apprehend the cohesion of harmoniously modulated qualities and the quality of that cohesion; and that we therefore respond positively to the value of the harmonious qualities of the aesthetic object in the culminating phase of our emotional and contemplative experience, *then and as a result of this aesthetic experience* we do feel a pleasure and an enjoyment that should, however, not be confused with those pleasurable experiences of excitement that we derive, for instance, from the cause which literary characters may defend, from the actions they carry out, and the fate they meet. These experiences have nothing in common with the aesthetic experiences we have described, in spite of the emotions they awaken in us and regardless of their relevance to the intellectual, social, or spiritual concerns of our practical everyday lives. The value that we apprehend through our intuitions of qualities modulated into a harmonious whole, and, we should add, the assessment of the value of any artistically treated object, capable of inducing our intuitions of its harmonious qualities, may be revealed to us only on the basis of an aesthetic attitude and experience.

All these considerations are pertinent to every aesthetic experience. There is no essential difference between the process of an aesthetic experience of, for instance, a statue, whose perceptible foundation is closely connected with the work of art, and a literary work of art, where we begin with word-signs and need to carry out complex mental acts before any of the presented objects can appear to us and an affective quality can induce our aesthetic experience. The reason why there is no essential difference in aesthetic experiences is that they are not experiences of sensory contents pertaining to perceived real objects. In fact, we must abandon the originally perceived object so that an aesthetic experience may set in. Moreover, we have already noted that no perceived real foundation is even necessary, because an aesthetic experience may be induced imaginationally. However, there are procedural differences, which allow us to apprehend the scope of the concept of the aesthetic experience, differences of orientation, complexity, and intensity in the acts by which we carry out an aesthetic experience. These differences ultimately depend on the relative closeness of the connection between the perceptible foundation and the presented objects of the work of art. Thus, when we first intuit an affective quality which leads us to the constitution of the aesthetic object on the basis of a perceived material object (e.g., a statue), and compare these acts with *essentially the same*, but far more complex acts we carry out before, during, and after a concretization of a literary work of art, we quickly recognize the immense procedural difference between these aesthetic experiences.

Not every literary experience leads to the constitution of an aesthetic object. A work may be concretized and, for instance, from an investigative attitude it may be assessed as a work of art capable of evoking intuitions of aesthetic qualities, without a full aesthetic experience on the part of the literary scholar who seeks to identify the work's schematic structure only. Likewise, if we are focusing on the work as, for instance, a social document, or if we are insensitive to the artistic directives of the work, an aesthetic experience may not set in at all. Also, the work may be of the kind that does not lend itself to an aesthetic apprehension if, for lack of an affective quality in any one layer or in the conjuncture of layers in any phase of the structural sequence, it cannot evoke an original emotion.

The artistic effectiveness of a literary work determines whether its aesthetic qualities can serve as a basis on which we may succeed in constituting an aesthetic object. However, not all articulated aesthetic qualities can be structured in a hierarchical order and lead to the constitution of a single aesthetic object. It may happen that several aesthetic objects coexist in one work without our being able to synthesize them into a harmonious unity. In some works all the relevant aesthetic qualities may be apprehended in only one layer (for instance, in the layer of sound-formations or in that of presented objects), while the aesthetic qualities in the other layers are of neutral value. In other works the relevant aesthetic qualities may occur in more than one layer or even in all layers, and their harmonious cohesion may thus found an aesthetic object that comprises some or all the layers. The aesthetic object also depends very much on the relative weight of the qualities that constitute its cohesion. For instance, if in a poem the qualities of the layer of sound-formations are *determining* and those of the layer of presented objects are merely *founding*, the aesthetic object that is based on this relation of its founding qualities will turn out to be very different if that relation of qualities is reversed in a translation.

If the intuition of aesthetic qualities is not to be a random occurrence, the reader must be capable of an informed and sensitive response to artistic elements in each layer and in the whole unfolding stratified structure. Of all the qualities of a literary work only those of the layer of sound-formations can be intuited on the basis of sensory data. Our intuition of the aesthetic qualities of all other layers depends on our imaginational acts, which are directed by our understanding of sense-units, by our apprehension of their correlates, and by our appreciation of their various—especially phenomenal—qualifications. Consequently, we must be able to actualize aspects with an appropriate regard for the qualifications by which they are readied, so that we may apprehend imaginationally the aspects themselves and the objects appearing phenomenally through them, and on that basis intuit their aesthetic qualities. Although our aesthetic experience is essentially the same whatever the art object may be, we can see in this instance one important variable—the imaginational foundation of the experience—which characterizes the intuition of most aesthetic qualities of the literary work of art.

Because our intuition of most literary aesthetic qualities has an imaginational foundation, and all our imaginational acts are directed by our intellectual apprehensions of sense-units, we must recognize that without this intellectual foundation a literary aesthetic experience cannot occur. However, our intellectual apprehension must not be identified with the aesthetic experience that is based on it. Our intellectual apprehension is, of course, directed at the layer of meaning-units, and this layer too may furnish important aesthetic qualities for our constitution of the literary aesthetic object. These qualities derive from the manner in which the relations between the correlates of meaning-units and of sense-units are projected, and that is the function (a) of the connections between sentences which result, for instance, in various compositional structures, and (b) of patterns of subordinate units in compound sentences. Clearly, these aesthetic qualities and those of the layer of sound-formations may be found in aesthetic experiences of literary art alone, which may be singled out also for the complexity and richness of heterogeneous aesthetic qualities.

Another variable in the aesthetic experience that characterizes the literary work of art is the effect of the structural order of sequence of its stratified phases, which is the reason why this aesthetic experience must unfold in the order prescribed by the structural order of sequence. This is also true of an aesthetic experience of a musical composition, whose order of sequence is, however, not stratified. During the unfolding of our aesthetic experience of a literary work of art, we can experience at any given time only one concretized phase as actual. This phase recedes into the past and is then complemented and modified by gradual accretions of aesthetic qualities and of intentional feelings that accompany these qualities. Consequently the qualities of every concretized phase that has already receded into the past, indeed the aesthetic concretion of the work as a whole, can be apprehended only in temporal perspectival foreshortenings. Thus the literary aesthetic object evolves necessarily in a sequence of partial and gradual phases of constitution. This is also true of the aesthetic experience of a work of architecture, except that a literary aesthetic object must be constituted in the structural order of phases, whereas an architectural aesthetic object may be constituted in various sequences of aspects.

2. The aesthetic-reflective cognition

When we carry out an aesthetic concretization of a literary work of art we constitute an aesthetic object through our discovery of its founding aesthetic qualities. Now we need to consider the feasibility of apprehending *cognitively* the aesthetic object which we have *intuited* in an aesthetic *experience*. This means that we must consider the process in which we reflect on the object of that experienced intuition, so that we may see whether an intuited aesthetic object can be described and analyzed as an object of cognition. We know that we can apprehend cognitively and *evaluate* in a series of judgmental acts a work's *artistic effectiveness*, which is its capability of carrying an aesthetic object, but we need to know whether that object can be made accessible to an *aesthetic-reflective cognition*, and if so, how. Because our intuitions of aesthetic qualities elicit our appreciative acknowledgment of their value, the results of an aesthetic-reflective cognition furnish the foundation for an *aesthetic evaluation* of a literary work of art, i.e., for an assessment of its aesthetic value (which must not be confused with its artistic value that we have just mentioned). This is the reason why the objective validity of aesthetic-reflective cognition is of great importance. Let us now consider some of the circumstances under which this reflective cognition may be carried out.

An aesthetic-reflective cognition carried out after only a single completed aesthetic experience is deficient (except when a work is very short), because we cannot preserve the quality of actuality of that experience long enough in our memory. Besides, the radical shift in our attitude from aesthetic experience to reflective cognition also represses our memory of that actuality. Moreover, our experience can be recalled only in a foreshortened form, because the structural order of sequence appears to us only from the final temporal perspective. If we interrupt our aesthetic experience to reflect on the phase of it that preceded the interruption, some of the same deficiencies just noted detract from the adequacy of our aesthetic-reflective cognition. Although some of these deficiencies may diminish when we focus our aesthetic-reflective cognition on individual phases of our aesthetic experience *while* we are constituting a work's aesthetic object, the aesthetic experience itself may be impaired because we are being distracted by our simultaneous cognitive acts directed at the results of that experience. In these instances aesthetic-reflective cognition does not hold out enough promise to provide a sufficiently solid foundation for aesthetic evaluations of literary works. To sum up, we should note (1) that our move from an aesthetic to a reflective attitude causes the literary aesthetic object to lose its actuality and recede into memory, where it may not be easily retrievable if our familiarity with it derives from a single aesthetic concretization, and (2) that ideally an aesthetic experience should not be impaired by interruptions and distractions. Let us remember these points, for they limit the circumstances in which an adequate aesthetic-reflective cognition may take place.

Before we can determine more favorable circumstances for such a cognition, we must also consider some problems that stem from aesthetic apprehension itself. An aesthetic-reflective cognition should focus on the evolving, and ultimately on the constituted, aesthetic object, but for this to occur we must not neutralize our *original and subsequent emotional responses to affective qualities*, for without these responses our aesthetic experience could not appropriately unfold and the aesthetic object could not evolve and be finally constituted. These emotions, since they elicit the pure feelings of our appreciative acknowledgments of the aesthetic value of each discovered affective quality and ultimately the value of the aesthetic object and of its *Gestalt*, are obviously moments of aesthetic apprehension. Consequently, if we are to intuit the harmony of the aesthetic qualities of the aesthetic object and its *Gestalt* so that they may at some point be conceptualized in our reflective cognition, those emotional responses must remain constantly engaged in the aesthetic experience. On the other hand, emotional "reactions," such as love, hatred, or anger, and the previously noted intentional feelings generated by intentional qualities themselves, and not by their values, need to be consciously excluded so that they may not falsify the object of our aesthetic-reflective cognition. But if the indispensable emotional responses that mark the aesthetic experience are not to be neutralized, if the aesthetic experience is not to be disrupted by interruptions needed for reflective cognition or impaired by simultaneous acts of reflective cognition, and if this cognition needs to be directed at the constituted aesthetic object and at the same time at the aesthetic qualities that found it, we must conclude that aesthetic-reflective cognition must *follow* our aesthetic experience. This very difficult task is in some short works facilitated by the phenomenal presence of the constituted aesthetic object in the final phases of our aesthetic experience and in vivid memory while we still savor the harmony of its founding qualities. In all other cases that phenomenal presence is bound to recede into ever deeper regions of our memory. If we tried to recall it, we would have no assurance that our acts of remembering have not modified the phenomenal presence of the aesthetic object as it was given in actual experience. We are thus led to the inevitable conclusion that aesthetic-reflective cognition *requires repeated aesthetic concretizations*. It is true that no two concretizations, even by the same reader, are quite the same, especially if the reader is concretizing the work without due regard to the artistic effectiveness, or if his readings are separated by long intervals of time. If, however, our repeated aesthetic concretizations are faithful to the directives of the work of art, we do in fact succeed in acquiring a better understanding of the layer of meaning-units, a more sensitive appreciation of the sound-formations, a fuller actualization of schematized aspects, a sharper objectification of presented objects, a more extended grasp of temporal perspectives—in short, we gain a keener sense of what is actually given in the skeletal structure of the work of art, and our aesthetic concretizations thus become increasingly appropriate. On the strength of repeated competent readings we can therefore apprehend the same aesthetic qualities and constitute the same aesthetic object. We may say that repeated competent aesthetic concretizations lead to typical (essentially identical) concretions.

It should be emphasized that our original and subsequent emotional responses to affective aesthetic qualities are elicited, circumscribed, and determined by these qualities to the extent to which we are sensitive to the effectiveness of the artistic elements of the work. Those emotional responses are not derived from fluctuating personal tastes, although they may be in harmony with our taste. Here we are not concerned with concretizations based on emotional responses that happen to be elicited by personal taste and show no regard for the artistic directives of the work. Adequate concretizations imply that our reading should occur in an aesthetic attitude, which means that we need to focus our attention on what is given in the literary work of art and that the aesthetic object should be constituted without coloration by inappropriate emotional responses. It is also necessary that our concretizations should not be colored by extrinsic insights derived from our knowledge of the life of the author, of the historical conditions which may have had certain determining effects on the work's genesis or on its material or formal features, or of literary models which may have affected them. Two assumptions underlie these requirements for an appropriate concretization: that a *work of art* is a sufficient foundation for a sensitive aesthetic concretization, and that the reader's *mastery* of the language in which the work is written (and of its "conventions") is an adequate tool for a concretization whose purpose is the constitution of a literary aesthetic object and not the determination of the work's relations to entities extrinsic to it.

We have seen that the most serious problem posed by aesthetic-reflective cognition is that of avoiding fragmentation of the unity of the aesthetic concretion of the literary work of art, i.e., the unity of the aesthetic object, and that this problem can be solved only through repeated competent aesthetic concretizations. How, one may otherwise wonder, can an appropriate cognition occur if analysis, which is essential to it, threatens to disrupt the object that is to be apprehended. An appropriate reflective cognition requires that we apprehend (a) the unity of the aesthetic object, which is the "harmonious unity" of the sum of the aesthetically valent (but also of aesthetically neutral) elements that found it and, as it were, shine through it, and (b) the *Gestalt* which emerges from that unity. In brief, aesthetic-reflective cognition implies the simultaneous apprehension of the *Gestalt* and of its founding qualities. Once again we should note what we have learned about the constituents of the square, which we can analytically apprehend as concretized equilaterality, rectangularity, and parallelogram-ness that constitute an individual square and thus found the quality (essence) squareness which emerges from the unity of the square. *Mutatis mutandis*, here is the extremely simplified model for the unified apprehension of the literary aesthetic object. We should note again that the aesthetic qualities of a literary work may be structured in articulations that do not yield a single unified *Gestalt* but several harmonious *Gestalt*-qualities, and that the articulations themselves may be structured in a multiplicity of patterns, depending on the type of the literary work.

One of the serious problems of aesthetic-reflective cognition concerns the difficulty of communicating the results we derive from it. There are those who maintain that aesthetic insights are unique, highly personal experiences that defy objective description. One could, however, develop a common language capable of conveying collectively achieved results if several individuals would focus at the same time on a given work and seek to communicate shared insights. They would realize that unlike the sciences, in whose discourse nominal word-meanings are determined in reference to purposely isolated and mutually independent elements and their complexes, aesthetic cognition needs to develop a language capable of projecting not only types and nuances of aesthetic qualities but also the reciprocal modifications that ensue from their polyphonic harmony.

As we look back at the reflective cognition of a literary aesthetic experience, we should briefly note that the aesthetic experience is creative in that it leads to the aesthetic concretion of a work, whereas an aesthetic-reflective cognition must focus on the aesthetic concretization and on the resulting completed concretion, i.e., on the aesthetic object and the qualitative harmony that founds it. The aesthetic experience does contain a chain of cognitive acts: we need to perceive the traits that carry the affective qualities which elicit our emotional responses and sustain the flow of our unfolding aesthetic experience; and we need to discover the qualitative harmony of the evolving concretion so that we may achieve the constitution and the valuative (*bewertend*, i.e., appreciative in the strict sense) contemplation of the intuited aesthetic object. But these acts of apprehension serve only the purpose of the aesthetic experience, and differ functionally from the acts of apprehension that lead to aesthetic-reflective cognition. The latter seek to fathom conceptually what we have intuited in our aesthetic experience: the manifold aesthetically valent and aesthetically neutral qualities that found the harmony of aesthetic qualities, the structure of this harmony, and the aesthetic object and its *Gestalt*. We can see that while in an aesthetic experience acts of apprehension are merely transitional phases leading to emotionally determined acknowledgments of the aesthetic value of affective qualities, in an aesthetic-reflective investigation they are soberly intellectual means leading to a knowledge that sheds light on the artistic effectiveness (value) of the work of art and results in the determination of the aesthetic value of the constituted aesthetic object. It is to be expected that we distance ourselves from the emotionally underscored intuitions of our aesthetic experience if we are to achieve a reflective cognition of the intuited object and its aesthetic value.

3. The preaesthetic investigation of the literary work of art

We have noted that no two concretizations of the same literary work of art are strictly speaking ever quite the same. Literary scholarship, in the sense of the science of literature as art, must therefore be able to determine the identity of the literary work of art as distinct from its concretions. To do so, we need to establish the properties of the schema of the work independently of the modifications which result from its concretizations. This means that we must be able to identify the properties of the work in their state of potential effectiveness as distinct from their being actualized and concretized, and we must determine whether these properties are those of a literary work of art, i.e., of a work susceptible of an aesthetic concretization that may lead to the constitution of an aesthetic object. However, it may seem that the very possibility of attaining objective cognition of a work's skeletal structure may be questionable, because (1) we concretize the work in the course of our reading, and as we have already noted, the concretization may veil the schematic work; and (2) we respond emotionally to its affective qualities.

First of all, some concretizations can be carried out without the emotional responses necessary for an aesthetic concretization. Secondly, falsifications that could result from concretizations and actualizations can be avoided as long as we are aware of these acts and recognize the elements of the work that serve as their foundation. Also, not all emotional responses falsify our reading. Certainly, there are the already mentioned emotional "reactions" of various sorts (anger, hatred, love) to which we may be incited by presented objects, but such reactions can be suppressed in an investigative attitude. Likewise, our emotional responses to affective qualities, which induce and sustain our aesthetic experience, can be neutralized even while they are alerting us—for the benefit of our investigation—to the artistic significance of those of the work's properties that are carriers of affective qualities. Moreover, certain feelings of sympathy (or "empathy") actually enhance our investigative cognition when, for instance, some of the aspects of a presented character are merely named, without being effectively readied, and if by our self-induced sympathy we live through that character's experiences and thus succeed in making him appear in our imagination. Of course, in such instances we must verify the accuracy of our procedure and see if the textual elements confirm our findings. We may say that as long as we suppress our emotional "reactions," neutralize our emotional responses to affective aesthetic qualities, and control and check our sympathetic responses that support our investigative task, we render the work of art aesthetically neutral. This means that we may be able to discover the actual and potential artistically effective elements of a work whenever they suggest their power to induce our aesthetic experience, which we must arrest, however, before it can evolve. Consequently, the necessary continuum of an aesthetic experience is not maintained in a preaesthetic investigation: every time the aesthetic experience sets in, we cut it short, so that we mean the aesthetic qualities merely as categorial formations, and ascertain them conceptually.

During the frequent interruptions in our reading we focus on the artistic functions of individual elements in individual layers or on the phases of all the layers in the structural sequence of the work. Every new step of investigation is first analytical, and we proceed from one discovered artistic element to the next. However, we must always follow up our cognition of analyzed data with a synthesis so that the identified artistic elements may be viewed from the point of view of the whole evolving artistic structure in its cohesive expansion.

Of the numerous instances of artistically effective elements that may be studied and identified we should recall at least a few. We remember that sentences which project states of phenomenal qualifications have a particular presentational efficacy by virtue of the manner in which they cause objects to appear through aspects which are thus readied. It may be most revealing to ascertain which objects in the presented world, and which of their features, are singled out for phenomenal appearance and with what effect on the aesthetic qualities of other objects that pertain to them in various relations. We may thus also study the types of aspects that are readied for various objects of a work or not readied at all for others, and whether the resulting aesthetic qualities are made to fit into a harmonious cohesion, and if so, how. We may also detect which objects are moved into the background and reduced to an inconsequential role or, on the contrary, kept there temporarily shrouded in mystery before they are made to appear prominently through a wealth of revealing aspects, sometimes in a flashback. We may, in addition, wish to establish whether these methods of presentation reveal one or several patterns and how those patterns affect our constitution of one or of several aesthetic objects in the same work. We may also wish to examine phases of presented time that are filled with events, or developing occurrences and other phases of presented time that are separated by cleavages which may or may not be appropriately filled in during a concretization. We may then wish to probe the aesthetic effects of these temporal presentations and of the suspension of the temporal development by a lengthy description of a single object, which is thus made to move into a protracted presence. All these instances entail important effects of temporal perspectives on the presented objects, and these effects, in turn, yield numerous interrelated aesthetic qualities.

We know that some of the aesthetic qualities that appear in presented aspects or in phenomenally appearing objects are ultimately founded in characteristics of the layers of sound-formations and especially of sense-units. This means that we need to go beyond *what* is intentionally projected in sentence-correlates, that we must also investigate the formal structure of the composition and connection of sentences and see which of their artistically effective features are the result of transparent or of complex compositions and connections. We also need to pay attention to the use of nominal expressions and assess their artistic effectiveness in determining the mode of appearance of presented objects, and to the use of verbal structures to assess their artistic effectiveness in determining the dynamic qualities of presented actions.

We should remind ourselves that all these investigations need to be put to the test at every step by means of various partial concretizations and should be followed by appropriate syntheses. Our analytical investigation serves to unlock the work so that we may discover within its skeletal structure the necessary objective foundation of all those possible concretizations which the elements of the work's schematic structure permit. Obviously no such problems are raised in ordinary reading and not even during an aesthetic concretization; they are the proper concern of preaesthetic investigations.

Because a literary work is a schematic structure, its *potential* elements are of special artistic significance and require particularly careful consideration in a preaesthetic investigation. Our actualizations of these elements lead to the discovery of aesthetic qualities that are not explicitly furnished, as are those which emerge from the work's actual elements. The potential elements need to be ascertained because their artistic effectiveness is important for an adequate concretization of a literary work of art. Such a concretization would not be achieved if our reading were to focus, for instance, on the destinies of characters or on the glorification of some view of life, because we should then be guided primarily by the actual elements of the work. Nor could we ascertain the artistic significance of potential elements if we sought to further our gratifying fantasies by concretizing them through free associations regardless of textual exigencies. Of course, our actualizations of potential elements need to be constantly verified in the light of their coherence with our previous actualizations of already ascertained artistically significant elements, and in particular in the light of the harmony of relevant aesthetic qualities which is emerging in the process of our partial aesthetic concretizations. This is how we check whether our so-called interpretations are appropriate or may need rectification.

Obviously, most of our concretizations and our actualizations of potential elements need to be applied to the great variety of cleavages and points of indeterminateness. In ordinary reading we do complement cleavages and points of indeterminateness by filling in some, although never all of them. Usually we carry out these complementations on the presented objects while the other layers are apprehended only peripherally and in perspectival foreshortenings. As we move from ordinary reading to investigative considerations, we focus on individual elements, and while we analyze them one by one we briefly abandon the total view of the work's structure. For instance, when we focus on a potential element, we objectify it, and consider how that particular element, that point of indeterminateness, is to be filled in. Taken singly, our acts of objectification, whereby actual and potential elements of the skeletal work become thematic, seem to break up the unity of the work. However, because these objectifications enable us to focus on the elements as constitutive of the work's total schematic structure, our objectifications ultimately serve the purpose of the *reconstruction* of the schematic work, which is an essential objective of preaesthetic investigation.

As soon as we have identified a potential element, e.g., a point of indeterminateness, and decide how it may be filled in, our analysis, which has led to the element's identification, is followed by the phase of synthesis, because the complementation—the filling in—must occur in the light of previous actualizations and concretizations. As we follow that process, we usually find in every instance a range of possible complementations that are textually admissible.

Although textually admissible complementations of potential elements are implicit in the context, not all implied states of affairs are points of indeterminateness. For instance, when a presented character shuts the eyes of another character, death is implied, but this implication is not a point of indeterminateness if the reader is familiar with what that action indicates. If there are several instances of similarly implied elements in the presented world, they should be noted for their aesthetic quality of suggestiveness, of toning down, of softening the implied harsh qualities of certain events or actions. Similar qualities may sometimes occur simultaneously with contrasting explicit aesthetic qualities, and each kind may serve as a means whereby, for instance, different characters are presented in the same work.

Every act of complementation by which we fill in points of indeterminateness contributes to the aggregate of actual elements in the layer of presented objects. Verifications of the appropriateness of our complementations are necessary because the resulting aesthetic qualities may not be in harmony with other already established aesthetic qualities, and this may adversely affect the constitution of an aesthetic object. Contextual indications usually furnish directives for our complementations; these may yield aesthetically relevant qualities and also qualities which are aesthetically neutral. The range of admissible complementations is indicated by the actual determinations of the elements, but even these are in some respects indeterminate. Sometimes the complementation of the points of indeterminateness of one element may be suggested by other elements within the same text.

The study of the problems raised by different types of points of indeterminateness should, according to Ingarden, prove fruitful in investigations of literary movements, styles, and also kinds, for they may turn out to be characterized by certain types of indeterminateness and may thus require certain types of aesthetic concretization.

We have already mentioned the important problem raised by points of indeterminateness that should not be filled in. This is found particularly in poems, where they fulfill the intended artistic function of hinting at the possibility of complementation but without in the least suggesting that it could succeed. The quality of opalescence is a strongly affective quality capable of thrusting us into an aesthetic experience; whereas an actual, positively determinate element attracts our perception, captivates it momentarily, satisfies it, and releases it, opalescence derives its sustaining power from the very indeterminateness of its material foundation. This indeterminate material foundation emits its quality of opalescence quite openly, and we are set free to experience that quality's haunting but ever-elusive secret. These, I believe, are the reasons for Ingarden's condemnation of clumsy attempts by "artistic dilettanti" to fill in such points of indeterminateness with "unnecessary babble." It is one of the tasks of preaesthetic investigation to make us aware of different points of indeterminateness, for this awareness is necessary if we are to reconstruct the work of art for appropriate aesthetic concretizations or—to put it differently—to establish the proper artistic significance of actual and especially of potential elements.

Although preaesthetic analysis, as we have already noted, seems to break up the unity of the literary work of art, such an investigation nevertheless succeeds during its phases of synthesis in reconstructing the skeletal structure of the work in such a way that many or most of its elements can be apprehended as artistically functional within the foreshadowed unity of any one admissible aesthetic concretization. They are also apprehended in their structural cohesion and as potential carriers of aesthetic qualities. These are the apprehensions that enable us to synthesize our data, which we have identified during analysis, that guide us toward appropriate exploratory concretizations and point the way toward constitutions of aesthetic objects. In saying that, we recognize that the fragmentations which occur during a preaesthetic investigation are in fact necessary so that—on the basis of constantly recurring phases of synthesis—the work can be reconstructed as a cohesive schematic structure and ultimately concretized in such a manner as to bring to light the polyphonic harmony of its aesthetic qualities. We also recognize that intermittent concretizations, by which we verify analytical and synthesized findings, are feasible and essential in a preaesthetic investigation.

One may argue, however, that such an "intellectual" analysis is likely to distort our aesthetic experience, especially of a lyric poem, because the emotional factors with which any aesthetic experience is permeated should not be conceptualized and also because an investigative analysis throws into relief certain details which ought to remain concealed. For instance, our aesthetic experience of facial skin would be distorted if we were to see it on a microphotograph. Similarly, our aesthetic experience could not be appropriate if it were based on individual perceptions of certain details of, for instance, the sound-formations of a lyric poem. However, no such distortions result from a preaesthetic analysis of artistically significant details, for our awareness of their artistic functions is a necessary condition for an appropriate aesthetic concretization, especially of a lyric poem, which cannot be read and analyzed only with regard to the presentative functions of its sentences. The lyrical subject does not project a world external to itself, but one of feelings. Words and their sequences are therefore not chosen merely because they can adequately project the presented world of the poem, but also, and in particular, because their phonic qualities endow them, for instance, with manifestative characteristics so that when they are uttered, as they are meant to be, the sounds can be intuited in their function of underscoring the word-meanings. The emotional characteristics of the poem's layer of sound-formations must be in harmony with the meanings of the words, but also with the other layers, and thus with the emotional state, the mood, of the lyrical subject. Even when this subject does seem to project a world external to itself, this world is actually only an intentional correlate of the subject's *experience* of that world: of that aspect of the external world that corresponds to the subject's lived-through experience of it. This means that the presented aspect of the world is a projection of the lyrical subject's mental and spiritual state, a response to a lived-through experience. For this reason the aspect is often presented through images, or barely sketched by emotion-laden traits. For these reasons one could hardly overemphasize the role of the layer of sound-formations (which resists translation) in its functions of capturing the mood of the poem, of eliciting our emotional and mental responses to its affective qualities, and of enabling us to constitute the aesthetic object. This brief exposition should suffice to show that a preaesthetic analysis that addresses itself to the apprehension of the artistic functions of the layer of sound-formations may provide needed knowledge of what we originally experience in an aesthetic concretization of a lyric poem. When we return to a renewed concretization of the analyzed poem, we do so with an enriched apprehension and a recognition of the artistic means that enable us to savor the aesthetic qualities we have discovered. It is true that during the analytical phase of our investigation, we are bound to disturb the hierarchical order of the elements of the poem, in that we pay equal attention to all the elements under consideration, but in the phases of synthesis—and especially in its last comprehensive phase—we do recognize their relative positions, which are determined within the poem.

We have touched on the problem of ambiguities in language, but a few remarks should now be added. Some aesthetic effects may be achieved only when the suggestive functions of literal word-meanings induce what we may call a double or multiple focusing in the reader's apprehension. The presented world appears to be projected on two (or more) levels simultaneously, and the literal projections serve as a foreground in which the other level—the one that is implied, but is not explicitly projected—is reflected. An analysis of this double focusing may in some instances demand that we pay equal attention to the layer of sound-formations (especially to manifestative characteristics and sound-configurations of higher rank) and to that of meaning-units, because the literal sense of the latter may sometimes derive its suggestive functions from the former. In some works the suggested meanings are meant to elude a single interpretive grasp, and we may therefore not achieve an unequivocal reconstruction. These remarks show that we may be expected to recognize the identity of the work by means of a faithful reconstruction of its multifunctionality. It would be a mistake to assume that we can grasp a literary work of art itself only if we can reduce it to a single explanation, a so-called definitive interpretation. In fact, we should recognize that we can never claim with absolute certainty that even our most careful reconstruction is in every respect faithful to the work itself. But this is true in all instances of empirical cognition, which can never remove all our doubts concerning the objectivity of its results. Nevertheless, this does not impair the scientific character of literary investigations.

We may conclude that the main task of preaesthetic investigation is a careful reconstruction of a work's skeletal structure and the judicious apprehension of its artistic significance on which our aesthetic concretization is to be based. Our propositions about the reconstructed work are valid if we ascribe to the work itself only the material and formal properties (and their interrelations) that are contained in it. This means that objective cognition presupposes that the object of cognition exists independently of cognitive acts. We know that a literary work is not an autonomous object, but that it does exist heteronomously and that this existential moment enables us to apprehend its transcendent identity. We have seen that the literary work's identical *subsistence* and direct intersubjective accessibility are grounded in a material foundation, such as the printed text, and in ideal concepts. This is the basis of our conviction that the identity of the literary work as a stratified structure is intersubjectively accessible. If one mistakenly assumed that the heteronomous subsistence of word-meanings is grounded solely in the acts of consciousness of the person who means them, one could apprehend them only on the basis of the fleeting experiences of the emitter. Consequently, if we wished to return to an uttered word-meaning, we would have to ask the emitter to repeat the intentional act and not only the uttered sounds. But how could we be sure that the new word-meaning is identical with the irretrievable past word-meaning if we cannot possibly effect their simultaneous presence? And how could we appropriately decode the printed word-signs if they are nothing but faint traces of the author's experienced (as distinct from intentionally projected and transcendent) word-meanings, which, we must conclude, cannot be reconstituted with unquestionable faithfulness even by the memory of the author, and never by the author who is no longer alive? No wonder if this conception ultimately leads to intolerably idiosyncratic so-called interpretations.

Only if we reject these notions can we recognize that the literary work continues to subsist long after the author's creative acts have ceased, that it subsists as identical and intersubjectively accessible. Only then can we begin to speak of objective cognition based on faithful reconstructions of the schematic literary work of art. In spite of the already mentioned reservations, we may say that a careful scholarly preaesthetic investigation, which comes to grips with the schematic structure of the work, may constitute so faithful a reconstruction that it can be called transparent, for the work itself shines through it. Under the most favorable circumstances a reconstruction of the work as a whole may not even take place, because we succeed in dealing with the work itself. In this case, the phases of reconstructive constitution serve only the purpose of testing the reliability of our investigation in the light of the conformity of our reconstructions to the text itself. However, even these favorable circumstances may be misleading, for we may assume that we have succeeded in constituting a perfectly transparent reconstruction and fail to be aware of our inadequacies. For the sake of scholarly integrity it must be stated again that however carefully we may refrain from filling in points of indeterminateness, actualizing potential elements, and imposing on the work elements derived, for instance, from "reading between the lines," so as to apprehend the work in its skeletal structure; that whatever precautions in analysis and synthesis we may take with due regard to all the layers and the order of sequence, we can never claim complete certainty that our reconstruction is absolutely faithful to the work itself and that the work has been unveiled with all its elements and moments laid bare. An investigative cognition, which must be guided by these and many other considerations, is ultimately based on, though by no means limited to, the proper apprehension of the layers of sound-formations and meaning-units. Omissions, misunderstandings of word-meanings, misconceptions of syntactic functions, inadequate objectifications, and a disregard for certain features of the order of sequence are among the many causes of variously significant distortions of reconstructed schematic works. Because we are not always aware of our shortcomings (and the literary work under investigation may have its own), we must have frequent recourse to synthesis of analytically established findings and thus refer at all times to the context of the text. A common language, intersubjectively accessible in its identity, is of course the basic condition for the direct apprehension of a text, regardless of how slanted that apprehension may be on account of our shortcomings.

We have dealt here with some problems pertaining to the validity of judgments we may formulate about the faithfulness of our reconstructions. These judgments assess the degree of similarity (or sometimes even the identity) between the reconstruction and the work. However, to be valid, this assessment must be based on our certainty that we have objective knowledge of the constitution of the work and of the reconstruction. We shall therefore briefly turn to the problems that pertain to the objectivity of that knowledge.[3]

Objective knowledge, as we have noted, implies that the identity of the object of cognition is accessible in direct apprehension. Knowledge is objective when—in *reflective cognition*—we ascribe to the object only those characteristics it possesses independently of the process of our direct apprehension, which means that we do not credit the object with any traits derived from this process. During the process of preaesthetic cognition of the literary work of art we apprehend directly the work itself, i.e., all its layers, its parts in the structural order of sequence, and the relative artistic significance of its actual and potential elements in the light of our comprehensive view of the work. In doing so we reconstruct the directly apprehended work as faithfully as possible, but as we know, we can never achieve a complete reconstruction of the work in its totality, and not even of the work in the fullness of our direct apprehension. Because even the most accurate reconstruction can never be carried out exhaustively, our reflective knowledge of the work is also necessarily incomplete. This deficiency by itself does not cause our knowledge of the work to lose its objectivity or to be erroneous, but it *may* result in misconceptions about the relative importance or the artistic significance of some of the work's elements. We may become aware of these misconceptions when after successive reconstructions we consider those elements from the point of view of increasingly comprehensive views of the work as a whole. We may also be alerted to these misconceptions when they lead to a dissonance or even to contradictions in the data obtained in reflective cognition. At that point we normally begin a new process of direct apprehension to find the source of our misconceptions. Sometimes the results of other investigators may alert us to our shortcomings, but the very formulations of their literary judgments may distort the findings of their reflective cognition if an appropriate terminology is lacking. This may be a serious problem, for if our literary judgments are to be valid, they need to be formulated in propositions whose content must be adapted to the *results* of our direct apprehension; i.e., the propositions are not supposed to repeat the text, they are meant to make valid affirmations about it. Consequently, literary judgments cannot be a substitute for the work; they must affirm the sense that reflective cognition derives from what we have directly apprehended.

We have just said that our literary judgments are no substitute for the

3. See Ingarden's "Betrachtungen zum Problem der Objektivität," in *Erlebnis, Kunstwerk und Wert*, pp. 219–55.

work, but they are not equivalent to it either. Literary investigations are carried out from one or more points of orientation within a distanced perspective, so that the work is seen in some of its "cross-sections," or we may fathom only some of its elements or structural features that emerge from exploratory probes. Enlightened by these insights, we return to a renewed direct apprehension of the work and are thus better able to appreciate those artistically effective properties and compositional patterns that have been brought to light and to engage in new exploratory probes. This, after all, is the function of literary investigations, for they are meant to lead us back to the work of art and enable us to savor the findings of continued investigations of its multiple facets.

Finally, it should be noted again that different sets of valid literary judgments may be formulated about the same reconstructed schematic work, i.e., a work that has not been in any respect complemented in concretization. When the different sets of literary judgments are true, they are reciprocally complementary. Obviously these judgments must be restricted to determinate and potential properties of the work and should not pertain to effected complementations; they must be judgments of strictly pre-aesthetic investigative cognition.

Chapter 6

1. Artistic and aesthetic values

A. General observations

The main function of preaesthetic investigation is, as we have seen, the determination of a work's manifold artistically effective elements that found aesthetic qualities which we intuit in the course of our aesthetic concretization. We have also seen that a work of art prescribes a range of admissible aesthetic concretizations. This means that when we have established the artistic effectiveness of the elements of a work we are in a position to assess their *artistic value in relation to* the aesthetic qualities that are founded in them. The artistic value of an element of a literary work of art must, however, be distinguished from the *aesthetic value* of the qualities that we constitute in an aesthetic attitude. Because the aesthetic concretion subsumes the elements of the work of art, it contains both the artistic and the aesthetic values. We are faced here with values of different kinds, and we shall have to establish where their difference lies and what distinguishes these from other values.

Before we turn our attention to artistic and aesthetic values, it may be appropriate to deal briefly with at least some of the problems raised by the so-called relativity of values and with those pertaining to the different kinds of values. The scope of the following observations, based on two of Ingarden's essays,[1] is limited to our immediate concern.

The concept of the relativity of values is broad, and we shall see that it is necessary to distinguish different meanings of relativity and to do so in the light of the distinctions between values of different kinds. For instance, the term "relative" is frequently applied to the value of beauty, excellence, or savoriness because these are not properties of an object. Even when there is an objective foundation in the properties of an object for our attribution of any of these values to it, there are those who consider them to

---

1. "Zum Problem der 'Relativität' der Werte," in *Erlebnis, Kunstwerk und Wert*, pp. 79–96; and "Was wir über die Werte nicht wissen," in ibid., pp. 97–141.

be illusory. Because these values are subjective in that they derive from responses of evaluating subjects, they are sometimes also called "subjective." Another type of relativity characterizes values by which an object (a thing, a process, or a person) is *valuable* to one object but harmful (or neutral) to another. For instance, a certain plant is nourishing to some animals and poisonous to others. We may say that this plant's value *as nourishment* is "relative" to different animals. However, we should distinguish this value of the plant from the value of its *nutritiveness*, a quality which the plant possesses because of its constitutive properties and regardless of whether it is nourishing to all or only to certain kinds of animals. The value of nutritiveness is *relational* when it is constituted by a relation between an object X (a certain plant) which has this quality and another object Y (an animal of a specific kind) to which that quality is valuable in that it serves a purpose. For that quality to acquire a relational value, object Y must have certain determinations that qualify it for a relation with object X. Thus the potentially *relational* value of a quality of an object becomes a positive or a negative value *relative* (in relation) to specific objects, although it may be neutral relative to different objects. Contrary to the supposedly "relative" values of beauty, excellence, or savoriness, which may be thought to be illusory, the relational value which we have just described cannot be considered illusory when it becomes a positive or negative value with respect to a specific animal.

On the basis of these few observations we may draw the following preliminary conclusions. Every value has the character of *valence*, i.e., of being a value. Every value is the value of some object, which means that a value cannot exist by itself; it is marked by *existential connectivity* to some object, and that is its *form*. However, a value is not an object's property because it is not its determinant, but it is derived from and determined by the object's properties. Some values are relational, but others, such as perfection, maturity, honesty, gracefulness, are not. Consequently, there must be qualitative (material) differences between values which make it possible (though not always) for us to distinguish one kind of value from another. For the time being let us say only that the qualitative differences between values are determined by the matter or rather by the *material quality of each value (Wertqualität)*.

Sometimes one speaks of the relativity of values because one naively assumes that to have absolute (and not merely "relative") existence, any object (including a value) must be accessible to everybody in the same way. It should be emphasized, however, that conditional accessibility to certain values in no way implies that they do not exist. For instance, the constitution of the value of an aesthetic object requires a knowledge of and a sensitivity to artistically effective elements of a work of art, and this value exists for every observer who acquires the competence to recognize it.

Let us now consider briefly some of the differences between values. According to their material quality we distinguish, for instance, vital values from ethical and aesthetic values. We have discussed the relational vital value of the plant and its "relativity," but it may serve our purpose to deal briefly with at least one other vital value, for instance, that of the eye. The properties of the eye endow this organ with the quality of sight, and because of this material quality the value of the eye, like all vital values, is relational in that it serves the realization of certain purposes. The eye, being a member of man's organic system, fulfills its function in serving the purposes of this whole system. The eye's value, derived from sight, is analogous to the value of the plant derived from the nutritiveness constituted by the properties of the plant. The value of the eye may become "relative" only in the sense in which sight may be more valuable, for instance, to a painter than to a musician, but this relativity does not affect the *valence* of the vital value of the eye. An analogous state of affairs pertains to all vital values, be they the values of organs, food, or tools, or of certain patterns of behavior that sustain life. The fact that some individuals do not or cannot recognize these values does not negate the valence of these values, nor does it render them illusory or merely "relative."

Vital values and, more particularly, values of usefulness derive the foundation of their existence from the determinations of their carriers, and their subsistence from the object with respect to which they do or may fulfill their functions. Aesthetic values, like vital values, have the foundation of their existence in the determinations of their carrier (the work of art), but the foundation of their subsistence lies in the constitution of aesthetic qualities by a human subject that intuits these qualities and acknowledges them with appreciation.

Many as yet unsolved problems are posed by all and especially by ethical values. According to some, they are classified under vital or, more exactly, under useful values, and their "relativity" is often justified by opposing ethical assessments of certain deeds according to social and cultural settings. Before we could establish the essential individuality of various ethical values, we would have to be able to intuit their different material qualities that derive from the particular constitutive elements of the actions and attitudes with which those values are existentially connected. It is sometimes very difficult to distinguish, for instance, courage from recklessness. The lines of demarcation between ethical values need to be clearly drawn. For us it is also important to establish distinctions between ethical and aesthetic values. We must assume that the mode of existence of the ethical values of certain actions differs from that of aesthetic values at least in that the former pertain to real persons, whereas the latter to purely intentional presented objects. Otherwise we may have to wonder, for instance, whether courage is only a social value within a human community or whether it is also an aesthetic value in a play or a novel. In this connection, it may be worth noting that we encounter equally puzzling problems within the category of aesthetic values. We need clear distinctions between the material qualities of, for instance, beauty, gracefulness, completeness, and magnitude. For example, beauty poses a problem because it acquires different meanings when applied to, say, churches built in different styles.

These observations show that every value is the value of something, that its mode of existence is that of connectivity and at the same time of existential derivation, because it is determined by certain properties of the object which is its carrier and its foundation. We stated earlier that an essential moment of every value is its valence, which characterizes its being a value, and not a real object or an essence. It is on account of the valence of the value of which an object is the carrier that the object acquires its worth and even the worthiness of its being. But every value exists individually as a particular value, and its particularity derives from a harmonious relation of congruous properties that constitute the object in which that value is founded. Consequently, it is the material quality of values that determines their different kinds, but it is on account of its valence that every value implies a summons to our appreciative acknowledgment and to our choice between a higher and a lower value. The relative height of a value is variable and results from the comparison of appropriately matching valuable objects.

One of the consequences of insufficient distinctions between artistic, aesthetic, and other kinds of values, i.e., between their different material qualities, has been a rather prevalent misconception of the essential function of art, of the specificity of aesthetic values founded in aesthetic qualities and of artistic values founded in artistically effective elements of a work of art. This misconception was compounded by the failure to recognize that the material quality of one kind of value is in a necessary relation to another kind of value (e.g., artistic and aesthetic values) or only in a coincidental relation with values of a different kind. These misconceptions may account for the failure to distinguish between the essential connection between artistic and aesthetic values in a literary work of art and the secondary connection between them and for instance, intellectual, social, or moral values which may also emerge from a literary work of art. Fundamentally, even if not quite consciously, the proponents of "art for art's sake" sought to establish a kind of "autonomy"—not in the sense in which we have used the term, but rather in the sense of a certain self-sufficiency—of the aesthetic values of a work of art. That motto meant to claim that "beauty" was a self-sufficient value, that it was derived from certain combinations of aesthetic qualities founded in artistic values, and that it did not derive from the "truth" of the presented world, or from some lofty ideals advocated in that world, and that it did not depend, as some claimed, on the need for the simultaneous presence of contrasting negative values (such as cruelty, vice, crime, or any disharmonious elements) whose concurrent appearance was meant to endow the presented world with the highly valued semblance of "real" life. Seen from the perspective of our insights, "art for art's sake" sought to establish the primacy of the material quality of aesthetic values, of that material quality which derives solely from artistically effective properties of the stratified structure of the literary work of art in its unfolding, and not from the very different properties of real life.

We must now turn to some observations that are based not only on *The Cognition of the Literary Work of Art*, but also on Ingarden's essays "Der ästhetische Wert und das Problem seiner Fundierung im Kunstwerk" and "Künstlerische und ästhetische Werte."[2] As we look back, we note that one of the important arguments underlying our findings has been that the literary work of art and the aesthetic object, constituted on the basis of the aesthetic qualities derived from the work, confront our acts whereby we apprehend and experience them. Therefore we must find the artistic value of the work in the work itself and the aesthetic value of the aesthetic object in this object itself, and not in the sphere of, for instance, our pleasurable experiences derived from reading. No doubt, we value the pleasurable feelings which some works elicit, but such experiences may be derived, depending on the reader, from works that lack artistic and aesthetic values. If we ascribe those values to a work on the basis of the pleasure it provides, instead of on the basis of its artistic properties, and if our tastes change according to the trends characterizing different periods, we are easily led to assume that the value of a given work is "subjective" and "relative." This is always so when we do not realize (a) that our necessarily subjective concretizations are supposed to heed the directives of the literary work of art or of an appropriate reconstruction of it, and (b) that our

2. *Erlebnis, Kunstwerk und Wert*, pp. 143–51; ibid., pp. 153–79.

appreciative acknowledgments of its aesthetically valent qualities must be founded in the work itself and elicited by the aesthetically valent qualities that constitute its aesthetic object.

When we ascribe a value to a literary work of art on the basis of the pleasure we derive from it, we are reducing the work to a mere tool and we judge it according to its capability of fulfilling its function of evoking pleasurable feelings. Seen as such a tool, the value of the work is relational with respect to the reader whom it happens to please because of *his* predisposition to be pleased by it, and not because of his recognition of the value inherent in the work, whose artistic and aesthetic values he may not even know or care about. All he does care about is his delight or pleasure, and the work derives its valence for such a reader only because he projects onto the work the value of his delight. So this relational value of a work ultimately depends on the attitude of a reader or of readers whose dispositions may change according to the tastes prevailing in various periods and places. The artistic and aesthetic values of a literary work do not change; they need to be sought and found by readers capable of fathoming them on the basis of the work. When a work has those values and the reader does not succeed in discovering them, it is the reader's lack of artistic culture that is at fault.

B. Artistic and aesthetic values in a literary work of art

Every value is determined by its material quality. Thus the artistic value of an object is determined by a material quality which consists of an assortment of artistic qualities. The aesthetic value of an object is likewise determined by a material quality which consists of an assortment of aesthetic qualities. For instance, an assortment or "set" of aesthetic qualities such as clarity, symmetry, naturalness, and genuineness may determine the material qualities of such positive aesthetic values as unity, beauty, completeness, or maturity. A set of opposite qualities such as asymmetry, confusion, and artificiality may determine the material qualities of negative aesthetic values such as ugliness, disjointedness, defectiveness, or rawness. We should note that some aesthetic qualities can appear in works of art of different kinds, but others can pertain to only one kind—as, for instance, the soft subdued shade of a color (in a painting) or the abrupt tones of a staccato phrase (in music). The aesthetic value of a work as a whole may consist of a variety of aesthetic material qualities or of one synthesized material quality, but in all instances that value is grounded in a multiplicity of aesthetically valent qualities. Thus the aesthetic value of a work is the correlate of our evaluation of the already constituted aesthetic object, i.e., of the evaluation which we carry out at the end of our aesthetic experience.

The material quality of the *artistic value* of a work must be founded in its *artistic qualities*. These qualities are the indispensable condition for our being able to discover relevant aesthetic qualities, to constitute the aesthetic object, and to recognize the *aesthetic value* of the work as it emerges from the constituted aesthetic object. Consequently, the artistic value is relational with respect to the aesthetic object which we constitute in an aesthetic attitude. The relational artistic value derives its valence from the absolute, nonrelational, *aesthetic value*. The aesthetic value is thus cofounded in the work's artistic value and in the constitutive acts of the reader, for it is he who constitutes the aesthetic object and acknowledges with appreciation the polyphony of its aesthetic qualities and its *Gestalt*. In a completed literary work of art all artistically effective elements are there ready for our constitution of all its aesthetic qualities into an aesthetic object (or aesthetic objects) and for our acknowledgment of its aesthetic value. However, any individual concretization constitutes only that aesthetic object (and leads to the acknowledgment of that aesthetic value) which the reader is capable of constituting on the basis of *his* arrangement of relevant aesthetic qualities. Consequently, we should distinguish the aesthetic object of the work itself from that which results from a particular concretization. These aesthetic objects and their values may differ more or less from each other, depending on the competence and sensitivity of the reader.

Not all elements of the work of art are artistically valent. Those which determine that it is a literary work, and not a sculpture or a painting, are axiologically neutral. Thus the skeleton of the layers and the structural order of sequence in a literary work of art are of neutral artistic value; they form the axiologically neutral foundation of the work of art in which the artistically valent elements and consequently the aesthetically valent moments of the work are grounded. On the basis of our discussion of the preaesthetic investigation of the literary work, in which we reconstruct the work's artistically effective elements, we may conclude that all those elements whose qualitative moments contribute to our intuitive apprehension of the aesthetic qualities of the presented world are artistically effective and constitute together the artistic value of the work of art. (Obviously, no isolated element can be properly assessed with respect to its artistic function; its effectiveness can be ascertained only in the light of its reciprocal relations to other elements with which it founds congruous aesthetic qualities.) Sense-units belong to the skeleton of the layer of meaning-units; artistically they are of neutral value, but the complexity of involuted sentence-structures, or the simplicity, clarity, or ambiguity of sentences affects the phenomenal appearance of the presented world and determines some of its aesthetic qualities. Word-sounds are artistically neutral, but they become artistically effective when the projected objects derive some of their coloration from aesthetic qualities founded in the word-sounds. Likewise, aspects acquire artistic value when they are readied to enhance the phenomenal appearance of presented objects and to further the constitution of the work's aesthetic object. Presented objects that are not exhibited, and a structural order of sequence, by which, for instance, the unfolding of the presented world through a skillful exploitation of temporal perspectives is not achieved, are all of neutral artistic value. However, all the elements of the neutral skeletal frame are indispensable, because they found artistically valuable elements and moments within each phase of the unfolding structural order of sequence and such elements and moments as need founding in antecedent phases. We may say, then, that the artistic value of a work comprises not only the value of artistically effective elements but also the value of the artist's skill which appears *within* the work of art through his selections, dispositions, and assortments of axiologically neutral and artistically effective elements.

We have repeatedly noted that the artistic value of elements of a work of art depends on their artistic effectiveness, which is assessed in the course of partial concretizations. The artistic value of a work of art as a whole is thus determined by a material quality which is constituted by manifold artistically effective elements whose particularity and assortment differ from one work to another and establish each work's unique artistic character. The artistic value of a work is relational with respect to the aesthetic object of that work in its concretion.

The aesthetic value of a concretized work of art emerges as the value of the aesthetic object. It is fathomed in the synthesis of manifold aesthetically valent qualities that constitute its material quality. This means that the role of the material quality of a positive aesthetic value (e.g., beauty, unity, completeness, gracefulness) is exhaustively fulfilled in being a *phenomenon*, which we intuit in an aesthetic stance. The purpose or the significance of the aesthetic value lies solely in that its material quality exacts our intuition and at the same time our delight which is inspired by our appreciative acknowledgment. We may wish to add that our intuition and appreciative acknowledgment of an aesthetic value do not lead us away from life; on the contrary, we return to life with a keener sense of its actual, and especially of its potential, qualities.

C. Systems of aesthetically valent qualities

One of the problems that we need to consider—at least for the purpose of drawing attention to its importance—pertains to the principle that governs the congruity of aesthetically valent qualities which determine the material quality of the value of an aesthetic object.[3] We are not directly concerned with the problem of how we should select, during a concretization, an assortment of aesthetic qualities so that they shall be mutually harmonious and lead to our constitution of an aesthetic object. What we need is the key to a more basic problem, in order to know which aesthetic qualities are harmonious so that they may constitute the stock of congruous aesthetic qualities in which the aesthetic object of the work itself and the value of this object can be founded. We need to know whether there are necessary dependences or desirable connections between certain aesthetically valent qualities and also whether some qualities exclude each other so that their simultaneous presence in the concretion of a work precludes the constitution of an aesthetic object or introduces a discordance in it. In brief, we need to know which aesthetically valent qualities are congruous and therefore capable of founding an aesthetic object of one or another aesthetic value. If we had the key to these problems, we would know which assortment of aesthetically valent qualities can, on account of their congruity, determine the material quality of the value of the constituted aesthetic object. We would also be enabled to check, during the concretization of a given literary work of art, our procedure in constituting several or only one aesthetic object, for we would know which principle of harmonious coherence we were following in each instance. Simultaneously, we could observe the functions of artistic elements and see how their assortments found sets of aesthetic qualities, which determine the coherence of several aesthetic objects or the cohesion of a single aesthetic object. At least theoretically, we can already see how and to what extent the *value* of an aesthetic object depends on the cohesion of its material quality, how the latter depends on the harmony of assorted congruous aesthetic qualities that determine it, and how these qualities must necessarily be

3. See Ingarden's "Das Problem des Systems der ästhetisch valenten Qualitäten," in ibid., pp. 181–218.

founded in a carefully selected set of artistically effective elements of the literary work of art. Conversely, we may see how the effectiveness of the artistic elements of a given work of art results from their being selected and arranged with a view to the expected harmony of aesthetic qualities which these elements are to found and to hold in readiness for a competent and sensitive concretization, and how the congruous aesthetic qualities lead the reader to a constitution of an aesthetic object. At this point, we should state that *unity*, as a fundamental value of the literary work of art and of its aesthetic object, is grounded in the reciprocal functions of the axiologically neutral stratified and unfolding literary work and in a judicious selection and assortment of artistically effective elements capable of founding a set of harmoniously cohesive aesthetic qualities. The particular material quality of the unity of an individual work must follow this general design.

When we refer to the *value* of the aesthetic object by designations such as "beauty," "completeness," "gracefulness," "excellence," or "powerfulness" (or their opposite), we do not refer to individual aesthetic qualities of the aesthetic object, but to the set of aesthetically relevant and congruous qualities that constitute its material quality. Consequently, we assign the value "beautiful" to the set of harmonious aesthetic qualities that constitute the material quality of that value. Because the same value ("beautiful") may be ascribed to different objects—for instance, to works composed in different styles—we must recognize that the material quality of that value may be constituted by various selections and assortments of aesthetically relevant and congruous qualities. In other words, there must be *a principle that governs the selection and assortment* of those aesthetic qualities which can found the material quality of the value that we call "beauty," even though these qualities are different in every individual aesthetic object. Since each set of qualities that can found the material quality of "beauty" must consist of qualities that are congruous, for otherwise they could not constitute the material quality of that (or any other) value, we must also ascertain *the principle of congruity* of aesthetically valuable qualities.

Ingarden does not offer solutions to these problems, but he provides a few designations for aesthetically valent qualities so that we may be guided in establishing principles of their congruity and of their assortments into material qualities that found the value of aesthetic objects. He distinguishes between designations of primary and of secondary aesthetically valent qualities. We shall enumerate only a few designations of positively and negatively valuable qualities from the groupings he establishes, for we are concerned only with an elucidation of the problems posed by the need to ascertain the principles we have mentioned, so that we may have at least a tentative basis for analyses that may guide the reader in individual aesthetic concretizations.

Ingarden divides primary aesthetically valent qualities into four groups:

(1) *Material-emotional*: melancholy, sad, desperate, terrible, horrible, atrocious, ghastly, joyful, gay, pleasant, charming, painful, grievous, pathetic, serious, tenacious, dignified, and also lyrical, dramatic, and tragic as they appear in certain human situations and occurrences and not in the sense of definite literary structures.

(2) *Material-intellectual*: witty, ingenious, impressive, wise, penetrating, dull, banal, silly.

(3) *Formal*: symmetrical, coherent, consistent, compressed, loose, fragmented, monotonous, slow.

(4) *Formal with respect to observer or reader*: transparent, clear, blurred, vague, distinct.

Ingarden lists seven different groupings of secondary aesthetically valent qualities, but we shall mention only a few samples such as: refined, simple, tender, tactless; soft, striking, discreet; new, original, fashionable, old-fashioned; natural, artificial, exaggerated, affected; genuine, specious; true, real, illusory; stirring, edifying, moving, soothing, indifferent.

All of these terms suffer from a certain ambiguity but they have the virtue of being drawn from everyday language. What matters is that we should fathom as clearly as possible the qualities of the objects and occurrences to which the terms refer, for it is they that carry the aesthetic values which found the aesthetic value of the concretized work and it is they that reveal the artistic means in which the aesthetic concretization is grounded.

Some congruous qualities that fall under the designations of both the material and the formal aesthetically valent qualities constitute the center of crystallization and the unified quality at the core of a given aesthetic object, whereas all other material and formal qualitative moments and some of those listed under the secondary aesthetically valent qualities must be essentially dependent on those at the center of crystallization whence the unity of the concretized literary work emerges. This is why the congruous material and formal aesthetically valent qualities at the center of crystallization are indispensable for the constitution of an aesthetic object and of its value. The system of *all* of a work's congruous relevant qualities, drawn from the material, formal, and the secondary groups, constitutes the stock of aesthetically valent qualities of the aesthetic object, but any individual concretization contains, as we have already noted, only a selection of congruous qualities from the stock.

The cohesion of that system varies from one work to another, but it is certain that without a cohesive system of congruous aesthetic qualities the *Gestalt* of the aesthetic object could not emerge. The same holds true for a metaphysical quality, which is the specific function of the layer of presented objects, and for the qualitative substratum that informs the view of life within the presented world. In conclusion, we may say that the aesthetic value of a work is linked to its aesthetic object, that this object has its ontic foundation and determination in the artistically effective elements of the literary work of art, and that the aesthetic object is at the same time intentionally constituted by the reader whose concretization conforms to the range of admissible complementations suggested by the work of art. Therefore the aesthetic object and its value are heteronomous.

It now remains to point out that it is one thing to affirm in an act of *valuation* (i.e., appreciative acknowledgment) the existence of an ascertained qualitatively determined aesthetic value (for instance, beauty), and it is another to *evaluate* the beauty of, for instance, two cathedrals and decide which is the more beautiful. In an aesthetic valuation we establish an aesthetic object's own value without comparing it with the value of a different object. Our acts of aesthetic valuation are anchored in our aesthetic experience, and they derive their substantiation from that experience. They are also founded in our recognition of the aesthetically valent qualities that constitute the material quality of that object's aesthetic value. Consequently, we should recognize that valuations derive from these cognitive operations and from our emotionally colored sensitive response to the affective qualities founded in artistically effective elements of the work.

During our valuation we may find that an aesthetic object may contain various cultural values which are of special significance, for instance, in a nation's history, but we have already noted that these values are secondary and do not constitute that object's primary values which we intuit during an aesthetic concretization. Primary values pertain to qualities which result, for instance, from various modes of presenting the destinies of presented objects, from special sound-formations, stylistic properties of sense-units, appropriately readied aspects, temporal and spatial perspectives, and the structural order of sequence. It is the polyphony of congruous qualities constituting the aesthetic object and this object's *Gestalt* that are of primary value.

If we wish to determine which of two works is more beautiful (or more powerful), we are really comparing the results of two different acts of valuation. This means that we are cognitively assessing the material quality of beauty of the aesthetic object of one literary work of art and comparing it with the material quality of beauty of the aesthetic object of another literary work of art. Evaluation depends on previous acts of valuation, and there is no aesthetic valuation without aesthetic concretization. Moreover, this means that our acts of evaluation must also be directed to factors stemming from the nature and functions of artistically effective, i.e., artistically valuable, elements of the literary work of art, and from the congruous aesthetically valent qualities constituting the material quality of the aesthetic object. No extrinsic criteria, such as those derived from social, economic, or political views of a period, or from artistic conceptions, norms, or fads prevalent at a certain time, can possibly take the place of the painstaking analyses which we have described and which are the condition for an evaluation of a work of art on the basis of its artistic and aesthetic values. It may be worth adding, however, that evolving conceptions of art may lead us to the discovery of artistically effective elements in certain works of the past, elements whose effectiveness may have gone previously unnoticed and may not have been consciously "intended" by the author. Such insights are, of course, extremely valuable, for they enhance our capabilities of constituting a work's aesthetic object and recognizing the aesthetic value it possesses, but which we may have failed to notice. This epistemological function of evolving artistic conceptions should, however, not be confused with the imposition of criteria for the evaluation—for approval or disapproval—of a work, since if we applied such criteria, we might assess a work's value merely on the basis of its conforming or not conforming to what may prove to be transitory norms. This occurs whenever extrinsic criteria are applied in evaluation. One of the consequences of the application of extrinsic criteria is the skeptical and relativistic attitude to aesthetic values which, as we have seen, Ingarden opposed. The other consequence of that application, which leads Ingarden to an expression of even greater sorrow, is that we are robbed of the deep emotions which our intuitions of aesthetic values arouse in us. The very purpose of genuine art, its essential role in human life, is not realized if our exposure to it leads to a mere knowledge of whether or not it conforms to criteria that are inconsistent with its essential nature. A criticism that leads

to evaluations of that kind tends to impoverish our life, for human life be-
reft of direct contemplations of value is an empty life.

2. Literary scholarship: its objects and branches

In its broad sense, literary scholarship consists of the findings attained in
varied investigations of literary works of different types: artistic, historical, religious, philosophical, political, etc. Depending on the object and
method of inquiry, literary scholarship may be divided, according to Ingarden, into different branches characterized by distinctive tasks. These
branches are: the ontology (or the theory) of the literary work; descriptive
literary scholarship and literary history, which together constitute literary
scholarship in the narrower sense of the term; and literary criticism. Ingarden calls *poetics* that branch of literary scholarship which deals only
with artistic literature; it is the theory of the literary work of art that
founds our constitution of an aesthetic object.[4]

A. *The ontology of the literary work*

The ontology of the literary work, which pertains to the philosophy of literature, and especially to the theory of the structure of the literary work,
has the task of arriving at general, intersubjectively valid, propositions. It
is not concerned with individual works but with the essential structure of
all literary works, the necessary connections of its elements and moments,
and the range of its variables. We have seen the results of this investigation
when we grasped the essential skeletal structure of the literary work: the
reciprocal functions of elements within the layers, the interrelations between layers, and the structural order of sequence. We have learned to recognize the applicability of those results to the preaesthetic investigation of
an individual literary work—as a schema—and on that basis to assess the
range of its potential concretizations.

We also dealt repeatedly with other ontological problems which are of
great importance to literary scholarship and criticism: the mode of existence of the literary work, its relation to the author, and the relation of the
reader to the work.

The solutions of the problems posed by the ontology of the literary work

4. See "Gegenstand und Aufgaben des 'Wissens von der Literatur,'" in *Gegenstand und Aufgaben der Literaturwissenschaft* (Tübingen: Max Niemeyer Verlag,
1976), pp. 1–28; and "Über die Poetik," in ibid., pp. 28–89.

have led to our recognition of the distinctions between the literary work and its concretizations, especially its aesthetic concretizations. Thus we have seen how these ontological explorations relate to the philosophical theory of aesthetic experience, to *aesthetics* in this sense of the term. We have also seen that the established heteronomous subsistence of the literary work relates these ontological explorations to the theory of cultural products, i.e., to cultural philosophy.

Considering certain features of contemporary literary scholarship and criticism, it is highly appropriate that we should heed Ingarden's admonition and distinguish the types of problems we propose to investigate; that we should recognize the results of ontological explorations; that we should fathom as clearly as possible the object of our investigations, and refrain from confusing, for instance, the literary work with our concretizations, derived in great part from our critical activity.

B. Descriptive and historical literary scholarship

One of the fundamental tasks of literary investigation is the descriptive characterization of individual literary works: the description of their essential determinations in a set of coherent affirmations, without which there is no scholarship in the sense of systematized knowledge. This knowledge is basic for the formulation and investigation of other literary problems, and even of those that do not properly belong to literary scholarship in the narrower sense—for instance, problems pertaining to the creative process or to the responses of readers.

Descriptive literary scholarship (literary "characterology") describes the literary work as the object of preaesthetic investigation, i.e., as a schematic structure. This means that the work must be reduced to its schematic appearance and removed from its historical setting. The investigator must aim at being objective and refrain from concretizations, except those that are strictly exploratory and intended only to measure the range of artistic effectiveness of various schematic elements. This means that he must limit himself to the description of each layer and pay particular attention to those elements and moments whose function it is to weld the work into a unity. He must ascertain the cleavages and points of indeterminateness and assess the range of admissible complementations. Finally, he must establish the structural order of sequence to verify the dynamics of the work's composition. In general, he must ignore whatever is not explicitly and implicitly determined by the *text*. Information about the life of the author or the circumstances of his creative process must not be brought to bear on this investigation, although this and other supplementary information are indispensable for the reconstruction of the concretization of a work of the past *when we wish to know how that work may have been concretized at that time*. Because the schematic work is intersubjectively accessible, it is useful for purposes of checking to consult the findings of other scholars whose investigations have followed strictly descriptive procedures.

Another task of descriptive literary scholarship is that of describing various types of literary works, of establishing a typology based on the characteristics derived from preaesthetic investigation. Regardless of whether we establish groupings according to periods, styles, or genres, or according to motifs, themes, or common authorship, our investigations must be based on a typological principle that governs the works which we describe, and not on a mechanical grouping.

The basic task of descriptive literary scholarship is the characterization of individual works as schematic structures. This branch of literary scholarship is founded in literary ontology, but it is a foundation for historical scholarship. A literary work participates in various historical streams which reveal its relations to its past and also to its present. For instance, some of its relations derive from the conditions and circumstances of its genesis and link it to its author and his intellectual and mental makeup, to antecedent and contemporaneous literary works and currents, and to the cultural atmosphere. Other relations link the literary work to literary communities of readers in various places and at different times. The problems of a historical investigation are determined by the particular relation of a work which we wish to explore. There are some investigations, ancillary to historical scholarship, that are absolutely indispensable—for instance, the complex philological and historical examinations of textual criticism that lead to editions of authentic texts. The modern methods used in this endeavor have raised textual criticism to a science. At present, the same cannot be said of investigations that seek to explore the psychology of the creative process, which is not a branch of literary scholarship but of psychology. However, to the extent that the process is traceable through its several phases on the basis of various changes recorded by the author on available manuscripts, the results of such an exploration are ancillary to historical scholarship.

One of the most important tasks of historical literary scholarship is to present, *on the basis of careful descriptive studies*, the development of literary conceptions and structural changes in the works of a given author, or, for instance, in works of a genre through successive literary movements.

Investigations of this type imply explorations of changes in the literary atmosphere in the course of time and of the general cultural atmosphere to which these changes are linked. The importance of this historical literary scholarship lies in that it traces the development of *literature* as a growing and changing *corpus*, as an evolving *unity* within the changing cultural, political, and social nature of society.

We have already discussed the "life" of literary works, and we saw how they subsist in their concretions during different periods. We are returning to this topic because it provides a basis for a special orientation of historical literary scholarship. Before its completion an individual work can, and normally does, undergo various changes that result from authorial interventions in the process of its creation. Once the work is completed, it cannot of itself undergo any changes, but it can be, for instance, shortened or translated. If we disregard such modifications, we may say that the completed work itself, or its faithful reconstruction, is an "extratemporal" object. Nevertheless, one may say that a literary work "lives" when it is brought to life in different concretions. Concretions vary not only because they are constituted by different individuals, but also because the responses of readers change as tastes change in the course of time, or because new artistic insights may allow us to discover unsuspected aesthetic qualities in previously neglected works. Thus the "life" of a work may be investigated through a series of its aesthetically significant concretions, or through a series of its concretions that are typical for different periods. One may also seek to assess its *impact* at different times and in different places, its popularity among different types of the reading public, and its position in the hierarchy of works coexistent with it, or one may wish to study the story of a work's successes and failures and explain the reasons for its destiny. While some of these investigations are literary in that they belong to the study of literary history, investigations of evolving literary tastes, of the popularity of works, and of responses of readers do not belong to literary history, but to the history of the literary life of cultural communities at different times and in different places.

Different concretions of one and the same work are possible only because every literary work is a schematic structure. However, because all the concretions are concretions of the same schematic work, they are in spite of their differences necessarily similar to each other. This is one reason why certain elements of an earlier concretion may be adopted during a subsequent concretization. This is frequently so when the two concretizations are carried out by the same person, or when we are influenced by previous concretions constituted by others. If the earlier concretization does not respect the range of admissible complementations, its errors may be perpetuated by subsequent concretizations. It is, however, also possible that each new competent concretization may lead to ever more adequate concretions. This happens when successive periods are marked by an increasing knowledge of and a deepening sensitivity to a work's artistic, aesthetic, and cultural values. An awareness of the history of concretions, based on careful preaesthetic studies of a work, may lead to ever more competent concretizations. Inappropriate concretizations are sometimes transmitted from one generation to another, especially when naive readers do not distinguish the work from its concretion. Appropriate or inappropriate concretizations may be associated with a prevailing literary atmosphere, which is normally linked to the cultural atmosphere of a period. A literary atmosphere is usually the result of a certain type of literary criticism that succeeds in stabilizing concretions which establish a traditional view of a work.

C. Literary criticism

Ingarden's conception of the task of literary criticism derives from his ontology of the literary work of *art*, in which the constitution of its aesthetic object is grounded. This means that literary criticism must be *based* on the distinction between the work of art as a schematic structure, and its concretion. The *purpose* of literary criticism must be the aesthetic concretization of individual works of art. The *task* of criticism must be an account of an aesthetic concretization and an artistic and aesthetic evaluation based on that concretization.

Although the literary critic is not expected to bracket the cultural and literary atmosphere in which he lives, he must nevertheless be aware that his concretization of a work does not have exclusive validity. In fact, he should explore various possible concretizations of the same work, the better to assess their range as it is determined by artistically effective elements, for it should be his task to draw the reader's attention to the richness of potentialities contained in the schema of a work. He must move from the aesthetic attitude, in which his concretizations are carried out, to the aesthetic-reflective cognition of the results of his aesthetic concretizations. Only thus can he fulfill his function of enlightening the reader about the artistic and aesthetic values of the work and making him sensitive to them. Only thus can the critic affect the cultural atmosphere of his time and create a literary atmosphere in which our grasp of the quality of literary art can make us aesthetically receptive and bestow a qualitative value on our lives.

Index

Absolutized concretization, 136
Active reading, 144, 145, 147, 153
Actuality: of nominal word-meanings, 44–46, 134; temporal (*in actu esse*), 85, 86
Actualization, 16, 17, 57, 76, 88, 126, 127, 128, 129, 134, 140, 144; admissible, 89; of aesthetic qualities, 120; of aspects, 104, 135, 147; temporal, 85, 157. *See also* Concept; Potentiality
Adaptation, 66, 113, 115
Adumbrational style. *See* Style of aspects
Adumbrations. *See* Aspects
Aesthetic attitude (stance), xix, 118, 119, 133–34, 160–71
Aesthetic concretization, xviii, xix, 160–71, 172, 173, 174, 181, 187
Aesthetic experience, 160–71, 172, 173, 175, 177, 181; differences between, 168–69
Aesthetic object, xiv, 119, 131, 151, 160–71, 172, 173, 174, 175, 180, 193, 195, 197–98; value of, 167–68, 189, 192–93, 194, 195–96, 197. *See also* Aesthetic-reflective cognition; Articulation
Aesthetic qualities, xviii, 119, 120, 122–23, 134, 145, 150, 187, 190, 192; of layer of meaning units, 36, 170; metaphysical qualities and, 119–20, 198; neutral, 175, 177; relevant, 165, 166; systems of aesthetically valent qualities, 196–97. *See also* Aesthetic experience; Aesthetic object; Aesthetic value; Cohesion of aesthetic qualities; Congruity; Harmony
Aesthetic-reflective cognition, 171–75
Aesthetic value, 171, 175, 187, 189–90, 191, 192–93. *See also* Aesthetic object; Aesthetic qualities
Affective quality, 163–66, 167, 172, 175
Affirmation, 9, 62, 67–68. *See also* Declarative sentence; Sentences
Ambiguity, 89, 141, 182–83
Analysis and analytical investigation, 174, 177–78, 181, 182, 184. *See also* Preaesthetic investigation
Anatomical structure, 119, 120, 122, 151
Apodictic assertion, 9
Appreciative acknowledgment, 190, 191, 194–95. *See also* Aesthetic value; Contemplation; Pure feeling; Valuation; Values
Apprehension, 90, 91. *See also* Perception
Apprehension of printed signs, 138–39
Apprehension of word-sounds, 138–39
Art for art's sake, 191
Articulation, 167, 169, 174. *See also* Structuring
Artistic effectiveness (Artistic elements; Artistic qualities), 169, 171, 175, 176, 177–80, 181, 187, 190, 191, 192–94, 196. *See also* Artistic value
Artistic language, 141–42
Artistic value, 168, 187, 190, 191, 192–93; neutral, 193–94. *See also* Artistic effectiveness
Aspects, xvi, 76, 91; actualization of, 104, 147; aesthetic qualities in ready, 109–11; based on sensory data (external aspects), 92–96, 110; described, 104; determinative functions of, 105–6; fulfilled qualities of, 94–95; functional dependencies